THE SOUTHERN REDNECK

THE SOUTHERN REDNECK

A Phenomenological Class Study

Julian B. Roebuck
Mark Hickson, III

PRAEGER

PRAEGER SPECIAL STUDIES • PRAEGER SCIENTIFIC

Library of Congress Cataloging in Publication Data

Roebuck, Julian B.
    The southern redneck.

    Bibliography: p.
    Includes index.
    1. Working class whites—Southern States.

2.   Southern States—Social conditions. I. Hickson,
Mark. II. Title. III. Title: Redneck.
HD8083.Al3R63 1982   305.5′63   82-9831
ISBN 0-03-059803-6   AACR2

Published in 1982 by Praeger Publishers
CBS Educational and Professional Publishing
a Division of CBS Inc.
521 Fifth Avenue, New York, New York 10175 U.S.A.

© 1982 by Praeger Publishers

23456789   052   987654321

Printed in the United States of America

PREFACE

Redneck is a popular term frequently found in the Southern vernacular that first designated poor white farm workers. Since ex-President Jimmy Carter's administration, this rubric has received more prominence (and notoriety) and so has its stereotypical referent. Middle- and upper-class Southerners often apply the term derogatorily to blue-collar, lower-class white memberships. Recently, however, the label has taken on a more positive connotation in some circles, particularly among Southern blue-collar workers themselves, denoting honest, hard-working, working-class men. Female equivalents of this traditionally masculine categorization have also surfaced—for example, *redneck women* and *women rednecks*. Though the sensitizing concept of the *redneck* has no precise definition in a formal sense, it connotes a category of people with a familiar rustic life-style recognizable by Southerners in their everyday lives.

We began discussing the redneck as a social-type referent for occupation and social class with one another and with others in 1971. Our interest in those labeled rednecks stemmed from a wider concern with the social class system in the South. Finally, we decided that a structural and phenomenological study of rednecks and redneckery in the Southern region would disclose the dynamics of social class therein.

During our informal discussions, the whole country began taking on an avid interest in the redneck topic for diverse reasons. Rednecks were portrayed in popular films such as *Smokey and the Bandit*. Country and Western music was heard all over the world by more people than ever before. Billy Carter, Jimmy Carter's brother, wore a tee shirt with "Redneck Power" printed across the front. Even more recently, "The Dukes of Hazzard" (a redneck serial) has become a popular television program. In 1982 Associated Press writer Phillip Rawls reported that John "Sweet Pea" Russel, Jr., had formed a national redneck club that required a $10 membership fee. Rednecks are in.

In 1975 we initiated our study in two parts using two methods. First utilizing a historical structural approach, we analyzed social class in the South with particular attention to the lower-class Southerner. Chapters 2, 3, and 4 analyze poor white Southerners, the redneck's progenitors, in terms of their folk culture. Chapters 5 through 10, the second part of the work, cover the phenomenological sociological study of the redneck. Chapter 1 explicates our phenomenological and historical approaches along with methods and procedures. We found that the social class structure in the South has changed little in form since the antebellum period and that the more the South appears to change, the more it remains the same. The poor white folk culture of the antebellum period persists and continues to produce rednecks and redneckery. The redneck's chief problem remains false consciousness.

Many people, including numerous rednecks, made this project possible. We thank the following at Mississippi State University for providing us with the time and resources to write: the Office of Graduate Studies and Research and Edward L. McGlone, Dean of the College of Arts and Sciences. Almost anyone we told about the book had a suggestion: Go over to so-and-so. Write about ol' so-and-so. Have you considered so-and-so? Some of our friends and associates, however, provided more professional information: John Shelton Reed, Professor of Sociology at the University of North Carolina, Chapel Hill, North Carolina, was one such person; Don Grierson, Harold Mullen, Glenn Vanderbeek, Rod Wenzel, and Kathryn Carter from Mississippi State are in this category. We also acknowledge and appreciate the able and patient assistance of our typist, Marietta Tubb, affectionately known as "V." Nancy Dorman provided valuable assistance on editing and indexing. Finally, we thank Lynda Sharp, our editor at Praeger, for her suggestions.

At this point most authors indicate that the entire responsibility of the manuscript is theirs. Phenomenological studies, however, are mosaics that are composed from readings, experiences, conversations, and involvements. The words here are ours, the impressions are ours, but the process reflects the cumulative mental mural of two lifetimes spent around (and knowing) Southern rednecks. The book is coauthored and represents coequal efforts in all respects. Finally, *we* do not use the term *redneck* anywhere throughout the book in a pejorative sense.

CONTENTS

THE SOUTHERN REDNECK

ONE

INTRODUCTION

This book is about the world of the Southern redneck and his place within the social class structure of the South. The *South*, as the word is used throughout the text, includes the 11 former Confederate States of America in addition to Kentucky and West Virginia unless otherwise specified. By *Southerner* we mean people born and residing in one of these states.

The ubiquitous Southern expression *redneck* resurfaced throughout the United States in the media and in everyday conversation during and after Jimmy Carter's successful presidential campaign. Generally, the term was used in a pejorative sense by outsiders stereotyping many white Southerners as poor, semiliterate, ignorant, provincial, reactionary, violent, bigoted fundamentalist hicks who hated blacks, Yankees, Catholics, and foreigners (non-Anglo-Saxons and the Scotch-Irish). Some outsiders of a more romantic bent utilized the term in a less benighted sense as referring to a group of working-class, hell-raising "good old boys" who spent most of their time drinking, fighting, and "screwing around" in honky-tonks, hunting, fishing, moonshining, and congregating at stock car races. The redneck, according to them, though quick to violence, was a rustic, simplistic, heavy-drinking, hell-raising, good-hearted macho who lived by a straightforward and "honorable" moral code; there is a right way and a wrong way, and if one is wrong, justice in the form of physical punishment follows. Jimmy Carter was not a redneck because he and his father before him owned land—besides, rednecks did not graduate from Annapolis. Nevertheless, Jimmy, by virtue of being a Southerner, had to have some

1

pink spots on his neck. On the other hand, his brother Billy, a self-avowed redneck, could qualify for the category despite family background because of his proclaimed stance on life and his hell-raising life-style. Still other outsiders combined elements of both of these perspectives in the usage of the term, *redneck*. The common denominator was being a low-class Southerner.

From our overall and over-time impressions and observations in the South where we grew up and now reside, the term *redneck*, when used by middle- and upper-class Southerners, specifies poor, working-class, uncouth, undereducated, disreputable whites—that is, disreputable either by being "from a poor class of folks" or by engaging in immoral, low-class behavior. To some of these Southerners *redneck* and *white trash* are synonymous terms. Other middle- and upper-class Southerners make a distinction and perceive the redneck as a poor, lower-class, uncouth working man, while the label *white trash* or *trash* is reserved for the more disreputable, irregularly employed, allegedly immoral and lazy, "no count" class (what Marx called the *Lumpenproletariat*). The crucial differential is the degree of disreputability. To some Southerners, all poor, working-class Southerners are not *totally* rednecks because some of them lead respectable life-styles and come from good plain folks, but all rednecks are low class and to some degree disreputable and disrespectable as a consequence of "poor family background" and/or reprehensible as a immoral personal behavior. The key criterion is being poor. Many Southerners apply the rubric to all poor people, whereas others use the term for poor people they do not like. Those who become labeled as rednecks find it extremely difficult to escape the category despite personal accomplishments unless they move to another community where they and their family backgrounds are unknown.

HISTORICAL AND GENERIC CONSIDERATIONS

Manual labor has been considered menial in the South since the establishment of plantation agriculture based on slavery, and it is sometimes referred to as "nigger work," especially if one performs it for someone else. Those who perform nigger work are said to share a rough-hewn life-style differentiated from that shared by genteel, quality Southerners. Significantly, the more democratic tradition of the "hired hand" system existing in the Midwest has never obtained in the South. Therefore, all those who work at manual labor, particularly for others, do not completely escape the disreputable redneck label. In fact, the term *redneck* was first used in the later nineteenth and early twentieth century Mississippi political literature to describe poor, white, subsistence farmers, sharecroppers, and tenant farmers. According to Mississippi folklore, the term *redneck* was first applied to those who literally had red necks, acquired from the long hours spent working in the fields. One did not acquire one from sitting in the parlor or on the front porch like the planters did (Hamilton 1958, p. 225, Kirwan 1951).

To many Southerners, including many self-styled rednecks, the term is used in a blue-collar generic sense to designate poor, indigenous, working-class white people who identify with Southern rural and small-town backgrounds who possess a distinctive regional ideology and life-style (including a racial, religious, political, and social world view). Occupational types frequently included within the rubric are service station attendants, construction workers, auto mechanics, factory hands, truckers, house painters, cab drivers, heavy equipment operators, miners mill workers, law enforcement officers, bootleggers, hunters and trappers, fishermen, farm laborers, warehouse workers, dock workers, off-shore oil rig workers, small farmers, and other manual workers usually remunerated by wages. Though the combination of working-class employment and lower-class status appear to be prime criteria connoting the redneck, some lower-echelon white- and blue-collar workers (such as store clerks, stock clerks, cooks, secretaries, clerical workers, waitresses, restaurant and theater employees, and many nonprofessional service workers) are generally encompassed as well, particularly in the case where those occupying these work roles are nonowners and products of working-class families.

Frequently, working-class Southerners call themselves rednecks in in-group situations. to them the term connotes a straightforward, un-pretentious, hypocrisy-hating, right-thinking, honest, and hard-working man who "stands on his own two feet and pays his bills." These rednecks are aware of and accept their lower-class position as well as the social superiority of middle- and upper-class Southerners. On the other hand, they consider themselves to be superior in certain ways to upper-class Southerners, for example, in honesty.

COMMON ELEMENTS AND THE STUDY QUESTIONS

Though some ambiguity is obvious in the way both insiders and out-siders utilize the term *redneck*, all definitions refer to components encom-passed by or subsumed under social class. The common elements of this *sensitizing concept* (Blumer 1969, pp. 127-53) of the redneck appear to be as follows: working class employment, relative poverty, regional ideology and life-style, and lower-class status and disreputability (Flynt 1979; Roebuck and Neff 1980, pp. 233-62). On this basis we decided to study the Southern redneck in terms of his place in the social class structure of the South. To this end we posed four major study questions: (1) Can the sensitizing concept of the redneck facilitate our identification of a subjective reality—that is, a definite set of socially constructed definitions that are real in the minds of Southerners? Do Southerners really carry around in their heads concepts of rednecks in their everyday lives; if so, how do they arrive at these conceptualizations? (2) What are the objective consequences of this subjective reality? To what extent do Southerners order their everyday lives, and especially their efforts, to maintain associations and intergroup boundaries on the basis of the meanings associated with this term? (3) Is there a distinctive and identifiable group of Southerners whose behaviors and personalities actually correspond in some degree to the meanings associated with this rubric? In short, is there a redneck type out there; if so, how does he perceive his social world? (4) Can we identify an underlying social dynamic (rural-urban conflict, North-South conflict, class conflict) that accounts for these various phenomena and the relationships between them?

METHODOLOGY

The study questions suggested the need for two approaches: first, the necessity for some historical structural analysis of social class in the South with particular attention to the lower-class Southerner, an area unfortunately awarded less attention by historians than the planter class and an area either neglected or glossed over by many Southerners when discussing their genealogies; and second, the need for a phenomenological sociological study of the contemporary redneck to understand his social world and social actions as experienced and interpreted by him in concrete social situations. A review of the literature disclosed that the term *redneck*, like other lower-class epithets, evolved from the more generic construct *poor white* and could not be understood apart from this social class entry. Therefore, we constructed a history of poor whites in the South from secondary historical sources. Chapters 2, 3, and 4 trace the history of this class and its folk culture from the eighteenth century through the 1970s and disclose a remarkable similarity and continuity in the parameters of the Southern class system, and those within it designated as poor whites or rednecks.

At this point, armed with the necessary structural class background material (the first page of the book), we attempted to reconstruct the contemporary social reality of the redneck in terms of his own actions, definitions, and interpretations (as presented or conveyed to us) to arrive at a phenomenological understanding of his world. This endeavor comprised the second part of the book.

While we realize that others can never fully "know" an individual as completely as the actor himself, we can reconstruct our own experiences as participants in the actor's culture, however, and also infer the actor's social reality from his observed actions, accounts, definitions, interpretations, and expressed feelings. One author grew up in rural, eastern North Carolina, and the other in small-town central Georgia. Both had experienced frequent and enduring work and social contacts with rednecks, middle- and upper-class Southerners, and blacks while growing up and working in all of the former Confederate States—and while traveling and visiting in all the border states including Maryland, Kentucky, West Virginia, and the District of Columbia. Our work experiences in the South included employment as a truckers' dispatcher, field hand, theater usher, soda jerk, tobacco warehouse worker, hotel clerk, bartender, playground supervisor, store clerk, church usher, public schoolteacher, secondhand clothing sales clerk, probation and parole laborer, radio announcer, enlisted military serviceman, door-to-door salesman, carpenter's helper, undertaker's helper, welfare case worker, and county health department venereal disease counselor.

The phenomenological data were gathered from a collective experiental synthesis over a lifetime and, since 1975, from directed participant observation, unstructured interviews, diaries and family histories, legal documents, and Southern folklore. Field notes were collected from January 1, 1975, through January 1, 1981. We recorded some of our explanations of the redneck's interpretations; however, we attempted to keep the two separate for purposes of analysis. All findings were examined within a historical frame of reference.

Following a comparative analysis of our team data, we discarded minor discrepancies, idiosyncratic materials, and cultural overlap contaminations from without the South (wherein possible). The remaining data, comprising the second part of the book (Chapters 5 through 10), were ordered according to the redneck's social world as reported to us.

TWO

THE SOUTH'S POOR WHITES FROM ANTEBELLUM TO 1920

THE ANTEBELLUM PERIOD

Introduction

The term *poor whites* as used in antebellum society connoted disreputability as well as a lack of financial worth. Over time, poor white manual workers without land of any consequence were referred to in the historical literature and in the Southern vernacular as *indentured servants, po' whites, buckras* (these last two primarily used by black slaves), *pecker woods, rednecks, hillbillies, sand-hillers, wooly hats, mechanics, crackers, sharecroppers, tenant farmers,* and *mill hands*. These terms, obviously, related to work status, geography, or clothing. Some farm laborers wore wide-brimmed wool hats to protect them from the sun; crackers were poor, rural, isolated people in Georgia and northern Florida; pecker woods lived in outlying wooded areas (Flynt 1979, pp. 8-11). Black slaves called mean, low-class whites *trash* or *white trash* (Genovese 1974, pp. 21-55, 91-95). Southerners of all classes were quick to pick up this latter epithet, which remains the ultimate derogatory category in which one may be placed.

Poor whites of the South have been portrayed and characterized by a wide assortment of Southerners and outsiders including travelers, so-journers, historians, government bureaucrats, economists, artists, photo-graphers, playwrights, novelists, journalists, and sociologists. Though these depictions have varied somewhat within time frames and from period to period, a common denominator persists—that is, poor whites comprise a segment of the Southern population set apart economically, socially, and qualitatively from the rest of the population of the region with a history and culture dating to slavery and persisting through the present.

Before 1970 there was opportunity for all the whites, including the poor, to become independent artisans or farmers in the colonies. In the eighteenth century, however, the establishment and development of the plantation slave system in the South made it more difficult for the freed indentured servants and other poor people to rise or maintain their own. As the tidewater section became dominated by a commercial one-crop plantation agricultural system (tobacco, rice, sugar, indigo, or cotton) based on slavery, the early homogeneity and mobility of the population gave way to a three-tiered white class system: the planters, the yeoman farmers (independent small-holders), and the poor whites at the bottom of the pyramid (Mell 1938).

Several scholars further subdivide this rough, but economically and socially feasible, classisifation. Eugene D. Genovese (1974, pp. 7-25) suggests the following breakdown: planters, solid yeomen, respectable subsistence farmers who supplement their incomes by working as day laborers, farmers and herdsmen in the up country in a world of their own, skilled and semiskilled mechanics (wage earners), and dissolute, déclassé "poor white trash." He documents the fact that slavery gave the South a social system and civilization with a distinctive class structure, political community, economy, ideology, and set of social-psychological patterns— for example, sectionalism, paternalism, noblesse oblige, and force and violence (Genovese 1965, pp. 3-30). Others propose additional minor modifications including large planters (200 or more slaves); small planters (less than 20 slaves); bankers, businessmen, and professionals (lawyers, doctors); yeoman farmers with no slaves; yeoman farmers with a few slaves; plain folks (herdsmen-frontier farmers and owners of hogs, cattle, and horses); day laborers and tenants on land owned by planters; and mill and factory workers (Fogel and Engerman 1974, pp. 57-234; Owsley 1949).

In the antebellum period, the North, unlike the South, through commerce, manufactures, and transportation offered a wage system to urban dwellers and a "hired man" status to landless agricultural wage workers, a status not derogated as in the South where labor performed for others was nigger work. In the South agriculture based on slave labor provided limited employment opportunities for white laborers and small landholders. The land tenure system, the one-crop system, and soil exhaustion caused the planters to move to new lands constantly, leaving in their wake worn-out fields. Small farmers found it difficult to prosper in plantation areas because the planters eventually through economic pressure secured possession of most of the desirable lands, leaving the barren fields to the yeoman farmers and poor whites. Therefore, many yeomen were forced outside the large plantation areas. Some small farmers, particularly those with a few slaves, managed to hold on to small tracts of land in plantation areas by hard labor and their families' help.

The poor whites "squatted" on worn-out land and unwanted tracts in the sand hills and pine barrens. Many pressured yeomen sold their small holdings to planters and moved out to the frontier, following the herdsmen, hunters, and traders, to start as farmers all over again. Some of the poor landless whites also moved along and became frontiersmen on public land. The planters followed this advance guard and quickly developed a plantation system similar to that left behind in the tidewater. Again, most of the small farmers were pushed on to a new frontier by the plantation system or to outlying hills where they grew some tobacco and cotton for the market with thier own labor. This ongoing "frontier process" left behind at various junctures a group of poor whites who could not move to a new frontier to hold on to their small farms within plantation territory. Downward mobility was the rule for many, as opposed to the upward mobility of the few. Consequently, the planters, yeoman farmers, and Negro slaves operated as functioning groups in the antebellum South's economic system, whereas the poor whites existed outside the system. The latter did not belong to a wage-earning system; and they were not a part of the nonfree laboring force that produced a market economy (Mell 1938).

Characteristics of Poor Whites

The poor whites were the economically and politically powerless, landless losers below the yeoman level, refugees from the world of competition. They commonly drifted as tenants or became squatters in wilderness clearings. Many were stranded on poor land in the sand hills, pine barrens, hills, and mountains throughout the South where they subsisted by hunting and fishing or by raising meager crops and a few hogs. Sometimes a few performed odd jobs for wages, worked as tenants on planters' land, or were employed occasionally as factory workers. For the most part excluded from the productive economic system, they were unable to attain this system's goods and services. Economic, physical, and social isolation removed them from respectable community life. They endured poor diets (ate clay), illiteracy, and a dearth of medical care, material goods, and security. Many suffered from general ill health, communicable diseases, malaria, hookworm, anemia, undernourishment, rickets, and pellagra. Black slaves received far better medical attention (from planters) than did this group. By 1860 one fifth of the total white population in the four states of Virginia, North and South Carolina, and Georgia were poor. Some few indigents received the meager "poor relief" provided by some counties (Flynt 1979, pp. 8-11; Phillips 1929, pp. 347-49).

Many cultural and physical traits attributed to poor whites by travelers, writers, artists, slaves, and some yeoman farmers must be viewed within the context of the Southern castelike class system and the accompanying injuries of class. They were frequently defined as violent, lazy, shiftless, ignorant, dull, dumb, degenerate, uncouth, sorry, trashy, degraded, common, immoral, violent, drunken, and biologically inferior people. Physically, they were often portrayed as ugly, lanky, slack-muscled, sallow, pale, bony, disjointed, and disfigured humans who moved awkwardly, jerkily, and indolently (probably a correct portrayal because of poor health). Poor whites were said to be naturally lazy, and they were lazy because they were poor whites. Actually, the poor whites of the nineteenth century were descended from the yeomen or, sometimes from slaveholders of an earlier time.

Downward mobility after 1800 was more frequent than upward mobility (Mell 1943). One's class position depended on a number of factors: talent, industry, resolution, luck, health, number of children (the more, the more division of wealth), and inherited wealth, but inherited wealth was hard to conquer (Phillips 1929).

The small but dominant planter class was primarily responsible for these negative definitions and the material conditions underpinning them. Though products of the yeoman class and the same gene pool (primarily English and Scotch-Irish) as most other whites in the South (of whatever station), the planter class proclaimed racial superiority to all blacks and even biological superiority to poor whites. Their physical and spiritual superiority verified by landownership gave them hegemonic rights over all other classes. This myth was shared by all throughout the social structure and served as the foundation for the plantation class system. Planters tried to prevent slaves from any kind of association with non-slave owners (except overseers), particularly with poor whites (with whom some slaves did associate). They expressed a disdain for poor whites to other planters and to slaves; however, they were less critical of them when talking to nonslaveholders. The white man, no matter how low, was never to forget that he was superior to all blacks. Otherwise, he might question the planter's class position and racial ideology (Genovese 1974, pp. 1-30).

The term *poor white* when applied by planters, yeomen, or blacks designated some moral and material degeneracy. Mountain people, even those impoverished, were usually spared this designation because, supposedly, they had ancestral and cultural pride and possessed a unique, worthwhile folk culture. On the other hand, many of the tidewater and Piedmont poor whites were considered "no count" people who were isolated socially from their own kind—and paradoxically enough at times, from their own kin. (Some members of the planter class had poor white relatives of whom they were sorely ashamed.) Respectable, hard-working, landless whites who did not perform field labor for others were not necessarily poor whites. These landless who did, and those landless who led an immoral life-style (drinking, gambling, fighting, hell raising, and being openly promiscuous) were poor white trash. The term *poor white* became a sociocultural term early on that described not only an economic condition but also a "moral condition" (Flynt 1979, p. 9). The planter, on the other hand, no matter what his morals or life-style, was still a gentleman. Yeomen were also permitted wide latitudes of behavior, though not as wide as the planter. The poor, the yeomen, and the planters were frequently hard-drinking, sensual, violent men.

The Dearth of Class Consciousness

By 1860 Southern society was dominated by a plantation-oriented, slaveholding system with conservative values, hierarchical relationshps, and authoritarian controls—a closed society, distrustful of ideas from outside and unsympathetic toward dissenters from within or without the region (Potter 1973, pp. 454-58). Wilbur J. Cash (1941) pointed to the South's "savage ideal" (antiintellectualism and hostility to new ideas). Open class conflict did not occur in antebellum society because the underclass (or classes) admired and monumentalized their social betters as natural leaders. Therefore, few developed an underclass consciousness. The planter class, on the other hand, was a class in itself as well as for itself, i.e. in a Marxist sense. The yeomen and the poor whites were indoctrinated with the racial and political ideology of the upper class, and all whites were irrevocably tied to the system because they believed in it and because they were afraid that structural change would result in racial amalgamation and further economic impoverishment. Some yeomen aspired to planter status. The Southerners' tendency toward concreteness rather than abstractness, their ignorance, isolation and racism, and their other worldly fundamentalist religion fostered the class system.

In 1859 Hinton Rowan Helper (1968), a native North Carolinian, wrote a book, *The Impending Crisis in the South*, in which he tried to tell his fellow plain folk how the planters were using them and how the slave system worked to keep rich people rich and the poor people poor. He contended that slavery was a class weapon in that the system allowed planters to operate their extensive acreage and bar others to both land and labor. In short, he tried to point out that the poor whites had no stake in slavery and that they had more in common with blacks than with planters. (Helper, in spite of this view, was a racist.) Most of the poor whites turned a deaf ear, but the planter leadership, a little wiser, suppressed the book (Thomas 1979, pp. 10-11).

Some poor whites, including yeomen, managed to elect a few of their class to state and national offices in the 1850s, but these politicians turned out to be demagogues who supported the business and planter classes after election. Some did call for internal improvements, tax changes favoring small farmers, public schools, equal taxation of property, and homestead legislation, though prior to the Civil War only two Southern states had public education (Flynt 1979, pp. 13-14). Those who had the money went to private academies. Most poor whites involved in politics supported the Democratic party, the party of the upper class. Between 1830 and 1860, white manhood suffrage, the popular election of virtually all county and state officers, and the abolition of property qualifications for office holding (in most cases) were incorporated into Southern states' constitutions. This was accomplished by public pressure exerted by plain folk (Owsley 1949, pp. 141-145). Pervasive power, prestige, and wealth remained with the planter and banking class.

Poor White Culture

Yeoman farmers and poor whites, whether in the coastal plain, the Piedmont, or in Appalachia, shared many elements of a Southern folk culture, and no rigid separation of the two is possible because they blended into one another. They were tied together by a direct and primal relationship to the land, kinship, race (white), ethnicity (English or Scotch-Irish), language, region, religion, extended family, poverty, isolation, hostility to outsiders, life-style, occupation, customs, traditions, and history. Most obtained food, clothing, and shelter from rural pursuits and lived in self-constructed cabins or houses of round poles or planks. An ax was used to fell trees, a froe to rive clapboards and shingles for the roof, a saw to cut apertures and boards, and a hammer to drive nails. They raised hogs and chickens, cultivated corn and other vegetables, and occasionally planted a small crop of cotton or tobacco. Some had cattle, horses, and a milk cow, which grazed frequently on open land. They also hunted, trapped, and fished for food. Animal furs and hides were sold at a town market (usually the county seat). Some also sold a little corn and tobacco there. All furniture was homemade. Some provided labor and products to planters. There was no reason to work too hard in a land of open resources, and after all, leisure was more important than hard work, which was the "niggers lot," but not that of the white man. Work and play were frequently united—for example, in corn shuckings, log rollings, woods burnings, house raisings, and quilting parties. Trips to town often involved marksmanship contests, horse racing, wrestling matches, drinking bouts, some gambling, courting, and fighting. The church was a community center where all day group singing occurred. Wedding parties at home often combined hunting, quilting, storytelling, feasting, courting, drinking, and dancing to music made by the guitar, banjo, and fiddle. Among the men, fighting, shootings, and stabbings occurred occasionally.

Poor whites and yeomen swapped seventeenth century English and Scottish tales and sang folk songs transmitted orally from one generation to another. The content, though not the form, was altered at will to fit in with the local situation. Lyrics and scenarios centered on everyday lives and environments—for example, animals, hunting, fishing, violence, courting, physical strength, humorous and tragic characters, preachers, traveling strangers, and hunters. Songs were sung and stories were told to entertain and not to moralize or to call for help or changes (Flynt 1979, pp. 16-32, Owsley 1949, pp. 90-133; Phillips 1929, pp. 339-53; Thomas 1979, pp. 9-16). In short, they appear to have enjoyed or at best endured their misery without complaint or a search for change.

The folk culture and physical circumstances encouraged the development of rule by men instead of law and institutions. Individualism, developed from a self-sufficient life on the frontier, was frequently expressed as a violent assertion of self and often led to bloodshed. Violence tended to be more acceptable here than in other regions because, for one reason, slavery depended on physical force or on the threat of force. The planters' penchant for violence was a model for the plain folk, if they needed a model.

In the rural South, often just beyond the frontier stage of development, the plain folk depended on and asserted themselves according to a personalized set of human relations (man to man) and a code of violent behavior based on the personal redress of wrong. They also shared responsibility with slaveholders for the internal security of slavery (and with planters, the legal sanction to discipline Southern blacks). Only about one fourth of the South's heads of families owned any slaves at all, and of these, an estimated 60 percent owned no more than five. Many poor whites had only tangential contacts with blacks, and some had no contacts at all. The population's rabid fear of slave insurrections, however, along with the constraints of the legal system, cast all whites into a disciplinary role where blacks were concerned. Poor whites compose the membership of slave patrols. Poor whites lived in a culture with other whites where they were supposed to be committed to human equality in political and religious principle but where they were actually committed to human servitude and aristocracy (Thomas 1979, pp. 17-20). Some scholars claim that such ambivalence resulted in a policy of "offensive defense," often violent in its expression (Potter 1968, pp. 18-23).

A Southern Folk Religion

The yeoman farmers and the poor whites, whether in the coastal plains or Appalachia, shared many elements of a Southern folk religion. They attended the same camp meetings, interdenominational revival services and Primitive Baptist, Baptist, Disciples of Christ, Cumberland Presbyterian, Church of God, and Methodist churches. Religious skeptics, Jews, and Roman Catholics (except in Louisiana and Maryland) constituted a small minority among overwhelming Protestant Christians; Quakers, Episcopalians, Unitarians, and members of liberal sects made up an even smaller number. The gospel, as poor whites perceived it, gave meaning, solace, peace, order, certainty, hope, reward, vindication, redemption, and salvation in heaven (another and better world) through and by repentence and the acceptance of Jesus. The fundamental emphasis was upon sin, the rejection of the ugly, unjust secular world, and salvation. Lay preachers (poor themselves) proclaimed a Calvinistic, puritanical, evangelical gospel short on theology and good deeds but long on individual guilt, repentence, and being saved through the acceptance of Christ, the right belief system, and baptism (rather than good deeds). Theirs was a highly personal and individualistic religion. One was admonished to live according to the demands of a strict father God, and whether one was an obedient or rebellious child, he acknowledged the existence of individual moral obligations.

Puritanism was combined with hedonism in the Southern religion. Sin could be enjoyed as long as one was aware of and admitted (to Him) one was sinning. The point was that one had to believe rather than act in the "right way." This otherworldy religion did not stress the social gospel, that is, changes in an imperfect society or in any social or political groups. Man was inherently evil, and therefore, there was little one could do about the sorry human condition. Because God was omniscient and onmipotent, there was an unknown reason behind one's miserable life. God permitted the poor and weak to endure and some to suffer and die. Christ, who had died for them, would eventually return and everything would be righted— at least, for those who had been saved (Flynt 1979, pp. 27-32; Owsley 1949, 96-104; Thomas 1979, pp. 21-23). And once saved, always saved. Churches were developed along individualistic, sectarian, provincial congregational lines (my church for my people). Therefore, the need for a universal social gospel and help for other Christians (strangers or outsiders) were not anticipated—and could not have been implemented even if they had been.

Some scholars claim that this simplistic, harsh, hellfire and damnation, antiintellectual, provincial, irrational, otherworldly, individualistic, sectarian religion was fashioned by the poor to compensate for their miserable, uncertain, hard, isolated, low-status, powerless, violent, disorderly, ignorant, and emotionally starved lives (Flynt 1979, p. 32).

Such a religion also sanctioned racial subordination (blacks were cursed as "Sons of Ham"), human bondage (from biblical accounts), violence, and devastating class exploitation—in short, a religion that helped keep miserable people docile and miserable. Southern churches were among the most enthusiastic advocates of secession from the Union and, with few exceptions, promoted the Southern militant cause throughout the Civil War. Throughout the Confederacy, clergymen regularly delivered patriotic sermons to spur onward the flagging and the faithful. (The vast majority of Confederate soldiers were plain folk.) Southerners, according to the churches, were the "chosen people"; Yankees were Philistines whom Jehovah would surely destroy in His time. Southern arms were like those of Joshua in times of victory; in the wake of defeats God was chastising and cleansing Confederates in preparation for eventual triumph (Thomas 1979, pp. 245-49). To a people who took their religion literally and seriously, political, military, and religious exhortations were united in a monolithic ideology that kept them fighting and dying in a lost cause. The Southern clergy supported slavery on the basis of religion and biology as well as the Southern class system (Davis 1975, pp. 523-56).

POOR WHITES BETWEEN 1865 AND 1920

The Poor Rediscovered

Following the Civil War, grim poverty became the lot of millions of Southerners of all classes. Neither the easygoing, indolent life-style on the plantation nor the freedom of self-sufficiency in agriculture in the backwater had equipped Southerners to meet such hard times. Many migrated from the Old South to Texas and Arkansas. Some flocked to Southern urban areas where a few found work and where most lived under squalid conditions. Others eked out a survival where they were. Many planters and yeomen lost their land and were reduced to tenant farmers on the land of their more fortunate neighbors.

In the late 1870s and 1880s, travelers from the North and native Southerners rediscovered "poor whites" in the South. They were said at times to live in the black belt, at others, the pine barrens or the sand hills. The local contempt for them was said to reflect the names by which they were best known: *hillbillies*, *crackers*, and *Tarheels*, all used by

Southerners indiscriminately to designate poor down-and-out fellow countrymen. Northern intellectuals used the concept of the poor white in a Southern sense to rationalize away the dire poverty of millions in an economically deprived region. Poor whites were again considered degenerate, lazy, and ambitionless. Affluent native Southerners referred to this "troublesome class" in the same sense as had the Southern planters during the antebellum period. We see here once more the attribution of a moral dimension to the status of poverty despite the fluctuation in class status of those derogated. To be affluent was to be respectable; to be poor was to be somewhat immoral (Woodward 1951, pp. 108-15).

Integration into the Economic System and the Return of White Rule

In the postbellum period, between 1865 and 1900, the poor whites were integrated into the economic system as one, dependent, lumpen lower class. They shifted from small subsistence farming, hunting, fishing, and herding to tenancy and sharecropping and to wage earners as mill workers, miners, and factory hands. Most poor whites and blacks became tenants and sharecroppers in a competitive situation. The poor white, in short, was for the first time reduced to an equal work status with the black, which intensified white racism.

One-crop agriculture (cotton), poor farming methods, declining crop prices, poor transportation, marketing problems, and the dearth of credit reduced many poor whites and yeoman farmers to sharecroppers. Tenants and sharecroppers (primarily blacks) lived on the landlord's farm or plantation in small dogtrot or shotgun frame houses. The "tenant" was really not a true tenant because he had no rights on designated strips of land that he and his family farmed for the landlord. Usually, he brought something to the agricultural situation besides his hands (seed, fertilizer, mules) and paid the landlord one third of his crop in so-called rent. The sharecropper, the most typical agricultural laborer, brought nothing to the agricultural situation but his labor and received one half of the annual crop. The landowner usually underwrote credit for both types at a country store. The landowner marketed the crop and subtracted his rent before passing on shares to tenants and croppers. In short, a plantation system continued with the use of sharecroppers for labor rather than slaves (Woodward 1951, pp. 175-93). Although sharecroppers and tenants did hae the freedom to move from one landlord to another, neither white tenants nor croppers enjoyed the freedom or work status they enjoyed before the Civil War as either self-sufficient yeoman farmers or marginal poor whites.

Millions of people were poor and hungry in 1865, and the Bureau of Refugees, Freedmen, and Abandoned Lands passed out rations to the hungry and provided hospital and health services to poor blacks and whites. During the Reconstruction period (1865-77) many poor whites rejected public welfare, public education, and health care provided by the U.S. government as "nigger programs." In short, they chose poverty, illiteracy, and ill health over integration. During the antebellum period they had nver received such services from their governments. Though the Southern poors' economic and political situation actually worsened following Reconstruction and the restoration of white Southern rule (state governments were returned by the United States to white Southerners in the 1870s), they supported (or acquiesced to) the new Southern aristocrats who took over after Reconstruction (planters, industrialists, merchants, textile mill owners, mine owners, bankers).

One by one, states of the old Confederacy passed new constitutions, disenfranchised blacks and poor whites, and set up the all-white primary. The Bourbons, called Redeemers, the new Southern white leaders and members of the Democratic party, reduced state budgets for public programs funded in the Reconstruction period by property taxes (primarily from landlords and industrialists). Welfare, health, and public school education programs were curtailed and turned over to the counties. Moreover, the Bourbons inaugurated the poll tax, the grandfather clause, literacy tests, and property qualification for voting, which removed many poor whites as well as blacks from participation in the political process (Stamp 1960, pp. 155-215).

Many yeoman farmers and poor whites helped bring these conditions about by their votes and by their physical violence against blacks and supporters of the radical Republicans (those in power during Reconstruction). Many from all social classes engaged in violence as members of the Ku Klux Klan and Knights of the White Camelia, two white hate groups organized primarily to deny blacks their legal rights (Stamp 1960, pp. 186-215). Race, rather than class identification, remained the poor white's problem along with his penchant for following his social betters.

The Mill Workers

The establishment of cotton mills throughout the South in the 1880s, 1890s, and early 1920s signaled a civic sectional "progressive" movement in the name of creating a new industrial South and furnished employment for the millions of white dispossessed and dislocated tenants and croppers who were sinking to the blacks' economic status. As many white tenants were faced with poverty and competition on the land with blacks (many white landlords preferred the docile black croppers), they responded to the Bourbon spokesmen's call for the new industrial order, the "New

South," which promised them a better life in the mill towns and mining camps of the Piedmont and Southern highlands. Thousands moved off the land and became wage earners in the 1880s through the end of the nineteenth century in textile mills, lumber mills, furniture factories, tobacco factories, coal mines, and iron- and steelworks. Most were exploited in a system combining private ownership, abundant raw materials, surplus labor, racism, political conservatism, and the lack of (or weaknesses of) labor unions. During the 1880s thousands of poverty-stricken white tenants moved into mill villages in the Piedmont region where they worked for no more than 50 cents per day. In many respects, the mill living and working situations were similar to those found in the paternalistic system of the antebellum plantation, and conditions of health and sanitation were worse. The conditions of other wage earners were little better (Woodward 1951, pp. 200-34).

Cotton mill workers initially lived in small, shoddy, segregated company houses and traded at company stores. By the 1920s many rented or owned their own modest homes in crowded slum mill sections of Southern towns—that is, they were still segregated in undesirable residential areas.

By 1900 the Southern mill worker was described as an inferior physical type similar to his ancestors, the poor whites, in antebellum times. A dead-white skin, sunken chest, and stooping shoulders were the earmarks of the breed. The women were stringy-haired, shrunken hags at 30 or 40. In 1900 they worked 68 to 72 hours each week as compared with 56 to 58 in New England. The incidence of tuberculosis, insanity, epilepsy, and pellagra was high. Middle- and upper-class Southerners referred to them as *the factory hill trash, cotton mill trash, lint heads, cotton tails,* and *factory rats.* Mill workers attended separate churches and schools, although the mill towns had adequate church and school facilities, because the upper classes snobbishly objected to association with them and because they felt uneasy and embarrassed among their social betters (Cash 1941, pp. 200-10, 250-70).

As late as the beginning of the 1930s, North Carolina textile workers were packed into squalid mill slums and were short of food and clothing. Many were suffering from pellagra, rickets, undernourishment, and other dietary diseases (Mertz 1978, pp. 4-5).

The Poor White Caste System

Poor whites lived under an institutionalized castelike social class system under the Bourbons. The middle and upper class and the political leaders did not believe in political equality among whites, and they feared the white masses as much as or more so than the black masses (Kousser

1974, p. 251). Poor whites and blacks were excluded from the political process and divided by racial animosity—an animosity exacerbated by the middle-and upper-class whites who dominated county and state government, including the legislatures, sheriffs' offices, and schools. These leaders felt no responsibility toward the needs of the poor, and class lines were strictly drawn along social and associational lines. Rarely, if ever, did wage earners or tenants socialize with or marry into middle- or upper-class families. Very few poor whites (sharecroppers, wage earners) became landowners or managers. Even churches became polarized along class lines within the same denominations—that is, members of the same denominations attended separate churches that were constructed for different social class memberships. Pentecostal and Holiness churches after 1900 attracted more lower-class folk.

Class rigidity stemmed from several sources: an indolent, get-by attitude; Bourbon rule following the Civil War; racism; one-crop plantation agriculture; poor farming methods, poor transportation services; the lack of credit and banking facilities; illiteracy; and poor health augmented by a lack of doctors, clinics, and hospitals (Flynt 1979, pp. 20-30). Finally, the antebellum plantation mind concerning class and caste persisted (Cash 1941, pp. 158-70).

Dissent

Finally, some class consciousness developed, as was exhibited by the Knights of Labor in the 1880s and the so-called Populist revolt of the 1890s. The Knights, an industrialized, integrated union, organized in Philadelphia in 1871, supported an eight-hour day, boycotts and arbitration, a graduated income tax, and consumers and producers co-operatives. This organization, with the help of local leaders, attempted to unite Southern poor white textile workers, farmers (including some tenants), and blacks in the 1880s. The Knights organized Southern locals, which included white and black farmers, textile workers, sugar cane workers, timber workers, and urban craftsmen. Though the memberships of some locals were interracial, most blacks and whites were organized in separate groups in the South despite the fact that the Knight's ideology was antiracist. They did foster some industrial integration in a common class cause, elected several city and state officials, initiated and won some strikes, and prepared the way for the Populist revolt and the creation of the Populist party in 1891. The failure of the strike as a weapon, conservatism, and reactive violence caused the Knights's decline after 1886 (Degler 1974, pp. 326-50).

The professed political strategy of the Southern Populists (the Populist party organized in 1891) was to form an alliance between the

South and West and to form an alliance between farmers and city and factory laborers within the South. In reality, the Populists constituted a conservative farmer's party, not a labor party. Despite a radical rhetoric, the principal concerns were to help the farmer get better prices for his crops, to reduce the costs of the things he had to buy, and to defeat the one-party system (the Democrats). The Populists failed to unite poor white Democrats and black Republicans because of racism (even among themselves), which proved stronger than economic considerations. Most white Southerners who voted Populist during the 1890s went back to the Democratic party from whence they came (Tindall 1967, pp. 5-7).

The so-called Progressive cause in the South, which was based on Populism, continued through World War I. Its cause, however, was founded chiefly on the aspirations of the middle-income groups to own and develop productive property; it drew its strength from merchants, mechanics, successful farmers, small manufacturers, and the bankers and factors who served the farm economy. Progressivism in the South was traditionalistic, individualistic, and conservative. Though Southern "Progressives" desired government programs to benefit farmers and to restrict big business, most opposed labor unions, restrictions on child labor, and social legislation. Their idea was that "God fixes man's lot and things were about right anyway" (Woodward 1951, pp. 229-34). The Southern Populists did very little, if anything, for the poor whites, and many were rabid racists. Most of the poor whites supported the Democratic party.

The Defeat of an Already Weak Movement

Despite labor unrest and strikes in the 1890s and the growth of labor unions in the South after 1900 under the primary aegis of the American Federation of Labor (AFL), the Bourbons via cooptation and violence (strikebreaking by city and state law enforcement officials, company guards, planters, townsmen, and conservative church organization memberships) weakened, if not destroyed, the poor white's stake in the so-called Progressive movement. Racism, a fundamentalist religious orientation (though a few preachers and church members in some mill villages supported the Populist cause), individualism, a distrust of outsiders, and a traditional economic dependency on the middle and upper classes militated against the development of strong class consciousness, labor unions, or any basic economic structural change. Even the AFL, the chief labor organizer after 1900 in the South, adopted a racial policy based on skilled crafts, that discriminated against black workers.

In this postbellum period (1865-1920), much of the pre-Civil War folk culture continued. Superstition and otherworldly religion persisted. Tall tales, home health care practices, and the lyrics to country music reflected a hard, painful existence. From 1880 to 1920 a series of black lynchings spread across the South. For the most part, lynch mobs consisted of poor, uneducated, landless whites who acted in the name of the protection of white womanhood. Actually, real or alleged rape was involved in only one fifth of the lynch cases during this period. Lynch victims were scapegoats and targets for a frustrated, powerless, white underclass. Despite the fact that some blacks and whites came to realize some mutual class interests during this period, racism prevailed, permitting the middle- and upper-class whites to divide and conquer (Flynt 1979, pp. 54-56).

Probably one of the chief reasons for the failure of Southern Populism to do much of anything for the poor whites was its leadership. From the farmers' movement in the South during the 1890s to the 1920s, a number of Populists claimed to be leaders of the poor whites—for example, Tom Watson, Ben Tillman, Coleman Blease, and James K. Vardaman. They flaunted upper-class proprieties, appealed to narrow prejudice against the rich, city folk, blacks, Catholics, and Jews, and made empty promises to the poor whites. Most of these so-called leaders were demagogues who became very conservative after election. Some of these leaders, such as Blease, stirred up racial violence in the region. Only in Texas and Oklahoma, the Southwest, where society and the economy were less bound by tradition and status, did a real Progressive movement (a Socialist party) make headway between 1909 and 1923. The membership and strength of this indigenous movement was based upon local tenant farmers (Tindall 1967, pp. 20-24).

Cash (1941) has claimed that the characteristic ways of thought and feelings formed in the antebellum period were reinforced between 1865 and 1900. The four years of fighting and then the "ordeal" of Reconstruction bound Southerners of all classes together in a nexus of common memories that strengthened Southern individualism and the lack of class awareness. The white Southerner, further, identified with the South the "Lost Cause," the power of the Democratic party, white supremacy, and Calvinism, along with hedonism, the romantic myth of the Old South, and the "savage ideal" (antiintellectualism, racism, sectionalism, sensuality, hostility to new ideas, unreality, parochialism, cruelty, violence, and fantastic mythology). To Cash the 1920s also witnessed a flowering of cultural demagoguery coupled with the savage ideal, which he likened to the prevailing ethos of Nazi Germany, Fascist Italy, and Stalinist Russia— as evidenced by demagogues, the revival of the Ku Klux Klan, the Scopes "monkey" trial (in Dayton, Tennessee, in 1925), religious fundamentalism, Prohibition, and expressions of opposition to new ideas. In short, Cash stressed the cultural continuity of the Southern mind through time and the failure of Southern leadership. To him the Southern mind was a collective mind so embroiled in the pathos of its own past that it failed to gain a tragic dimension (Cash 1941, pp. 319-42). Southerners were quick to resort to violence and cruelty to defend and maintain a narrow religious, class, political, and racial ideology. Unfortunately, this penchant continues.

Many have assumed that the Southern savage ideal evolved from an aristocratic ideology traceable to the English manorial system as evoked by the chivalry of the English gentleman and his overseas counterpart and cousin, the Southern planter. There never was a Southern aristocracy in the more refined European sense. An aristocracy cannot be established within a period of less than 50 years (circa 1820-60). Moreover, so-called Southern aristocrats, planters, unlike the English gentlemen, fashioned an ideology derived from a rugged and cruel frontier life, an agricultural system based on slavery, and a fantastic ambivalent mythology. To the authors the ideology of the so-called Southern aristocracy was more similar to the credo and behavior of the ancient Celts and Iberians or at best the Spanish and German knights of the fourteenth century.

However, as W. I. Thomas, a famous social psychologist, once remarked, "If men define situations as real, they are real in their consequences." Certainly Southern planters defined themselves, and were defined by other Southerners, as aristocrats. And many, if not most, likened themselves to characters from the novels of Sir Walter Scott. To this authorship they resembled more closely characters in the more recent Gothic novels. On the other hand, as Tuchman points out in her book *A Distant Mirror: The Calamitous 14th Century* (1978, pp. 62-64), the *prime essentials* that made a *chevalier preux* were courage, strength, and physical prowess. Honor, loyalty, courtesy, and "courtly love" were the lofty ideals far removed from the actual reality that hopefully sustained chivalry— even in its breach. Fighting was something to do or a substitute for work, and hunting and jousting were the knights' (gentlemen's) leisure time pursuits. A necessary Christianity and cruelty undergirded the whole savage ideal. The Southern planter qualified on the prime essentials and did not fall too short on some other criteria. Like the knight, he was a romantic, violent, sensual, Christian man of action whose loyalty and "code of honor" functioned only with coequals. The lower classes were to be used and abused if necessary. Both, of course, were avid womanizers and often exploited women. The yeoman farmers who became planters turned their backs on their former peers and eagerly embraced all components of their new class status in similar fashion to those commoners who achieved nobility in fourteenth century Europe.

THREE

POOR WHITES IN THE 1920s AND 1930s

THE BENIGHTED SOUTH AND THE POOR

The South remained a poor, "benighted" region during the 1920s, characterized by underdevelopment, racism, Protestant fundamentalism, antiunionism, sectionalism, and violence (Tindall 1967, pp. 184-218). The revival of the Ku Klux Klan between 1915 and 1925 signaled and authenticated a mass folk social movement including militant Protestantism, fundamentalist antievolutionism, nativism (anti-Catholic, -alien, and -Jew), antiunionism, antimodernism, antiliberalism, and anti-intellectualism. Southerners reacted negatively to social change and feared new and alien ideas; the loss of white supremacy, Southern religion, and morality; the status of Southern womanhood; and Southern hierarchical social arrangements; further, they feared the loss of the South's identity and the traditions and mythologies of the past. Blacks were lynched, strikers were beaten and sometimes killed, "modern" books were removed from public schools and university libraries, and the preachers railed against all new ideas and heretics from the pulpits. Poor whites were held responsible for most of the violence, particularly participation in lynch mobs. The major responsibility for the whole reactionary social movement and the attendant violence rested on the shoulders of the white upper-class membership that supported nativism and permitted (and, in some instances, abetted) the lynching. Poor whites followed their leaders and did their bidding without having to be instructed (Cash 1941, pp. 334-39).

23

World War I brought relative prosperity to some Southern poor whites in the form of industry jobs and higher farm prices (especially cotton and tobacco). The wartime demand for cotton, lumber, coal, and textiles improved employment opportunities and wages. This relative prosperity of a few, however, glossed over the squalid conditions of the millions of poor. The 1920s brought argricultural surpluses, reduced farm prices, and decreased the demand for textiles. Consequently, foreclosures, bankruptcies, and unemployment followed. Many yeoman farmers were reduced to tenants. Rural poverty persisted. In 1930 the South was still 67.9 percent rural, and 42.8 perent of its work force worked on farms at a per capita income of $189 in contrast to the $1,484 for nonfarm occupations. Average earnings in industry for 1927 were $671 in cotton goods, $748 in lumber and timber, and $823 in Southern industry as a whole (Tindall 1967, pp. 111-15). The Great Depression aggravated rather than caused Southern poverty in the 1930s. In 1929, the end of a "booming" decade, the average per capital income for 12 southeastern states was only $368 and that of Texas was $487, compared with $703 for the nation. The average per capita income of the Southeast was $204 in 1932; it was $262 in Texas and $401 in the nation (Schwartz and Graham 1956). In 1929 the per capita income of the Southern farm population averaged $183 in the Southeast and $298 in Texas. Per capita wealth in 1930 was below $1,110 in Mississippi, and it was $2,620 for the nation (Odum 1936, pp. 46, 48, 75).

Before the crash in 1929 there was widespread depression in the old cotton belt as well as a decline in landownership and a loss of farm animals by share tenants. After 1929 the tenancy system began to decline, either driving many sharecroppers out of agriculture or reducing them to irregular wage hands. By October 1933 depression conditions had forced on relief more than one eighth of the families in seven southeastern states. The Federal Emergency Relief Administration found in the early 1930s that many blacks were living better off in the South on relief than they had in their usual agricultural employment, and they were difficult to remove from the relief rolls. Urban relief case loads were crowded with chronically poor whites, many of whom were migrants from the country. Poverty was widespread in the South prior to and after the 1930s, but it was most evident among several million tenant farmers, sharecroppers, and agricultural wageworkers (Mertz 1978, pp. 4-18).

Tenants and Sharecroppers

In 1930 tenants and sharecroppers comprised 1,091,944 white and 689,839 black families, accounting for about one quarter of the South's population and half its farmers. They included about 8.5 million individuals (5.5 million whites and over 3 million Negroes) in a nonurban population of about 18 million. The birthrate was the highest of the country's regions (Odum 1936, p. 463). These tenants and the share-croppers were the largest single block of the nation's rural poor.

In 1880 tenants operated 36.2 percent of all Southern farms; by 1920, 49.6 percent; and by 1930, 55.5 percent; by 1930 they operated 60 percent of the cotton farms. In the decade before 1930 white, landless farm families increased by 200,000 or about 1 million persons, compared with only 2,000 additional black families (Johnson, Embree, and Alexander 1935, p. 1). Cash tenants—in the minority and numbering about 205,000—leased land for a specified period and paid as rent a specified sum of money or a stated amount of the crop. They provided their own utensils, work stock, fertilizer, and the like and financed the farm operation. These farmers were independent of the landowner's supervision and were better off financially than tenants and sharecroppers. Share tenants (about 0.5 million farmers) provided at least some of their own utensils, farm equipment, and goods (for example, all or part of the fertilizer, work stock, feed, and/or livestock). Landlords furnished a stated amount of farmland (parcels of their farms), a house, and equipment the tenant lacked. Cash, food, and subsistence goods were provided the tenant during the year, or the landowner "stood for" the tenant's credit (underwrote) at one or more stores. Some planters owned plantation commissaries, which furnished the tenant his goods on credit. Share tenants worked on a yearly verbal contract under the landlord's work supervision. The landowner marketed the crop and gave the tenant three-fourths or two-thirds of the cash returns minus advances and credit costs. Sharecroppers (383,000 whites and 393,000 blacks, 44.6 percent of all black farmers) comprised nearly half of all Southern tenants (the poorest category among renters). Sharecroppers, propertyless workers, brought nothing to the agricultural work situtation but their hands and were paid with a portion of the crops they raised—usually half the proceeds of the crop minus the cost of all furnishings plus interest (Raper 1936, pp. 146-48).

The landlord held a statutory lien on the tenants part of the crop, which entitled him to market it and deduct the costs of all advances plus interest. The landlord kept the books, and frequently many ignorant and illiterate tenants did not know the amount of their indebtedness or the interest rates, which varied from 19 to 71 percent. The landowner generally engaged several sharecroppers and/or tenants on his farm, depending on the size of his holding and the number of tenant houses. He usually had to borrow money from the bank to finance farming operation and his tenants' subsistence. To this end he frequently borrowed money himself on a lien system and in very lean years had to mortgage his land. He claimed that the tenant had at least lived at his expense even if he, the tenant, did not come out with any cash at the end of the year—that he, unlike the tenant, had to pay off his heavy debts. Many landlords claimed they had to exploit their tenants to profit from the "furnish" or tenancy system because of fluctuating farm crop prices, the weather, a credit squeeze, and the laziness of some tenants. Many felt that low-class tenants deserved only a bare existence, and some were just plain greedy and dishonest. During the 1930s tenants' average cash per capita income was about $200 per year, and that of sharecroppers was about $122 annually. Some tenants and many sharecroppers came out with no cash return at the end of the year. Moreover, some found themselves in debt to the landlord (Woofter 1936, p. 36).

The economic conditions of agricultural wageworkers were worse than those of tenants. Throughout the 1930s the ranks of these day laborers grew with the decline of the furnishing system. The effects of the New Deal crop control measures and increased farm mechanization pushed many tenants off the land. By 1933 an estimated 200,000 dispossessed rural families received federal relief in cotton counties from Arkansas and Louisiana eastward. In 1940 these laborers in the same general area numbered 842,000. They lived in unoccupied shacks on farms but received no furnishing from the landowner. The etimated annual earnings of all these family members averaged no more than $160 in 1934 (Woofter 1936, p. 36).

Croppers' Life-Style

Housing and Furnishings

In the 1920s and 1930s the typical tenant lived in a small (two- or three-room), dilapidated, unpainted frame clapboard house supported on stone, logs, stumps, or concrete blocks, loosely constructed with inferior lumber. Roofs were made of tin or rough-hewn pine shingles. Sometimes doors and windows were without glass in the 1920s, and in most cases they were unscreened. Interiors were frequently unceilinged. Walls were not plastered but covered with several layers of newspapers and old magazines for insulation. There was no inside plumbing, running water, pumps, or electricity. Kerosene lamps provided light. Sometimes outside privies existed. The floors were bare, and heat was provided by open hearths and crude wood stoves. No dwellings were weatherproofed, and many had cracks in the walls and roofs through which the wind and rain poured. They were unbearably hot, smelly, and full of dust and flies during the spring, summer, and fall and very cold and dank during the winter. Frequently, the occupants slept in their clothes on beds without springs or mattresses. Household furnishings were sparse and crude. Often there was not a complete set of dishes, and glasses and pots and pans were at the minimum. Those without kerosene stoves cooked on the open hearth. Many drank from Mason jars. Scraps from the table and dirty dishwater were thrown from a back porch window onto the hard-packed and grassless backyard. Bath water had to be heated in a dish pan and wash rags and towels, always in short supply, were made of old rags and old bed sheets.

Privacy and the necessity for cleanliness were not appreciated. Therefore, few baths were taken, usually no more than one per week. Infants were infrequently bathed for fear that they might catch cold. Dogs and cats slept under and in the house, which was frequently infested with fleas as well as flies and other insects. Dishes, forks, spoons, and kitchenware were seldom properly cleaned because of the inconvenience of heating water.

Diet and Health

The poor white's diet was indeed poor. The furnish system rarely consisted of more than a few foods: fat salt pork, hunting and fishing game meat, lard, flour, cornmeal, molasses, sugar, salt, and dried beans and peas. Landlords and bankers discouraged gardens because the precious land was needed for cash crops (cotton and tobacco). Tenants, in any event, displayed little interest in gardening after spending long hours in the cotton, sugar cane, or tobacco fields. The farm owner showed more interest in gardening and appreciated a more varied diet consisting of fresh vegetables. Tenants concentrated on pork and chicken (when they could get it), potatoes, and bread. Few croppers had cows, pigs, or poultry.

These sordid and deprived living conditions undermined the health, disposition, and economic and social productivity of the poor. Malaria, rickets, pellagra, hookworm (many rural people could not afford shoes), childhood diseases, dental diseases, tuberculosis, and various communicable disorders prevailed at a high incidence. In 1938 *The National Emergency Council's Report on Economic Conditions of the South* to the president described the cotton states as a "belt of sickness, misery, and unnecessary death" (Hopkins 1934, pp. 29–32). Trips were seldom made to the doctor and only if one were seriously ill. Patent medicine and folk home health care practices prevailed—for example, herbs, poultices, asafetida, and sassafras tea. Lay conjurers, faith healers, practical nurses, pharmacists, and chiropractors were frequently utilized. Doctors, clinics, hospitals, registered nurses, and licensed pharmacists were scarce in small towns and outside county seats.

Land Tenure and Education

Land tenure was based on one-year verbal contracts between tenant and landlord, and tenants moved every year or two in search of better landlords and living conditions. This mobility and frequent disagreements with the landlords did not make for conservation or improvement incentives related to the land, farm buildings, farm equipment, houses, and other property. The cropper owned little, frequently felt exploited, and cared for little—certainly little that belonged to the landlord.

Southern rural schools were poorly equipped and run. There has never been enough money per schoolchild available in the South in comparison with other parts of the country. Family mobility did not make for school adjustment. Illiterate and semiliterate parents did not prepare their children for school or help them much after they got there. Tenants, for the most part, did not stress education for their children. They and the landlord needed them in the fields. Landlords picked croppers in large part on the number of field hands they could bring to the farm situation. School attendance was infrequently enforced. Schoolteachers in the rural and urban South paid very little attention to the lower-class poor pupils. In many cases, croppers and mill workers' children were automatically considered dumb trash and dismissed from attention in or out of the classroom during the 1930s, 1940s, 1950s, and even the 1960s. Rarely did poor children take part in school plays and extracurricular activities in the 1920s through the 1940s. Many dropped out of school, a punishing situation, before graduating from high school—and many earlier on. Illiteracy rates were high among croppers and mill hand workers during the 1930s, 1940s, and 1950s.

Recreation and Church and Social Relations

Recreational pursuits included hunting and fishing, an occasional attendance at a country or revival meeting, a monthly or bimonthly trip to town, and visits to neighbors. Hunting and fishing also provided much needed food. Card playing and dancing violated the religious views of most of the respectable poor and remained primarily a middle-class thing. Many without motor transportation in the 1920s and 1930s traveled to small towns and villages (rural area service centers) in mule-driven wagons and two-wheeled carts on Saturdays for an outing—and to shop for staples, whiskey, candy, snuff and tobacco, and patent medicine. Sociability took the form of tale swapping and gossip in general stores, street drinking and camaraderie, courting, flirting, drinking, gambling, and fighting; there was also movie going and pool shooting after the late 1930s, 1940s, and 1950s. Model T's and A's and trucks served as transportation in the late 1930s and 1940s. Traveling medicine shows and an occasional carnival also provided entertainment. The whole family usually came to town, but the adult males wandered off from the womenfolk and children who gathered in knots on the street to socialize among themselves.

White and black croppers segregated themselves in separate milling areas and ate, drank, and fraternized in separate cafés and bootlegger joints in or nearby town. Often the bootleg operation was fronted by a service station or a private house and provided a focal point for male gossip and an occasional white or black whore for those who were interested. A few croppers both black and white wound up in local jails on drunk or assault charges and were usually "paid out" by landlords on Monday morning. They were known to the police or sheriff by the name of the landlord they "belonged to,"—for example, "The man in the first cell belongs to Mr. Jones, the 'nigger' in the second cell belongs to Mr. Tom."

Small groups of young couples managed to cluster and walk up and down the streets together away from the prying eyes of the adults. There was little open display of affection and sex play among the young or older couples. Secret sex activities occurred in dark corners, on vacant lots and the back lots of stores, on school, church, and graveyard grounds, in wagons and carts, and often after the late 1930s, in the movie theaters and back seats of cars and trucks. Heavy alcohol drinking (whiskey or wine) by males (straight out of bottles and Mason jars) accompanied sociable encounters and the courting and sex play scene. Condoms (middle-class devices) were rarely used, and therefore pregnancy usually followed by marriage ensued at an early age (15 to 19).

Middle- and upper-class whites, especially women and children, stayed off the streets on Saturdays to avoid any contacts with the throngs of white and black croppers and their families. Sex appeared to be a hit-or-miss perfunctory sort of thing among croppers, who were quite puritanical in this area. Men and women bragged about never having seen their spouses naked. Sexual foreplay was rare among them. Sex was something necessary, but one had to get it over with quickly in the dark. Middle- and upper-class whites and blacks enjoyed sex, which became an art form among many, particularly among white men and some black women in strict secrecy. Many white men left small pieces of property to their black female lovers, and many black families live on these small farms throughout the South today.

Cropper women and children and occasionally adult males attended small, one-room, frame fundamentalist country churches usually of the Primitive Baptist, Holiness, Church of God, Church of Christ, and Baptist denominations serviced by itinerant, uneducated, working-class preachers. Services were characterized by the emotional singing, swaying, weeping, shouting, hollering, amening, and open testimonials of members of the congregation and by the loud, rasping, hollering, and frenetic exhortations of an ignorant, bitter, bombastic, racist preacher man. No middle- or upper-class Southerners were in attendance. Middle- and upper-class whites attended separate churches of the missionary type (main-line Baptist, Methodist, Christian, Presbyterian, and Episcopalian) that were serviced by seminary ministers and tied in with denominational associations, colleges, and other similar church congregations. Poor white churches were (and still are) more oriented toward a local, isolated congregation.

Croppers and other poor whites had no social contacts with the middle and upper classes. They lived in separate neighborhoods, went to separate churches, shopped at different times, avoided the same social space, attended separate parties and dances, and were even, in most cases, buried in different cemeteries. When buried in the same graveyard, croppers were interred in marginal sections—that is, along the borders or in low-lying sections away from middle- and upper-class whites. Croppers and working-class whites were looked down upon as social inferiors by their betters who did little to disguise their contempt and felt superiority—for example, middle- and upper-class members frequently called croppers by their first names.

Factory and Mill Workers

Economic Conditions

Many poor urban whites worked in textiles, lumber, furniture making, tobacco processing, coal mining, and iron and steel production as cheap labor (without labor unions until the late 1920s) throughout the 1920s and 1930s. The oldest and most numerous single group of Southern industrial workers were cotton mill hands who numbered about 400,000 in 1930, a fifth of the total Southern factory workers. Most were new arrivals and former croppers from nearby agricultural areas. During the first three decades of the twentieth century, the average annual wage reported by the census for ten Southern states fluctuated between 60 and 70 percent of that for the rest of the country except during the postwar boom of 1919 when it reached 73.9 percent. The average annual wage per production (nonagricultural) worker in the South in 1937 was 63.2 percent of that in the non-South; in 1939, 64.9 percent; and in 1947, 74.1 percent. Government-imposed minimal wage standards, rather than unionism, were responsible for this improvement. Throughout the 1930s Southern wages ran at least 25 percent below Northern wages in lumber, furniture, rubber, fertilizer, soft drinks, and food (Tindall 1967, pp. 319-20; 535-38).

From the 1880s onward through the 1930s, thousands of tenants moved into the cotton mill villages of the Southern Piedmont. White male mill workers made $1.75 to $2.50 a day in 1920, and white women made from $1.34 to $1.84. When the Fair Labor Standards Act applied to a 32.5 cents minimum wage in July 1940, 55 percent of the workers in the men's clothing industry and 43 percent of the workers in the shirt industry were earning less than this minimum. In the late 1920s through the 1930s, strikes for higher wages occurred in mills throughout the Piedmont South, but they failed for a number of reasons: the textile industry's poor economic state, a surplus labor supply, the lack of leadership, the lack of knowledge about industrial relations, and a poor white folk culture (that is, individualism, other worldly religion, self-sufficiency, orientation to the present, a history of getting by, and hostility to new ideas).

Southern workers were mobile, apathetic, mercurial, and ignorant about the need for permanent unions to protect their industrial relations with management and owners. They would strike for specific reasons but did not exemplify staying power. The presence of strikebreakers and the dearth of, or weakness of, labor unions did not help. Many were turned off by labor leaders and members whom they deemed too radical or socialistic. The New Deal in the 1930s tried to protect the workers' rights to collective bargaining, but the mill employers found ways around these efforts (Cash 1941, pp. 243-80; Flynt 1979, pp. 69-74). Throughout the 1920s and 1930s, particularly in the textile industry, the Southern middle- and upper-class political leaders, the bankers and businessmen, the corporations, the schools, the press, the clergy, and the local and state law enforcement personnel and administrators of criminal justice fought labor unions (Cash 1941, 296-300).

Social Relations

In the 1920s Southern cotton mills were increasingly owned and operated by absentee Northern owners. Southern foremen were employed to keep the workers more docile. Paternalism ended, and mill workers on their own in terms of housing and shopping. During the 1920s and 1930s they lived under slum and semislum conditions in segregated white neighborhoods and attended separate schools and churches from the middle- and upper-class Southerners. Many belonged to the Holy Rollers, the Church of God, and Baptist churches where they became sanctified and hollered, jerked, and spake in unknown tongues and listened to hellfire and damnation fundamentalist preachers. A wide social gulf separated them from the upper classes and from non-mill town neighborhood dwellers.

Mill worker children and other town children did not associate outside the classroom even in public schools where both groups were in attendance. Frequently, two annual, separate senior class plays were staged, one for the "lint heads" or "mill trash" and one for the other children. Despite these economic and discriminatory social conditions, the urban wage earner fared better in the 1920s and 1930s than did agricultural workers.

Discovery of Poor Whites and the New Deal

Growth of Awareness

J. Wayne Flynt (1979, pp. 74-75) points out that Americans became aware of Southern poverty in the 1930s when poor whites became part of a national crisis, the Great Depression. Actually, widespread poverty had always prevailed in the region. Several Southern novelists and journalists portrayed the destitution of poor white Southerners from the 1920s through the 1940s, calling the national public's and the federal government's attention to the problem. Unfortunately, most dealt with the conditions and consciousness of individuals rather than with the underlying class structure. Though these writers described the conditions of poverty and the characters involved in relationships to the unique Southern scene, among other things, very little was said about underlying causes or answers to the problem. In fact, most of the poor were ennobled for their forbearance, endurance, fatalism, dignity, and valor in the face of poverty. The Southern sensual, nonintellectual mind, as Cash would have put it, produced sensual, nonanalyzing writers and characters. A few illustrations follow: Edith S. Kelly in *Weeds* (1923), Erskine Caldwell in *Tobacco Road* (1932), Marjorie Kinnan Rawlings in *The Yearling* (1938), Thomas Wolfe in *Look Homeward Angel* (1929), William Faulkner in *Light in August* (1932), James Agee in *Let Us Now Praise Famous Men* (1941), Lillian Smith in *Killers of the Dream* (1949), William Percy in *Lanterns on the Levee* (1941), Elizabeth Maddox Roberts in *Time of Man* (1926), Caroline Miller in *Lamb in His Bosom* (1933), and Jonathan Daniels in *A Southerner Discovers the South* (1938).

Several Southern reactionary writers adapted a more sanguine approach to the region and took a stand against its critics, particularly toward those such as H. L. Mencken who defined the South as the "Sahara of the Bozart" (King, 1980, p. 53) in 1916. For example, in the late 1920s a group of poets at Vanderbilt University recruited several academics and social scientists and published a number of essays in a book entitled *Twelve Southerners, I'll Take My Stand* (Ransom et al. 1930). These essayists called for the return of the South to the so-called Jeffersonian ideal: to a "democratic" organic hierarchical agrarian order that had once allegedly existed in the antebellum South—an order based on private property held together by cooperation between planters and yeomen, an order at best committed to an aristocratic class society and to a separate but equal racial policy. These writers claimed that Southern poverty had produced a culture of great value that was jeopardized by "progress," capitalism, and communism and held that tenants felt life on the land was not all bad despite the poverty. The so-called Jeffersonian agrarian ideal probably never existed, certainly not after 1820 with the entrenchment of the plantation system.

Some of the writers in *Twelve Southerners, I'll Take My Stand* and in other published pieces fashioned what could be called a literary agrarian movement, but their ideas neither reached the masses nor were they part of any practical program. To the contrary, many Southern intellectuals rejected the thesis of a neoantebellum society in a capitalistic machine age, as well as the idea that the best life for the South's poor and common folk was subsistence agriculture. The agrarians were nostalgically interested in planters and yeoman farmers and had little thought for the landless poor whites, other than the fuzzy idea of doing away with the rural proletariat, which could only have been accomplished by taking land from the planters, an unheard of radical thought by Southerners though a feasible one that had been considered by some radical Republicans in the Reconstruction period—no land distribution, no real reconstruction.

Some other writers, primarily sociologists and human geographers, adopted a so-called scientific approach to poverty in the South. Howard Odum, a sociologist—along with Rupert Vance, Guy B. Johnson, Guion Johnson, and Harriet Herring, among others—published a series of works in the 1930s and early 1940s consisting of plans for the Southern poor and the South's revitalization. Odum's chief work and the benchmark for the group was *Southern Regions of the United States*, which was published in 1936. Actually, the published works of this University of North Carolina group, called the "regionalists," contributed more to scholarship about the South's people, culture, geography, history, and economy than to any immediate plan to help the poor. The Odum group's findings and planning suggestions did call attention to the "problem South." The regionalists proclaimed the need for regional harmony and the integration of the South into the nation. Their numerous publications centered on social, geographic, and economic data on the South, diversification of agriculture and the economy, academic and vocational education, industrial development, regional planning boards, farmer's cooperatives, efforts to keep educated Southerners in the South, and the beloved Southern folk culture (customs, music, handicrafts, language, and religion) to which poor whites had made important contributions.

Though regionalism was *for* the people, it was not to be *by* the people.

According to the Odum group, the social problems of the poor were to be solved by scholarly technocrats within a capitalistic racially segregated society without any analysis of the class structure or any redistribution of the wealth. Odum abhorred political conflict, conflict theory, and socialism. To him and most of his followers, education, a gathering of the facts, sweet reasonableness, separate but equal facilities, and the implementation of economic planning procedures within the system could and would solve the South's problems. Obviously, the regionalists were naïve, wrong, and too conservative. However, most Southerners in the 1930s and 1940s, including the professionals and academics, considered the regionalists to be dangerous radicals, "that socialist crowd at Chapel Hill that didn't have any religion or respect for the South." Odum never understood this, nor could anyone else but a nonsociologist Southerner. Many of the regionalists' research findings and planning ideas were adapted in the New Deal program and thereby helped some of the poor. The most lasting detriment of the Odum program, in our view, has been his and others, insistence that we maintain a Southern folk culture even though it is clear that certain elements therein (religion, clannishness, provincialism, antiintellectualism, racism, fantastic historical mythology, and a savage ideal) perpetuate the region's problems.

A few Southern scholars saw that small farmers, tenants, mill and factory workers, and blacks were being exploited as an underclass. For example, Broadus and George Mitchell in *The Industrial Revolution in the South* (1930) described the dire poverty and working conditions of mill workers and called for an "industrial revolution" by the unions to do away with paternalism. Arthur Raper and Ira Reid in *Sharecroppers All* (1941) described the deplorable conditions of tenancy and pointed to racial division and attendant class inequalities as the cause of poverty and the depressed wages among blacks and whites. They noted the racial and social class inequalities and the deprivations that were the real causes of the South's low economic position and its social problems, that is, in comparison with other regions. They advocated racial equality and strong labor unions.

Herman C. Nixon in *Forty Acres and Steel Mules* (1938) called for a class analysis of the South, which directed attention away from attributing its problems to a colonial status. He depicted the grim life of tenant farmers and laborers and interpreted the South's past ills in terms of class conflict (a very radical position at that time). According to Nixon, since the Civil War the South's colonial economy had been run by a commercial gentry in cooperation with the merchant and the planter who were both tied to the financial East. He recommended rather vague land reform and rural cooperatives such as those in Scandinavia—for example, planned communities and rural villages. Negroes were to be included as equals.

The plan was to be financed with capital from the U.S. government rather than from the private capitalist sector. To Nixon, class division and inequalities were at the seat of the South's problem, and he called for interclass justice among united blacks and whites.

With the exception of Nixon, Cash in his book *The Mind of the South* (1941) probably explained the class position of the poor whites in the South with keener insight than anyone before or since. The poor white, despite his individualism (developed from a caste-bound, harsh, semi-frontier society), identified with *the Southern destiny* as embodied in the planter class that exploited him daily: the "Lost Cause," white supremacy, racism, provincialism, and anti-Yankee liberalism, modernity, and new ideas. In short, the poor whites lived by the dictates of a fantastic, unrealistic Southern myth. Incapable of detachment, often illiterate or semiliterate, fearful of threats from blacks below and Yankees outside, misled by political demagoguery, and possessed by a harsh Calvinistic religion and a sensual nature, the common white man suffered from false consciousness, a lack of social responsibility, and a "savage ideal." The savage ideal was likened to the ethos of Nazi Germany, Fascist Italy, and Stalinist Russia.

Unfortunately, Cash provided no program for changing the South's class structure. He did note the weakness of Southern leadership and the chasm that existed between the few liberal Southern intellectuals and the masses, and the politicians. Cash indicated the need for a higher caliber of political and economic leadership, a sense of social responsibility, and the end of violence, intolerance, and racism. He defined *mind* as a mental pattern associated with a certain social pattern—a complex of relationships and habits of thought, values, sentiments, prejudices, and ideas common to white Southerners. The Southern mind was flawed because it was too sensual, romantic, pristine, and childlike. It could feel but not think. Therefore, the gallantry, manners, generosity, whimsicalness, hospitality, warmth, interpersonal charm, gushing affection, and exaggerated patriotism as well as the gothic touch, chauvinism, racism, narrowness, rigidity, staunchness of "moral principle," self-righteousness, ethnocentrism, and cruelty were used as justifiable and sometimes necessary devices to maintain the Southern way of life.

Along these lines the authors have noted that Southerners of all classes can do almost anything they want to other people, including physical harm, so long as they do it within their sense of propriety. They can also completely ignore the physical or mental condition of the person or persons they have punished with a feeling of rectitude. In short, "the bastard got what he deserved anyway, or maybe not enough." Such action and feelings are particularly prevalent among middle- and upper-class Southerners in their dealings with rednecks.

In her autobiography, *Killers of the Dream* (1963) Lillian Smith supported Cash's thesis that the cardinal feature of the mind of the white South is its mythological transmogrification and denial of reality. To her the problem of race tied in with sin—that is, sex—and segregation was the South's chief problem. Southern policy, according to her, was founded upon a tacit agreement between upper-class whites and poor whites that blacks were to be excluded from power in society and that poor whites would not challenge upper-class rule.

Additionally, like Cash, she traced many of the South's problems to poor leadership and an inadequate religion. Fundamentalism and its preachers stressed the fear of eternal damnation and the sins of the flesh rather than the quest for justice, the social gospel, and the joys of the senses. Spiritual equality was separated from political and social equality and individual responsibility from social responsibility. Christianity was (and is) convoluted in the Southern tradition, which resulted in psychic and emotional confusion and guilt. Guilt was transformed into hate for those (blacks) toward whom whites felt guilty, which resulted in aggression against the oppressed. Deep down the whites knew they were wrong. Poor white women envied the high status of upper-class white women. Poor white men accepted the white upper-class male's sexual fantasies about black women (supposedly more sensual and comforting than sexless white women). Things intellectual and humanitarian religion became feminized and the province of white women. God remained a powerful and vindictive father to all, but men resented the religious asceticism and its "civilizing" goal. Smith called for the abolition of the poll tax, the white primary, discrimination in defense jobs, and segregation in the public sector. She was a liberal publicist who advocated moral, psychological change within the existing economic system during the 1940s, 1950s, and early 1960s (R. King 1980, pp. 174-93).

The New Deal

Though the foregoing works reached a national audience and a few Southern social scientists and college students (who, for the most part, ignored or laughed at them) and intellectuals, the poor whites were not a part of such an audience, nor did they have much to say about politics and economic planning during the depression era. The middle and upper classes, government technocrats, and political planners ran the show. The poor whites who did not supported Franklin D. Roosevelt's policies along with the small businessmen, a small group of professionals, farmers, clerks, and wage earners. New Deal policies were put together without the South by the federal government in Washington. Some Southerners (particularly a few liberal ones such as Lister Hill and Hugo Black from Alabama, Huey

P. Long from Louisiana, Sam Rayburn from Texas, and Claude Pepper from Florida) helped Roosevelt engineer his program through Congress. Roosevelt had strong Southern political support as well as some Southern opposition when his program swung from recovery to reform (Works Progress Administration, social security, the Wagner Act, tax policy against the rich, and the Farm Tenant and Housing Acts of 1933). After this he encountered increasing strong Southern political opposition (Tindall 1967, pp. 607-49).

SOME SPECIFIC NEW DEAL PROGRAMS

Parity

President Roosevelt and his progressive administration became involved in the South's problems in May 1933 with the passage of the Agricultural Adjustment Act. The goals of the price parity programs under this act in the South were to reduce cotton production, thereby raising the price and diverting land to other crops; to reduce the dependence of croppers on landlords; to free croppers from an exploitive credit system; and to improve tenancy conditions or enable tenants to escape it. The act actually injured tenant farmers. In 1933 some landlords plowed up their share of the crops and received government subsidies, while their tenants were denied such aid. The cash payments made to the farmers to plow up cotton and to reduce cotton acreage (take land out of cotton production for government "rent money") were not distributed fairly. The cotton contracts awarded the lion's share of the benefits to the landowner, who received the checks and then supposedly distributed them to his dependents (croppers on a share basis). Tenants were supposed to receive larger shares than sharecroppers. Wage workers received no benefits. Frequently, the landlord did not pass on any payments to the croppers. Furthermore, landlords often evicted their croppers despite their legal obligation to keep the normal number to avoid the division of government cotton payments with them.

The displacement of croppers was massive as planters converted croppers to wage labor because it paid to do so. The total number of sharecroppers in the South declined between 1930 and 1935 for the first time in more than five decades. Many tenant farmers became agricultural laborers or unemployed rural squatters. Planters moved some marginal lands from production and through the use of heavy fertilization of the remaining tracts of land produced almost as much cotton as before (Mertz 1978, pp. 44).

Rural Rehabilitation

The second major New Deal approach to poverty in the South was rural rehabilitation. The Federal Emergency Relief Administration (FERA) that began operations in 1933 was the New Deal's first real program to improve the condition of the rural poor in the South. The FERA granted funds to Emergency Relief Administrations (ERAs), which furnished weekly direct relief ($4 to $6.76 per family). In 1935 the Resettlement Administration began lending propertyless croppers and laborers money to acquire work stock, implements, and equipment in an effort to raise them to the status of share tenancy. Furthermore, under the Farm Security Administration (FSA), loans were made to 20,748 tenants for the purchase of land with the aim to convert tenants into small landowners. The lack of funds required the denial of 20 applications for every 1 granted.

The rehabilitation programs were limited primarily because of Southern conservative politicians, but they did reach more than 0.5 million cases in the South with functions ranging from subsistence grants to the very poor and dependent to assistance that permitted a few capable tenants to buy farms. The programs proved inadequate to reach the bulk of the region's poor. With more funds, a more radical approach, and congressional backing, more could have been done to help the landless poor (Mertz 1978: 260-61).

Failure of the New Deal

At the end of the 1930s, the tenant problem was still not solved. Mechanization of Southern agriculture after the late 1930s and the phasing out of the FSA (by political enemies who sniped at it as a socialist agency) in the 1940s killed the ideal of transforming the rural poor to small land-holding farmers. Appropriations for World War II took precedence over the FSA as well as other New Deal programs. Southerners' as well as outsiders' attention to the poor was diverted to the general economic development of the region following the return of relative prosperity after 1936. The needs of the poor began to be neglected in favor of programs for industrialization and the diversification of agriculture in keeping with the 1938 *National Emergency Council's Report to the President on Economic Conditions of the South* (Mertz 1978: 232-40). This report, though documenting the millions of Southerners in poverty with attendant health, education, and income problems, focused on the general question of what could be done to stimulate economic programs, rather than centering on how to help and uplift poverty-stricken individuals directly.

The New Deal agencies did not solve the tenancy problem or, for that matter, poverty in the South, but millions of the poor received some form of New Deal agency aid. Many would not have survived without New Deal assistance. Conservative politicians, many of them Southerners, impeded New Deal efforts in behalf of the poor by promulgating the false and ridiculous notion that many New Deal agencies (for example, the FSA) were socialist or communist. Needless to say, middle- and upper-class whites dominated the Southern scene and the politics of the New Deal, and many of them could not see "all the government aid to the poor. A man should get with God and support his family; and, there had to be something wrong somewhere with losers—poor whites, trash, rednecks." Many Southern journalists, community leaders, big businesmen, big farmers, and members of the clergy expressed bitterness and resentment toward the federal government for berating the region and meddling in its economic, political, and social affairs. In short, many claimed there was nothing really wrong with the South that Southerners could not straighten out themselves (an ancient and false song).

Southerners, including some of the poor, denied the region's, as well as their own, impoverishment. Many of the poor accepted their condition fatalistically and looked for solace in their religion and folk culture. They were poor but proud of their customs, race, historical heritage, region, and religions. The ineffectiveness of the New Deal era, then, stemmed from several sources: the lack of basic social class structural change (which it never attempted to affect), the failure of Southern leadership, self-serving class interests, and false consciousness tied to otherworldly religion and racism. The impoverishment of millions of Southerners continues (Mertz 1978: 221-62).

THE RADICAL GOSPEL MOVEMENT

Ideology and Goals

The most radical Southern progressive program to help the poor was proclaimed during the 1930s in the name of a "radical gospel" movement. A small group of radical Protestant preachers developed its ideology, Christian socialism, based on the teachings of Christ and Marx. Individual leaders and followers of this numerically small movement varied in political stance from pacifistic Christian socialists to outright revolutionary communists. Most, initially, espoused eventual governmental ownership or control over the basic sources of wealth and the means of production, though there was no agreement on how or when this was to be accomplished. All agreed that the world could not be redeemed through man's good works or beliefs but rather through the rising up of the poor. Revolution was imminent and the poor needed *their* leadership. The participants may have only occasionally viewed themselves as part of a single movement and their political strategies differed, but they did have many things in common: youth; formal or informal religious, educational background; idealistic resistance to racial and economic injustices; a religious calling; and the precarious style of life imposed upon them as a result of their "revolutionary" activities (Dunbar 1981, pp. 60-62).

The membership was active in three major fields. They sought to help the South's poorest people—sharecroppers, textile workers, and the unemployed—through community and labor union organizing and education. They fought racial segregation in all forms and attempted to get liberals to stand up and fight on this issue through the courts and by personal behavior. Finally, they sought to draw the mainstream of Southern churches into the struggle for social justice through the expression of a biblical message of human liberation (Dunbar 1981, pp. 73-75). They won some battles and minor concessions regarding the first two goals but failed in the third because the overwhelming number of Protestants and their leaders maintained a conservative, individualistic, and otherworldly stance.

Leadership and Associations

Many indigenous leaders were Protestant ministers representing both the liberal and fundamentalist persuasions, with the liberals affording most of the enduring leadership roles. Several politically left-wing national organizations acted as a nucleus and support base for action, including the New York-based Fellowship of Reconciliation, whose Southern secretary was Howard A. Kester; Reinhold Niebur's Committee on Economics and Racial Justice; the Emergency Committee for Strikers Relief, chaired by Norman Thomas, a prominent socialist; the Church Emergency Relief Committee, chaired by Alva W. Taylor, a Disciples of Christ minister and professor of social ethics at the Vanderbilt University School of Religion; and the Socialist party. The Vanderbilt University School of Religion, directed by the Reverend James Myers (industrial secretary of the Federal Council of Churches), served as a mecca for the training of radical ministers durings the 1930s. Alva W. Taylor was the academic mentor of several active members in various movements, though he remained aloof from many of their "radical" exploits: for example, Howard A. Kester, a socialist preacher, educator, and union organizer from Virginia; Ward Rodgers, a socialist preacher and union organizer from Texas; Claude Closey Williams, a socialist preacher, educator, and labor organizer from

Tennessee; and Don West, a socialist preacher, educator, and labor organizer from Georgia (Dunbar 1981, pp. 19-82).

Myles Horton from Tennessee and James Dombrowski from Florida were also two important socialist preachers in the movement. Horton and West organized the famous Highlander Folk School near Monteagle, Tennessee, in 1932. Initially, it was a "settlement house" in a rural setting where neighbors were welcome to visit the farm and attend workshops where they heard a blend of religious talk, discussion about agricultural problems, and criticisms of the establishment. The staff later trained Southern labor leaders and civil rights leaders and organized unions, cooperatives, and left-wing political activities. The school's staff also extended assistance to strikers' activities and to strikes and labor organizing drives in the South as well as to strike victims and victims of racial disturbances. Christian socialism was taught in classes. By 1947 Highlander had trained 6,900 unionists despite opposition from Southern antiunionists, newspapers, politicians, and vigilantes. Another radical school, Commonwealth College at Mena, Arkansas, founded in 1925 as a workers college, served as a training ground for strikers and supported a strong militant cause during the 1930s (Tindall 1967, pp. 633-34).

Though Southern radicals solicited the power and help of the federal government, national organizations, the national press, church organizations, the Socialist party, and the Communist party, they developed several indigenous radical organizations of their own: Sharecroppers Union, Southern Tenant Farmers Union, Highlander Folk School, Commonwealth College, Fellowship of Southern Churchmen, Southern Conference for Human Welfare, Southern Conference Education Fund, and the Southern Regional Council, among others.

The Southern Tenant Farmers Union

Organization and Goals. The radicals were distinguished from other groups by their keener desire to organize the victimized group (for example, the poor, and racial and labor victims) than outside do-gooder groups. In this endeavor a few radical leaders organized the Southern Tenant Farmers Union (STFU), the largest and most effective radical organization during the 1930s. A small group of socialists (Harry L. Mitchell, Clay East, Ward Rodgers, Joyce Williams, J. R. Butler, and Charles McCoy) met in Tyronza, Arkansas, in February 1934 to discuss the deteriorating situation of the black and white sharecroppers and tenants on the cotton plantations in eastern Arkansas. Croppers and agricultural wage earners' children missed three or four months of school each year, where there was school, and few adults could read or understand the foreman's arithmetic. Wages were low for agricultural laborers, 40 to 80 cents per day in 1934. Sharecroppers were lucky to come out of the year free of debt. The people lived in shacks, they were hungry, and they did not vote because of the poll tax. Many wage workers were disenfranchised croppers who had been pushed off the land under the Agricultural Adjustment Administration (AAA). Cut loose from the land, many sought day-by-day wage work on the plantations. These farmers knew that the landlords had illegally pushed them off the land to collect cotton land subsidies. With proper leadership they were ready to organize (Dunbar 1981, pp. 82-91).

In the spring of 1934 Hiram Norcross, the owner of a 5,000 acre plantation near Tyronza, evicted 23 of his 248 tenant families to avoid lending them money to get through the planting season; 11 white and 7 black men from among those evicted met with Mitchell and East in a schoolhouse near the Norcross place. Though the AAA refused to intervene in this case (because the evicted sharecroppers were not parties to the contract between Norcross and the government), the STFU was organized ostensibly to establish cropper bargaining power with landlords and the equitable treatment of tenants under the AAA regulations. The real goal of the biracial union was landownership, which was spelled out in the preamble of its constitution—the demand for the return of the land to the landless.

STFU activities became a sacred Christian movement, and union meetings included hymns, prayers, and sermons about a richer life on the land. Many labor leaders were socialist preachers. All leaders believed in the principles of Marx and Jesus and considered themselves to be Christian revolutionaries. Their radical plan called for the U.S. government to buy up all farmland except tracts smaller than 160 acres, producers' co-ops, and farms operated by local governments. Public land was to be leased to tenants and cooperatives on the basis of need for a period of 99 years. In short, the STFU wished to do away with the plantation system of farming and supplant it with socialized cooperative agriculture. At its peak this union had 328 locals and over 30,000 members in Texas, Oklahoma, Mississippi, Tennessee, Missouri, North Carolina, and Arkansas. Croppers who desired to join the union were chartered as community councils under the leadership of one who could read and write. The membership fee was ten cents, and the dues were ten cents a month. A deficit of funds was one of the STFU's greatest problems (Dunbar 1981, pp. 83-160, Tindall 1967, pp. 416-24).

Weakness, Failures, and Victories.   From its inception throughout its history, the STFU was hampered by powerful political opposition from middle- and upper-class whites throughout the social structure, particularly in the black belt of the cotton South. Members were lynched, beaten up, and sent to jail and prison on trumped-up charges. Politicians, governors, and state and local leaders cooperated with law enforcement officers, vigilantes, and strikebreakers in the disruption of their meetings and strike activities. This organization rapidly lost membership, prestige, and influence following its unification with the Congress of Industrial Organization (CIO) in July 1937, a union that did not respect its autonomy. It split from the CIO in 1939 to avoid a communist image, but by this time the zeal and the purpose of the organization had past.

Several specific factors, in the authors' views, were involved in the collapse of the sharecroppers' movement under the aegis of the STFU: the inability of its leaders to work together because of ideological differences; its refusal to combine with the radical Alabama-based Sharecroppers Union and the Commonwealth College leaders (that is, the more radical elements in the movement); and its inability to combine the necessary power and force of collective socialism with the pacific Christian ideas. More general factors include the pervasive power of Southern political reactionaries, conservative Protestantism, the prevailing racism and antiunionism, the failure of aid and support from the national labor unions, conservative pressure within and without the organization, and the impending World War II (which caused millions of rural workers to move northward from plantations and small towns to cities with booming war industries).

Though it fell short of a successful and enduring labor union, it achieved several things for poor people. It won a few strikes and elevated wages; exposed the situation of peonage and forced labor in Arkansas; precipitated government investigations of tenancy conditions; gained greater recognition for the constitutional guaranties of civil liberties; brought government benefits and grants, Works Progress Administration (WPA) jobs, and fairer contracts with planters; elected union members to New Deal committees (for example, AAA committees); gained free textbooks for black schoolchildren; exposed the sharecroppers' plight to the public and the federal government; and contributed to the establishment of the FSA (Mertz 1978, pp. 31-32).

The STFU called for the establishment of collective bargaining, old-age pensions, workmen's compensation, unemployment insurance, abolition of child labor, educational facilities and opportunities for children of farm workers, and equal pay for equal service regardless of reace, sex, or nationality (Dunbar 1981, pp. 164-65). Finally, it proved that whites and blacks could work together in labor unions. Unfortunately, a lack of funds, public support, and steadfast militancy and revolutionary zeal in the face of great odds tore it apart. Certainly the national power structure would never have accepted its revolutionary land policy.

The Southern Conference for Human Welfare and the Fellowship of Southern Churchmen

In the 1930s the last major radical endeavor of Southern dissenters for the poor was the Southern Conference for Human Welfare (SCHW) established in Birmingham, Alabama, in November of 1938. This organization's main task, with the knowledge and encouragement of President Roosevelt, was to ensure the passage and implementation of New Deal measures. The political spectrum covered by its membership varied from moderate liberals such as Frank Graham, the president of the University of North Carolina, and Christian socialists such as Howard A. Kester to those with close ties to the Communist party such as Joseph Gelders, the Southern representative of the National Committee for the Defense of Political Prisoners from Alabama. This organization fostered civil liberties (particularly those pertaining to the abuse of communist and union organizers in Alabama), the elimination of state poll taxes (which prevented poor whites and blacks from voting), civil rights, prison reform, the easing of farm tenancy problems, playground facilities for Negroes, women's bureaus in each state, and the eradication of racial discrimination. The committee blamed the House Un-American Activities Committee (HUAC) established in 1938 by Congress to investigate un-American activities for discrediting New Deal policies for the poor.

Martin Dies, chairman of the HUAC, charged that the SCHW had been organized and dominated by the Communist party immediately following its first conferences in Birmingham. Howard A. Kester, the best known and probably the most respected and influential of the Christian dissenters in the South, identified several members of the organization as communists, including Joseph Gelders from Alabama, its chief organizer, along with other Christian colleagues. Further, he publicized his opinion that the Highlander Folk School staff, tied in closely with the SCHW, was communist. These statements by Dies and Kester caused many moderates either to leave the organization or withdraw support. The committee lived on until it was dissolved in 1948, fighting the poll tax and lynchings. Accusations of being communist, congressional investigation, internal ideological battles, and the lack of President Harry Truman's administration support finished it off (Dunbar 1981, pp. 187-200).

Kester's reports about communists in the SCHW and the Highlander Folk School broke up a tight circle of radical gospel activists (including himself, Claude Williams, Don West, Myles Horton, and James

Dombrowski) who had established the Fellowship of Southern Churchmen (FSC) through, and by, the Conference of Younger Churchmen of the South in 1934. The FSC, a regional ministerial fraternity, was the radical Christian fulcrum of the 1930s. Its original program called for a socialist political party comprised of all races. All natural resources were to be held in common, poverty and class were to be eliminated, and capitalism was to be done away with. At the same time, it called for a greater commitment to a Christian God and more justice for the disinherited and oppressed.

The problems and struggles among capitalists, fascists, and communists in Europe preceding and following World War II and the split among Christian liberals, socialists, and communists in the United States splintered the membership of the organization. It lost its revolutionary fervor in the late 1930s and, for all practical purposes, was through by 1939. But it lingered on until 1963, promoting the cause of labor, racial equality, and rural life improvement. The organization's loss of the national Socialist party's support, internal ideological conflicts, and its withdrawal from a socialist economic program were its undoing (Dunbar 1981, pp. 216-27).

Expectations Denied

With the drift into World War II, government investigations, ideological in-fighting, a retreat from radical economic principles, the loss of national organization support (including that of the Socialist party), and the adamant resistance of main-line Christians and churches, many Southern dissenters dispersed—and their once radical organizations became attentuated and dissolved, or they were coopted by less regional and militant associations. The New Deal, which the Christian radicals had fostered and supported, actually coopted and transformed their radical programs into a conservative mode. The Southern Farmers Tenant Union (SFTU), for example, was tamed down by New Deal measures such as the FSA created in 1937. Finally, the SFTU was renamed the National Farm Labor Union, now a part of the American Federation of Labor, and moved to Bakersfield, California, in 1948. This marked the end of the agricultural union movement in the South.

The Highlander Folk School, the cradle for Southern labor organizers, was finally closed in 1961 by a Tennessee court on the trumped-up charges of peddling beer and whiskey and practicing racial integration in violation of Tennessee law. Small quantities of beer and liquor for personal staff purposes were found on the premises; integration had always existed. Previously the school had been investigated by the Central

Intelligence Agency (CIA), the Senate Internal Security Subcommittee, and the Internal Revenue Service (IRS). Many of its staff members were investigated by the Federal Bureau of Investigation (FBI).

Socialism did not resurface in the South following World War II because of a prevailing conservative mood, the cold war, and the aggressive investigatory programs of the FBI and the CIA. Part of the radical gospel program died in the 1930s and a part lived on in the Civil Rights movement (1950s, 1960s) and in the 1960s War on Poverty. The fatal error of these latter two intertwined movements was the separation of racial equality from economic equality. The enduring interests of both programs had been voting rights, desegregation, and equal employment opportunities without any challenge to the economic system. In short, the blacks and whites could now be poor together. Neither movement proposed an economic plan calling for structural change. The radicalism of the 1930s had passed on.

The Radical Gospel Movement in Retrospect

In retrospect the explanation of the radical gospel movement in the South during the 1930s is difficult but necessary. Succinctly put, How could such activism occur in a "benighted," traditional society? The answer to this question is essential to an appreciation and understanding of the most enlightened and noblest undertaking in Southern history. (The happenings in Louisiana under Huey P. Long were generated from the same bag.) Moreover, the answer might prove valuable to those interested in future social change in the South. The stage was certainly set for attempts at radical social change. An increasing number of white people were dispossessed, underemployed, unemployed, destitute, and hungry. Additionally, the two pivotal traditional institutions, the agricultural system and the church, no longer met basic human needs. But what was new? We suggest that the synchronization of three conditions was critical: the cataclysmic dispossession of and separation from the land in a traditional agrarian society; an increasing knowledge of and interest in socialism and the "Russian revolutionary experiment" in academia and among intellectuals (including schools of religion and liberal ministers); and the appearance of a small group of zealous, humanitarian, poor country preachers who experienced a spiritual compelling drive to action for the poor.

The first two elements are well known; however, the third necessary constituent has often been wittingly or unwittingly overlooked. The small coterie of preachers who led the radical gospel movement were not Southern gentlemen nor the sons of the planter or professional class but rather the products of tenant farmer, yeoman farmer, and blue-collar families. The "call to preach" served their religious, educational, mission-ary, and leadership aspirations. It was very difficult for any but middle-and upper-class folk to go to college in the South until after World War II. However, religious education in this region then (and now) was heavily subsidized by various Protestant denominations at both the four-year and seminary levels (the Disciples of Christ Church was especially helpful). The preacher man, of course, held a high status in the Bible belt.

This explanatory attempt is a reconstruction of past social reality and therefore vulnerable to oversimplification. All history, however, is written from the viewpoint of the present—there is no other way. Finally, the Christian message does contain many socialistic principles. Who is to say that the prophets "against the grain" were not sui generis and *right*?

FOUR

POOR WHITES SINCE THE GREAT DEPRESSION

POOR WHITES IN THE 1940s AND 1950s°

Poverty and Dislocation

During this period many reasoned erroneously that New Deal measures, World War II prosperity, and some unionism had eliminated poverty in the South. Certainly economic conditions among the poor in this region had improved on the basis of per capita income and improvement in housing, employment, health conditions, public services, and educational facilities, though a wide gap remained (and still remains). The South is perennially said to be "catching up." After the 1930s several factors contributed to this relative prosperity and a reduction in the numbers of poor whites: out-migration (2.5 million, mostly poor, left for the North and West during the 1940s), technological change, the expansion and dispersion of industry, diversification of agriculture, and urbanization. The mechanization of agriculture, industrialization and city jobs, urbanization, and technological change contributed to the out-migration of the rural poor (the most significant and enduring poor group). Many found factory and unskilled labor work in the urban South; many migrated to the North (Flynt 1979, pp. 94-101).

°Official poverty statistics were collected in the United States in 1959, for the first time since the Great Depression. Since this time poverty standards have changed, depending on stipulated real income, thresholds based on minimum income, number in the family, and inflation rates. We utilize the official definition existing in the time period referred to. We also include the characteristics associated with poverty—for example, poor housing, inadequate diet, hunger, unemployment, poor health conditions, and lack of educational facilities.

49

The large majority of those who migrated to the urban South found employment in low-wage industries. The AFL-CIO achieved success in organizing a few (especially the highly skilled) but failed with the many unskilled and semiskilled workers, particularly those in the textile industry where many women were employed. Overall unionism failed during this period because of the same old historical reasons. Southern workers, nearly all with rural backgrounds, were individualistic and, at the same time, geared toward paternalistic relations with their social and economic betters. They preferred a Southern boss to an outside labor organizer. Rural impoverishment and a perennial labor surplus situation rendered them employable at a much lower wage scale than workers in other regions, and racism prevented many from joining integrated unions. Institutionalized religion, for the most part, opposed unions, especially that religion promulgated by main-line, middle-class Protestant churches. Southern newspapers, politicians, and businessmen were antiunion. Finally the South's basic industries—namely, textiles, food products, lumber and wood products, apparel, and chemicals—employed many woman, who were difficult to organize (Flynt 1979, pp. 96-102).

Those poor whites who migrated to Northern cities were frequently discriminated against in seeking employment and housing because they were considered unreliable, dirty, lazy, undereducated, unskilled, and overly independent in spirit. Outside and self-discriminatory patterns also occurred in social relations, for example, in friendship associations, work contacts, bar and tavern sociability, and church membership and at-tendance. To Northerners white Southerners, regardless of regional background (coastal plain, Piedmont, mountain), were (and are) all hillbillies by definition and therefore ignorant, clannish, slum, unskilled "poor white trash" from the South. Moreover, they were dirty (without standards of hygiene and sanitation), immoral, heavy drinking, violent people. Hillbillies were not accepted into other white community groups, formal and informal associations, and institutions and therefore remained isolated as ethnic Southerners. Our respondents in the North, both locals and migrant Southerners, tell us this exclusionary process still operates and that migrant Southerners to the third generation perpetuate a Southern life-style.

Exclusion and self-segregation reinforce one another.

Migrating Southern blacks, on the other hand, were (and still are) accepted by the Northern black community. Furthermore, blacks suffered less industrial employment discrimination (Killian 1970, pp. 102-13). This is not to say that Northern blacks do not make some distinctions between themselves and recent black migrants from the South. They do, but recent family and friendship ties with Southern blacks, the brotherhood of race regardless of class (because of universal discrimination against all blacks), the large numbers of lower-class Northern blacks, and the recency of middle-class status among many Northern blacks preclude the degree of discrimination toward their Southern brothers as that found among Northern whites toward white Southern migrants. Finally, on this point, Northern black communities were (and are) more long-lived than the more recent white Southern migrant communities.

In actuality many Southern migrants to Northern cities were (and are) semiliterate, provincial, ignorant, unskilled workers who found themselves isolated and discriminated against in the big city where neither their customs, accents, dress, religion nor their rural view fitted in. Many expect to stay just long enough to find work, save a little money, and leave when things got better "down home." Many compose a transient group (from and to the South) that usually find things worse than ever in the South upon returning and remigrate again and again to the North (Bruns 1973, pp. 102-08).

Millions of poor whites who lost agricultural employment during the 1940s because of agricultural mechanization, crop diversification, and technological change did not migrate. They eked out an existence in backwater rural areas where they were often forgotten by affluent society in and outside the South. They remain the unfinished business of the New Deal (Mertz 1978, p. 97). Millions of these poor whites were overlooked until the beginning of the John F. Kennedy administration—they lived in Appalachia, the rural cotton South, along the coastal plains and in the urban South where they were either blue-collar workers in small enterprises or industrial workers. The total number of people affected by agricultural dislocation was appreciable during the 1940s and 1950s. White farm families comprised only 7 percent of the total number of families in the United States in 1960, while they included 16 percent of the poor. Of the 16 million rural persons in poor families in 1960, three fourths were white, and over half of these lived in the South, over 6 million people (Flynt 1979, p. 97).

Political and Intellectual Mood Shift

A conservative mood and political stance has prevailed in the United States and in the South since the Great Depression, especially prior to and following the presidencies of John Fitzgerald Kennedy and Lyndon Baines Johnson. A measure of prosperity during the post-world war years led many politicians to grow more conservative on social and economic issues. Many Southern writers (for example, John Temple Graves, Virginius Dobney, Willie Morris, Cleanth Brooks, and Robert Penn Warren) moved to the Right, if in fact they were not already there (R. King 1980, pp. 243-50). Southern politicians reacted strongly against

Negroes who tried to assert their rights (for example, voting and employment rights) after World War II, the New Deal measures still persisting, and organized labor. From 1941 through 1950 all Southern states passed "right-to-work" laws and union registration laws, which have crippled the labor movement to this day in all Southern states (Tindall 1967, pp. 687-731). The post-1954 realignment of Southern politics proceeded under a conservative and/or racist dispensation—that is, the Republican party, conservative Southern Democrats, and third-party (for example, George Wallace) splinter groups grew while Southern "liberalism" disappeared. With the exceptions of the black movement in the late 1950s and the 1960s and the anti-Vietnam War movement, there has been no liberal or class movement in the South through the 1970s and into the 1980s. Poor whites in the South joined middle- and upper-class whites in attempts to thwart the Civil Rights movement and the War on Poverty in the 1960s. The little Southern liberalism that existed in the South during the 1930s appears to be dead.

No liberal or radical political or social movement in the South can ever be successful without the unification of lower-class whites and blacks on specific goals and implementation procedures. The first requirement for any meaningful structural change requires, first, the unification of strong white and black leaders along class rather than race lines. Then the masses might be persuaded to work for the common good—whatever that is decided upon.

REDISCOVERY OF POVERTY IN THE 1960s

The War on Poverty and Some Aftermaths

During the 1950s the problems of economic inequality, poverty, and discrimination in the United States were considered to be outside the realm of public policy with the exceptions of social security and unemployment insurance. This national position, under the aegis of President Dwight D. Eisenhower, a hero and popular president, marked a shift from governmentally controlled and regulated capitalism, which was advocated in the 1930s under the New Deal, a shift historically in keeping with the prevailing American traditional position. The Eisenhower presidency ended with a serious economic recession. During the 1960s inequality, poverty, and discrimination moved to center stage, and the South again became the nation's number one economic problem. Poverty was rediscovered in the South.

The first official stirrings that eventually led to the War on Poverty began with President John F. Kennedy's Council of Economic Advisors under Walter Heller, which proposed several ways to combat poverty including full employment, economic growth, the end of discrimination, better health care, education and training, regional and community development, and direct cash assistance to the aged and disabled. President Lyndon B. Johnson followed and expanded the Kennedy lead. He declared war on poverty in 1964 to expand, among other things, health, housing, education, and training programs and to increase transfers in cash and in kind. Johnson converted state and local governments into federal instruments for achieving these goals by federal aid formulas to mayors, governors, and state agencies.

Statistics Relating to Income and Wealth in the United States during the 1960s

The most comprehensive statistics relating to poverty available during the 1960s were figures on the distribution of income, which showed no year-to-year change in the distribution of income from 1948 to 1960. The bottom fifth (quintile) of families and unrelated individuals received between 3 and 3.4 percent of total U.S. income, while the top fifth received between 43.4 and 50 percent. This pattern remained through the 1970s. Little has been made of, or done with these statistics, which disclose the persistent relative poverty (Aaron 1978: 15-22; 148-50; Kolko 1962, p. 14).

A small group of individuals and families hold an unusually large proportion of the total income and wealth in the United States. Dominated by about 2,000 family fortunes, 1 percent of the total population owns and controls high concentrations of property including real estate, cooperate stock and bonds, family trusts, capital goods, unrealized capital gains, and inheritances. Property is the foundation of wealth much more so than is income; property changes hands to produce profits, while incomes (mostly wages and salaries) are usually applied to the satisfaction of basic human needs such as food, clothing, and housing. About 30 percent of the nation's private wealth is held by 1.6 percent of the adult population (Lampman 1962, p. 23); 1 percent of the population holds 80 percent of the total corporate stock, and the top 5 percent of this 1 percent (.0001 percent of all adults) holds 40 percent of the total (Anderson 1974, p. 144). This concentration is due largely to the fusion of industrial and banking assets and finance capital. Through family trust funds, banks have reached out singly or in combination to gain controlling interests in almost 30 percent of the top 500 industrial corporations (Patman Committee 1972, p. 74).

Stock ownership is concentrated in the hands of corporations (that own other corporations) rather than in the hands of individual stockholders, frequently multinational corporations. For the majority, on the other hand, income and wealth are widely diffused; 80 percent of the population owns only 24 percent of the nation's wealth (Turner and Starnes 1976, p. 23), while 86 percent of the population is propertyless by virtue of owning no stock whatsoever (University of Michigan, Survey Research Center 1960, p. 474). Based upon a detailed review of government documents concerning property distribution, Ferdinand Lundberg (1968, p. 23) claims that 70 percent of Americans are poor. Gabriel Kolko (1962, p. 101) claims that half the households in the United States have incomes inadequate for the maintenance of minimal standards of comfort and well-being. When the worth of all families is tabulated, 56.9 percent of families make only 66 percent of the total net worth (Turner and Starnes 1976, p. 22).

Certainly U.S. society is a class society wherein the system of production is owned by one segment of the society to the exclusion of others. Most of us are relatively poor, but the Southerners are poorer.

POVERTY—SYMPTOMS AND SOLUTIONS

The War on Poverty came to encompass Office of Economic Opportunity (OEO) programs plus such traditional programs as social security, public assistance, veterans' benefits, public housing, urban renewal, Medicare, and Medicaid. Following the Johnson administration, OEO programs have been either terminated, reduced, and/or transferred to other federal or state agencies.

Most of the OEO War on Poverty education and training programs were by-products of projects directed primarily toward the middle class. They were poorly planned, passed in haste, and inadequately funded, and, therefore, they failed to transform the poor through education and training. Unfortunately, a great deal of the program expenditures for the poor lined the pockets of middle-class professionals who directed poverty programs rather than the pockets of the poor. Evaluation studies of OEO programs for the poor following the mid-1960s were inconclusive and functioned primarily as political instruments to either support or derogate one or another political group who favored or disfavored particular programs. We do know that legislation enacted from 1964 to 1975 in the behest of the poor strengthened the system of cash assistance and in-kind benefits for temporarily or permanently needy households within and without the South. The apparent failure of transforming the poor by education and training programs was signaled by structural unemployment and inflation, which continue through the 1970s (Aaron 1978, pp. 39-45) and into the 1980s.

When attention shifted from the War on Poverty to the war in Vietnam and later away from both, the dollars targeted for the poor did not decline but, in fact, increased until the mid-1970s—that is, in-kind benefits provided by the federal government to low-income households increased in the form of food stamps, medical benefits under Medicaid and Medicare, housing assistance (under a variety of federal programs including low-rent public housing), and the Legal Services program's legal assistance to the poor in civil cases. In short, what has been achieved is a massive income in cash and in-kind assistance that has made it possible for those unable to earn their way out of poverty to secure a modest or survival living standard. This shift from educational and training programs for the poor to transfer in kind alleviated some symptoms of poverty but did not deal with its causes. Officially tabulated poverty declined from 22.4 percent of all Americans in 1959 to 17.3 percent in 1965 to 12.1 percent in 1969; in 1975, however, it climbed to 12.3 percent (Aaron 1978, pp. 38-39).

Under the Ronald Reagan administration the modest gains of the War on Poverty are in jeopardy because of the budgetary cuts in all programs including cash assistance and in-kind benefits for the poor. Moreover, Reagan's economic and tax policies (the reduction of corporate and business taxes and the taxes of the individual rich), based on supply-side economics and the "trickling down theory," are making the rich richer and the poor poorer—thereby increasing the relative poverty level as well as the absolute number of poor people by shoving middle-class people down into the lower class. A 10 to 25 to 30 percent decrease in income taxes for those making between $10,000 and $50,000 will not remove the substantial sums from the U.S. Treasury that would be required for the provision of essential public services, including services to the poor. Such tax reductions for the rich will make an appreciable difference. Additionally, capital gains and all sorts of tax loopholes and tax credits are showered on the rich and on corporations—for example, tax credits to big oil companies (Roebuck and Weeber 1978, pp. 152-62).

The grossly unequal and unfair distribution of wealth previously mentioned has been upheld by the structure of the tax system, which draws revenue mainly from income and salaries (small potatoes) rather than from wealth, which should, on any fair basis (even in a capitalist society), be the base for major taxation. The Reagan administration has just made tax matters worse with the erroneous belief that corporations when taxed less will gain more money in profits to expand and to invest in new projects, thereby employing more people, gaining more profits, expanding, and so on to infinity. Less corporate tax does not necessarily mean further corporate investment in required essentials either for scarce products (for example, oil) or for employment needs (for example, manufacturing). Corporations invest for profit, and financial institutions only lend money on profitable projects. Both have quick returns in mind. Diversification is the name of the multinational corporation game, not the provision of necessary goods and services and employment opportunities, even when given tax breaks to do so. For example, the big oil companies invest very little in the search for new oil; smaller oil companies with less governmental tax aid take this risk.

Poverty in the South during the 1960s and 1970s

In 1964 the President's Council of Economic Advisors found that one fifth of America's 47 million families (9.4 million families) had incomes of less than $3,000 annually, the poverty level. Nearly half of all Southern families (47 percent) fell below the poverty level, compared with one fourth of the families in the North Central United States, 16.3 percent in the Northeast, and 12.4 percent in the West. There were over 3 million poor white families in the Southern states. Rural residents (farm and nonfarm) constituted less than a third of the U.S. population but accounted for almost half its poverty ("Sudden Drive on Poverty—Why?" 1964, pp. 36-40).

The President's National Advisory Commission on Rural Poverty found that in the 1960s most of the rural South was a vast poverty area plagued by a lack of physicians, hospitals, and dentists; hunger, high rates of disease, early death, high unemployment, poor education, and inadequate housing. Most poor whites and blacks were nonfarm residents who lived in rural areas. As late as 1968, 70 percent of the Southern poor were white. The various OEO programs in the 1960s provided temporary employment and job training for many individuals, but most projects were primarily geared toward urban whites and blacks rather than toward rural folk. During the late 1960s employment in the South did rise, welfare rolls declined, there was a decrease in out-migration from the land, and new hospitals, roads, parks, and water and sewer systems were constructed. Nevertheless, the war on poverty, despite some gains, did not reach the Southern poor in any effective measure. The poor came out of the 1960s as a more alienated ethnic group than they had comprised during the 1940s and 1950s. This situation, which will be explained later, was in part a consequence of the persistence of the poor white indigenous culture (Flynt 1979, pp. 108-13).

By way of example, Senator Ernest F. Hollings of South Carolina testified concerning the extreme poverty conditions in his state before the Senate's Select Committee on Nutrition (U.S., Congress, Senate, Select Committee on Nutrition 1969). He claimed that substantial hunger, squalid housing, primitive sanitation, illiteracy, lack of skills, illness, and unemployment existed throughout his state, and he pointed out that masses of poor people needed food, health care, housing, sanitation and education but that local people would resent outsiders' drawing attention to these conditions. Many of the poor were ignored by the state and federal government and consequently received no public assistance. Many never sought help. Hollings's remarks indicate that the poor and the culture in which they reside have not changed much throughout Southern history. The authors have observed similar conditions in several other Southern states. In spite of these observations, sophisticated opinion polls in the 1970s showed that large percentages of people in the South, when compared with other regions, had unfavorable opinions about the poor— for example, the poor were poor because of lack of effort or because of lack of effort and circumstances (Wohlenberg 1976, 491-505).

Several studies in the 1970s show that relative to the population in other regions the Southern population is characterized as being more rural and more poverty-stricken. The average AFDC (Aid to Families with Dependent Children) recipient in the rural South during the 1970s was a female-based household head with dependent children, who tended to be middle-aged, to have little, if any, work experience, and to have had a low level of educational attainment. The majority of AFDC recipients were not in the labor force. Those who did work were employed in occupations and industries that pay the lowest wages (unskilled, domestic, or agricultural occupations). Less than a quarter of those eligible participated in the Food Stamp Program because welfare officials lent no encouragement and provided no outreach program. Other reasons were the cost of the stamps, extensive red tape, incorrect information, and transportation problems. Additionally during the 1970s, there existed in the rural South many households with an employed head that remained below the poverty level (the working poor). The working poor are not eligible for any welfare programs per se, although they are eligible for food stamps. Because so many impoverished families were (and are) excluded from local and federal aid, and because of the low benefit levels now existing for those who do receive aid of some kind, there is little likelihood that the present system can be restructured by local and state initiatives to meet the needs of the poor of the rural South (U.S., Bureau of Statistics 1978, pp. 28-30).

The South, An Underdeveloped Region

According to the statistical measure of economic well-being utilized (for example, per capita personal income, distribution of income, poverty rate per person and per family, physicians and dentists per 100,000 population, hospital beds, housing conditions, et. cetera) and the period considered, the South has been (and still is) a relatively poor and underdeveloped region in comparison with other regions in the United States. In 1970 the South's average per capita personal income was $3,062, 78.3 percent of the $3,910 average for the nation as a whole. This was up from 50.7 percent of the national average in 1900, and 60.1 percent in 1940. Although the South has made progress in "economic catch-up," per capita income in the non-South was still 38.2 percent higher than that of the South as recently as 1970. Not a single Southern state had an income level that reached the national average in 1972 (Naylor and Clotfelter 1975, pp. 10-12).

Virtually half of America's poor lived in the 16 Southern and border states in 1968, an area that held less than a third of the total U.S. population (*Time*, May 17, 1968, pp. 28-29). According to the 1970 census, 43.3 percent of all U.S. families living below the poverty level (2,343,000 families) lived in the South ("Measuring Poverty Now" 1976, pp. 57-58). The 1970 census figures show that 14 percent of the families in the South in 1969 had incomes of less than $3,000 in comparison with 7 percent for the Northeast and 8 percent for the North Central and Western states of the country. The definition of poverty then was an income of $3,000 for a family of four, plus increments of $500 for each additional member of the family when the family size exceeded four. In 1969, 11.2 million (46.1 percent) of the 24.3 million people in the United States living in poverty were located in the South. Equivalently, 18 percent of the people in the South were still living in poverty in 1969. Of the black families living in the South in 1969, 36 percent had incomes below the poverty level. Median family income for Southern whites in 1970 was $9,240; the corresponding figure for Southern blacks was $5,226; for the United States the median family income was $10,236 for whites and $6,279 for blacks (Naylor and Clotfelter 1975, p. 12).

Of the 26 million Americans living at the poverty level in 1970, 11.5 million (13 percent of the total population) were Southerners, who comprised 45.0 percent of all the poor in the nation and 18.5 percent of all persons in this region; 59 percent (3.4 million) of the poor living in the rural South were white (Ryscavage 1970, pp. 20-21). In 1970, 16.2 percent of Southern families lived on an income below the poverty level compared with 10.7 percent for the United States, 7.6 for the Northeast, 8.3 for the North Central, and 8.9 for the West (U.S. Bureau of the Census 1973). In 1970, 50.9 percent of poor families lived in metropolitan areas, and 49.1 percent lived in nonmetropolitan areas. About two thirds of poor black families were in the South, while 38 percent of poor white families lived in this region. Overall, the South had 46 percent of the poor families in America. The next highest proportion lived in the North Central States, with 22.4 percent designated as poor ("25 Million Poor in the U.S.— Really" 1971, pp. 40-43).

A 1981 Report of the Southern Regional Council

In 1981 the Southern Regional Council in Atlanta reported that President Reagan's new welfare policies will cause more human suffering in the South than any other federal action since the Civil War.

> Forty percent of individuals receiving welfare payments under the Aid to Families with Dependent Children Program will be cut from the rolls by mid-1982, and an additional 20 percent will have their benefits cut if all of Reagan's proposals are adopted, the council charged in the report. As the home of one-third of the nation's poor and half of the country's black poor, the South will be especially hard hit by changes in welfare policies, according to the nonprofit research corporation. The report stipulated that the numbers of those affected by the cuts, "add up like a casualty list in wartime." "Indeed the numbers suggest that the national government has now transferred the War on Poverty of 15 years ago to a war on the poor today." The Council's report claims that not since the Civil War era, "has the national government instituted deliberate policies and practices that will likely cause so many human casualties among blacks and whites on Southern soil."
>
> The document said 10 percent of the more than 2.1 million AFDC recipients in 11 Southern states will lose their benefits in the next five months because of new federal eligibility regulations. Further, the document maintained that an additional 20 percent could be removed if requirements to report income on a monthly basis were enforced strictly, and an additional 10 percent could be removed by the president's proposed 1982 budget cuts. The 11 states covered by the report are Alabama, Arkansas, Florida, Georgia, Louisiana, Mississippi, North Carolina, South Carolina, Tennessee, Texas, and Virginia. [*Clarion Ledger* 1981]

Weak Labor Unions

The weakness of Southern labor unions has probably been the greatest detriment to solving the region's poverty problems. Employers have provided barriers to union organization, and in many instances, the workers have been reluctant to ally themselves with national unions. For example, the nation's percentage of unionized workers was 26 percent in 1977, whereas South Carolina had only 8 percent and North Carolina had only 7 percent ("Latest on Unions' Drive to Organize the South" 1977, pp. 72-74).

Another barrier to strong unions is the Taft-Hartley "right-to-work" law. Most unionists are aware that Southern states are not likely ever to repeal this crippling labor union law. The unions' hopes have been with the Congress, where chances have been faltering with the increase of Republican members. Because the unions lack enough support from Congress, the Taft-Hartley Act will remain in effect in the South. The net result is that most unions will remain out of the region, thereby fostering comparatively low wages and low job security among Southern wage earners.

The fact that blue-collar union workers in similar plants in the North make significantly more money than unorganized rednecks in the South appears to make little difference to the home boys. Rednecks do not want to be obligated to the union. They wish to maintain their independence, and they can accept the paternalism of the local "bossman." Southerners are not generally educated at any level about collective bargaining. Many view unions as socialist organizations. Therefore, the low credibility of labor unions is difficult to overcome.

The following table from *U.S. News & World Report* ("Latest on Unions' Drive to Organize the South" 1977) illustrates the status of labor unions in the South:

	Union Membership at Latest Count	Percentage of State's Nonfarm Jobs
Tennessee	295,000	19
Alabama	223,000	19
Arkansas	108,000	17
Louisiana	194,000	16
Georgia	264,000	15
Virginia	247,000	14
Texas	567,000	13
Florida	354,000	13
Mississippi	84,000	12
South Carolina	82,000	8
North Carolina	140,000	7

Not only has unionization in the South lagged far behind that of the North, but the expected wage levels in Southern communities are considerably lower than in other parts of the country. These normative elements reflect, of course, the relative power of workers and employers. The most disadvantaged workers experience the greatest regional inequality.

Whites, especially the well educated, and those with higher-status occupations are better able to "bargain" with employers on terms that essentially represent national standards. Perhaps this is because of common knowledge of relative pay levels for professionals (and other highly skilled workers) throughout the nation. Blacks and blue collar workers appear to be more constrained by their position and relative lack of power. Their pay seems to be conditioned more by local job market than by the national standards. Although regional differences have been reduced, Southern workers continue to experience a significant disadvantage in their paychecks. [Hirschman and Blankenship 1981, pp. 388-403]

Task Force on Southern Children

The Task Force on Southern Children of the Southern Growth Policy Board in Raleigh, North Carolina, reported a number of negative findings to the 1981 Southern Governors' Conference (Madigan 1981, p. 16A). Their data were based on a comprehensive look at census data and detailed reports on education, welfare programs, state budgets, and poverty levels. More impoverished children reside in the South than in any other area of the nation. Infant mortality rates are higher, welfare programs provide less support, and spending on education is lower than in any other region. Southern poverty was found to be persistent, and Southern children were the poorest in the country. Millions of poor Southern children were reported to be painfully vulnerable to risks of poor health, poor housing, poor nutrition, and the lack of basic education and other opportunities. The South has more children than any other region, 4 million of whom live in poverty. On an average, the South spends about 25 percent less educating each pupil than the rest of the nation, and it depends far more on federal funds for school than the rest of the country. Average test grades fall below national figures, and more Southern students have been "held back" a grade than in any other region. For every 100 children who graduate, there are 38 dropouts. For every 100 students who graduate from high school in Mississippi, there are 58.5 dropouts, compared with the national average of 29 dropouts for every 100 graduates. In the South 42 percent of the parents did not complete high school, compared with 34 percent in the nation as a whole. For Southern-born children, the chance of survival during the first year of life is less than in other areas of the country; 72 percent of the nation's high infant mortality areas are in the South. These include major metropolitan areas as well as remote rural counties. Outside the South, there are 15.3 infant deaths per 1,000 live births. There are 17.7 deaths per 1,000 live births in the South. Among nonwhites, the infant mortality rate for the South is 25.8 deaths per 1,000 live births.

The report also touched on one area that is not likely to receive much attention, given the current federal emphasis on welfare cuts. The South gives welfare aid to fewer of its poor children than the rest of the country and gives less money to those it does aid. Of the 4 million children in families below the poverty level living in the South in 1975, less than 2 million received Aid for Dependent Children grants. In other parts of the country, 8 million of 10 million poor children receive grants. Those Southern families that receive such benefits get about "half of the U.S. average" and try to make up the difference with food stamps.

FIVE

THE SOCIAL TYPIFICATION OF
THE REDNECK

METHOD

We began with an attempt to "get inside the head" of the self-identified redneck to arrive at a grounded, albeit working, definition. That is, we attempted to probe into rednecks' *own* descriptions of themselves to effect entry into their social worlds and world views.

Conceivably, we could have attempted to obtain such self-definitions by launching into a series of intensive interviews with some type of probability sample of working-class Southerners. However, apart from the improbability of obtaining open or candid responses by such a method, we are obviously middle-class in speech and manner; therefore, barring suicidal tendencies, we would have been ill-advised to approach Southern white, working-class strangers with questions about rednecks. When used by a middle-class person in the presence of working-class Southerners, the term *redneck* connotes an epithet and an insult of the worst order.

Alternatively, we relied on informal discussions with "rednecks" (and upwardly mobile ex-rednecks) with whom we had previously established ongoing acquaintances—ranging from relatively superficial tool-borrowing encounters to relatively close relationships (for example, card playing, pool shooting, hunting and fishing, funeral and wedding attending, drinking and storytelling) with many self-identified "necks" of both the ex- (upwardly mobile but "I'm still a neck") and the nonmobile varieties.

These casual interviews, encounters, and observations soon disclosed some commonalities and agreements. Self-identified rednecks are (or have been) working-class whites with an expressed value system (religious, racial, political) and a commitment to the maintenance of a Southern ideology explicitly identified with virtues peculiar to those "close to the land," that is, of a rural or agriculturally based, small-town background. We found that many of these values were persistently clung to by many urban working class Southerners who were removed in space and time from rural areas (see Reed 1972). However, there were also ambiguities and definitional disagreements, as the following self-definitions indicate:

We're violent and proud tuv it.

We ain't no more rough th'n nobody else, but we gots to protect what little we got the only way we know how, an we got mo' guts th'n 'niggers', yer classy whites, and yer Yankees.

The gov'ment and the big companies had done ripped us po folks off. Fact is, we done been raped. All we got lef is a lil respect.

Well, us necks ain't so bad off. We're honest workin' men. Let the big shot whites carry on. Tain't nothin' we can do bout that.

Let the niggers suck in the welfare. Won't do them no good cause they're still gonna be niggers. We're gonna put food on the table and git by som'a how.

Us rednecks probably need more book learnin'. That way our chillen might could make it.

Hell with that ejacation shit. I seen too many ejacated men. All phonies and blood suckers. Me, I'd druther work. And alla my kids I'ma hoping will go to work early. Don't tell me about no future bullshit. My family's gotta eat today.

Them outside people come down here from th' North and treat us like dogs. They wont ta change everthin'. You know, bring unions in. Piss on 'em all. I'd druther work at my own pace. I don't wont no foremen on my back alla time. Yankees love niggers and wants to give em our jobs with all that union stuff.

Them foreigners, and the gov'ment, and the uppity whites wont all that desegregation cause their chillen don't hass to to go school with "niggers," like us rednecks.

Well, us rednecks gotta understan' that the world is a changin'. Maybe we gotta lissen to sum them outsiders. To git somewhere maybeso we's got to take that union shit. I ain't talkin bout no communist unions but sumpin we can live with. The damn big shot whites has allus taken everythin way from us necks. We allus suckin' the hind tit. Hell, if the niggers git a little more, O.K. That's the way things go. But we otta git sumpin, too.

Us rednecks are a holdin' the South together. Without us the rest of the whites and the niggers, too, would git et up.

I might be a redneck, but my chillen won't be. I ain't justa talkin cousin. There ain't much difference tween us necks and other people here-abouts—'cept money. All us live bout alike. I mean none us is a goin' hungry.

Some big shots is necks, too. All us come otta the same bag. Fact is, it's hard to tell who be and who ain't a redneck.

Shit, anybody can be a redneck; it ain't who you be—but how you think.

Such diversified and partially inconsistent self-identifications brought us to the realization of the multiple reality of the redneck, the question-ability of a pure type, and the probable merging and overlapping of some redneck characteristics throughout the Southern white social structure. Finally, we learned that the redneck defines his characteristics and thinks of the meaning of being a "redneck" in explicit opposition and contrast to other social categories.

The meaning of *redneckery* to the redneck himself (and, for that matter, to others as well) exists only in his relationship to a specific set of other actors within the Southern social milieu. In short, as the inter-actionist perspective suggests, the redneck's views of particular "others" are fundamental to his view of "self." Ultimately, the redneck defines himself in antagonistic juxtaposition to three other groups: "outsiders," non-Southern immigrants and visitors; "the big shot whites," middle- and upper-class white Southerners, all of whom he perceives as essentially one group; and blacks (all). We emphasize that this tripartite categorization is taken from the redneck himself—these are his typical categories in use rather than our imposed secondary constructs.

In sum, our procedure that allowed self-identified rednecks to describe themselves opened up a multiple reality of mutually antagonistic, yet mutually embedded, social worlds. It is not surprising, then, that rednecks are somewhat ambivalent and inconsistent in self-descriptions. A person's self-concept is always in part a reflection of the way others respond to him. We find that the redneck is responded to quite differently by the various groups in his world. His own group (fellow rednecks and their wives and children) respond to him in one way; other groups in the Southern milieu react to him from their vantages. To understand him, therefore, one must consider how each of these other groups—namely, outsiders, middle- and upper-class Southerners, and blacks—views and interacts with him and how he, in turn, views and interacts with them.

SOCIAL WORLDS AND INTERACTION PATTERNS—OUTSIDERS

People who visit, travel through, or migrate to the South without durable previous experiences in the region initially express diversified, truncated, and mixed views and feelings about the area and its people. To some outsiders, the South is a traditional plantation section still characterized by the class, racial, and romantic themes not too far removed from those featured in *Gone with the Wind*. For others the South approximates the *Tobacco Road* model, that is, rural redneck country where ignorance is bliss and 'tis folly to be wise, especially for "wise" outsiders. Southerners, for the most part, are envisioned as a bunch of fundamentalist hicks who hate blacks, Yankees, Catholics, and foreigners (everybody but Anglo-Saxons and the Scotch-Irish). Southerners are pictured as bigoted, reactionary provincials who oppose civil rights and most democratic ideas, practices, and institutions. Still others have heard of the "New South" and are somewhat aware of regional, class, and rural-urban differences therein. To them the highly urbanized South is gradually being homogenized into the United States, while small towns and the rural countryside remain impacted. Many outsiders incorporate an amalgam of these images. Regardless of preconceptions, most outsiders are aware of their stranger status as newcomers to the South and approach the area with a tentative, cautious, ambivalent, and typically condescending attitude. Whatever the South might be to Southerners, for most outsiders it is preconceived as an economically, educationally, and culturally deprived territory marred by a tradition of race conflict, aggressive religiosity, intolerance, and reactionary politics. There is, of course, some truth in this stereotype.

Outsiders' views and descriptions of the Southern working-class man closely resemble the redneck as presented via the media (stage, screen, radio, newspapers, magazines, novels, and television). That is, the redneck is a rough, gut- and sex-centered roustabout who lives in a physical world; he wolfs down coarse, greasy food; he drinks large quantities of beer and cheap whiskey; he speaks in an idiomatic, regional hick language punctuated with crude, obscene, and profane expressions; and he carouses, frolics, gambles, and fights with his peers and cheap women in rough-hewn redneck bars affording loud country and Western music. Arrogant, hostile, bigoted, chauvinistic, stubborn, and belligerent, these rustic machos are portrayed as quick to fight, especially if their sensibilities are impugned in any way—for example, a denigration of their physical or sexual abilities or proclivities. Additionally, they are defined as particularly touchy regarding any off-color remarks about or references to their wives or female relatives. Allegedly, they pick fights with outsiders, whom they enjoy beating up (Boney 1971).

Outsiders, when traveling, visiting, or conducting business in the South, avoid interaction with the redneck insofar as possible, because they think non-Southerners particularly are perceived by rednecks as hated Yankees, foreigners, liberals, and "nigger-lovers," who pose a threat to the Southern way of life. Additionally, social class differentials between outsiders and rednecks typically inhibit open or relaxed contacts between them. Direct contacts with rednecks are usually fleeting and segmental. For example, travelers may purchase such things as gas from service station attendants, food and soft drinks from employees of small-town and country stores, liquor from package stores, and souvenirs and fruit from roadside markets. Travelers also interact with motel desk clerks, bellhops, waiters, waitresses, and auto mechanics. Social visitors to the South usually stay with middle- and upper-class Southerners who shield them from encounters with rednecks. Outside businessmen negotiate and socialize with Southern middle- and upper-class executives, managers, and owners. Transplanted outside factory managers usually steer clear of indigenous factory workers, even at the work site, and direct the redneck's activities through, and by, local Southern lower-echelon foremen. White residential migrants to the South tend to accept quickly the prevailing folkways and mores relating to class, race, and politics as the most effective means of accommodation to the Southern scene. White outsiders (other than civil rights workers and educators) avoid contact with Southern blacks because of racial and class differences and the prevailing etiquette of race relations (Roebuck and Neff 1980)

Outsiders claim that rednecks are impolite, stupid, arrogant, inconsiderate, gruff, dirty, and bigoted; and they tell many stories about the shabby treatment (for example, verbal and sometimes physical abuse) they have received from rednecks because of their Northern license plates, dress, and speech.

Visitors are typically middle class and hence prefer to socialize with middle- and upper-class Southerners with whom they share certain status characteristics and interests rather than with rednecks or black Southerners. However, they accuse the upper classes of being hypocritical and evasive in social interrelationships among themselves and with others. Outsiders report that middle- and upper-class Southerners gloss over all but their most intimate relations with a facade of informality, openness, trust, and personal involvement. Actually, these interactions are studied and impersonal. Though loquacious, polite, and seemingly gregarious and friendly, the genteel Southerner's social meanings and background expectations are hard for outsiders to decipher. For example, following a chance social encounter, open invitations are extended to everyone to "come visit us at the house," but such wholesale invitations are only polite social forms unless a specific time and place is designated and the invitation is extended by the wife to her counterpart. As outsiders report, the middle- or upper-class Southerner talks a lot but says very little. In this vein, Southerners claim that impolite and pushy outsiders have not learned how to read them.

Talk and conversation to the middle- and upper-class Southerner, according to outsiders, is often a form of sociability (Simmel 1950) whereby the dialogue becomes its own purpose. Stress is on the form or manner in which one converses. The content may be interesting, witty, and even important, but it is not the purpose of the discussion. Therefore, rarely does conversation pursue an objective result but tends to ramble easily from one topic to another in an unserious, charming, and often purposefully pointless fashion. Outsiders report that even serious negotiations are conducted in a seemingly disarming, informal, polite, chatty, and familiar manner, frequently camouflaging hidden agendas. Outsiders also point out that middle- and upper-class Southerners are great long-story tellers and that the patient person who likes non sequiturs and allegories enjoys them. Many times, conversation is relatively free from the consequences of the real world, though it certainly reflects and is anchored in such a reality, that is, in the allegorical mind of the Southerner. In formal and informal negotiations with these affluent Southerners, outsiders often wonder if and when the dialogue will center on the issue at hand.

MIDDLE- AND UPPER-CLASS SOUTHERNERS

Social World, Life-Style, and Proper Conduct

Middle- and upper-class Southerners live in a highly protected, relatively affluent, and segregated social world, removed from the everyday lives of rednecks and blacks. As owners, executives, bosses, professionals, managers, and administrators, they share the class rewards and perquisites of a semitraditional society. Class demarcations are sharply drawn, as exemplified by an emphasis on family background, residence, race, occupation, correct demeanor, and speech and dress patterns. They live and exert their energies in a practical world of business, professional, and political affairs. Intellectual pursuits (the arts, philosophy, the classics, and non-Southern literature) are viewed as useless frills that do little for one professionally, monetarily, spiritually, or socially. Middle- and upper-class Southerners see themselves as superior individuals who enjoy a justly deserved life-style based on social background, breeding, superior personal characteristics (industry and intelligence), and a special set of skills that sets them apart from the lower classes (rednecks and blacks). The validity of this claim is highly questionable (Collins 1979). Middle-class people, unlike rednecks, possess the wherewithal to teach children all sorts of skills and social behaviors necessary for success in a stratified society. They also possess, unlike rednecks, the means to send children to the right schools where they may acquire the credentials necessary to obtain occupational or professional status, skills that anyone of average intelligence could attain with little difficulty, given the motivation and opportunity that rednecks do not have because of cultural and economic deprivations.

Middle- and upper-class Southerners in serious behavior settings (for example, business offices, churches, doctors' and lawyers' offices, schools, banks, and funeral homes) and not-so-serious behavior settings (for example, social gatherings, parties, beach resorts, restaurants, cocktail lounges, weddings, and sports events) present a self-contained, self-satisfied hauteur to inferiors and a good old boy front to insiders and outsiders of equal status. Their children assume a similar mien, among peers and others representing different age, sex, and class affiliations. By age six, the children meet even strangers in a calm, cool, and collected manner—that, is, they make direct eye contact with them and converse with poise. Verbally and nonverbally (facial expression, posture, gestures), they approach strangers in a quizzical, insouciant fashion, which may be paraphrased as follows: "I know who I am. I am somebody. Who are you? What are you doing here? Are you somebody or nobody?"

Middle- and upper-class Southerners prefer personal and informal interaction only with peers and family. They have learned how to qualify, moderate, simulate, and neutralize verbal as well as facial expressions, thereby controlling the emotions of happiness, surprise, fear, anger, disgust, sadness, and so on. They have been taught not only what to say in particular situations but how to camouflage feelings of fear and anger in public places.

They are also taught what things they should not say and what expressions they should not allow on their faces, particularly in the presence of teachers and strangers. Vocabulary is mixed with both concrete and abstract content and suffused with regional and biblical metaphors and allegories. Voice quality is low and softly pitched, drawly, and marked by relaxed articulation, smooth rhythm control, full and rich resonance, and slow tempo. Correct mannerisms negate the expression of strong emotion in public. No aggressive movements of the hands, feet, or limbs are permitted. Exaggerated body movements of any type are frowned upon as lower-class expressions. Hands must be kept away from the mouth and out of pockets. The whole mien must express self-containment, body balance, and relaxed attentiveness. Speech and gestures are synchronized and complementary. Much emphasis is placed on what you say to whom (in what social class) and how you say it. One must always speak and act with good manners to all. It is not so much what you think of others, or what they think about you, but rather the correctness or the proper behavior that transpires in social encounters that counts. Though you might hate another's guts, you act like a gentleman or a lady in his presence while in public. You may literally destroy him later, providing you have justification and providing you do it in an "honorable" fashion.

A few illustrative parental admonitions follow:

Always be nice and polite to everybody.

Love your enemies to death until the time is ripe.

Be friendly to everybody at work, especially your superiors, and underneath compete like hell to get their jobs.

Associate only with those at your social level or with those above you.

Never challenge authority or tradition openly.

Go to church whether you want to or not.

If you have to sin, do so discreetly.

You must fight when it's necessary, even if you are outpowered.

Never discuss your sexual relationships, and never carry tales about the sexual relationships of others.

Give to all women, even whores, the utmost respect.

Girls never should play the role of a big sister or one of the boys with eligible males (these roles lead to always a bridesmaid but never a bride).

All men have standard equipment, so marry someone who's got something going for him financially.

Love and seek out winners—leave all losers alone.

Never invite people of different levels to the same party. Dress in style for the occasion. Drink only what you can handle. Never take advantage of a woman when she is highly intoxicated.

Date only men you would consider marrying.

Don't be too smart around men because they like to feel superior.

Suggest things to the male—never challenge him head on and lead him to believe that many of your ideas are really his.

All males want to be tigers, so help them to be tigers—tigers you have tamed.

Upper- and middle-class Southerners place much stress on kinship ties and family lineage. For example, they habitually recite the exhalted genealogical histories of Southern brides and grooms at wedding receptions throughout the Southern region. These recapitulations constitute an important part of the symbolic nuptial scene where the two fortunate young people are invariably exhalted for coming from "good stock" (a stock-in-trade Southern term that is no euphemism). *Good stock* has a real "biological" meaning for the Southern cast of social actors. Of course, outsiders and sociologists with some knowledge of history know that the term *good stock* used in this particular context is a shaky, if not spurious, social reconstruction of reality. Most Southern social actors are unaware of this or gloss over it and could care less about what outsiders, sociologists, or historians have to say about Southern lineage (F. King 1975). And what is more significant, many Southerners interact with one another on the basis of these biological meanings. Actually, Southern working-class people have swelled the ranks of "quality" Southerners (structural mobility) for years (Genovese 1974, pp. 15-30), though certainly it is harder to climb the class ladder today than during past generations. A naive Northern friend of ours once questioned some Southern wedding party guests about their interminable genealogical accounts of the married pair at hand. Later he confided to us that it sounded to him like a genetics course in veterinary medicine that he was prepared to practice in a Southern context sans marriage, i.e., stand at stud.

Recreation

Middle- and upper-class Southerners' reacreational activities center on the church, the golf course, the hunting lodge, the country club, and the home. Although all Southerners live in the Bible belt, where strong proscriptions still exist against drinking, sex, and "sin," most middle-class Southerners have graduated from the fundamentalist denominations to the more permissive and modernist denominations (Methodist, mainstream Baptist, Presbyterian, Episcopalian). To them, religious form is more meaningful than religious content.

Most compromise their sensual appetites and the prevailing external asceticism by balancing conforming public behavior (for example, attending church, presenting a conservative moral front) with "deviant" private behavior in the areas of sex, drinking, and gambling. Unlike the rednecks, this membership generally drinks behind closed doors at home, at private house parties, in exclusive cocktail lounges, or at the country club. Rednecks say they drink to get "high" or drunk, whereas middle- and upper-class Southerners claim to use alcohol as a social lubricant. Actually, both groups drink to get "high" or drunk, frequently drunk. Most Southerners view alcohol as a magical substance tied in closely with manliness, sin, and sexuality. And Southerners really enjoy sinning because it is so forbidden! While Rednecks sin openly, their social "betters" sin secretly for two reasons, paraphrased as follows: veiled sin protects their reputations; secret sin is more fun not only because it is forbidden, but because it provides the raison d'être for a secret society of superior, annointed fellow elites. Middle- and upper-class Southerners can sin all they want at most anything they want, as long as they do it in secrecy with panache, style, élan, and camaraderie.

Views of the Redneck

Middle- and upper-class Southerners denounce the redneck as a lesser breed of Southerner, whom they term the spiritual, if not the physical, descendant of the seventeenth century colonial English poor— that is, indentured servants who worked alongside black field hands on the plantations and farms of the upper South (Virginia and Maryland). In fact, however, only a very few cavaliers and members of the English landed gentry came as settlers to the Southern colonies. Much of the planter class arose from indigenous yeoman farmer origins. A small, but not insignificant, portion of the yeoman farmer class (sometimes starting out as day laborers) was derived, in turn, from the indentured servant and free working class. Accordingly, large numbers of middle- and upper-class Southerners today are products of yeoman farmers, and some derive from working-class backgrounds. Still others are only a few generations removed from one or both of these classes. Yet to hear them tell it, the "bad seed" (ancestors of the rednecks) were planted in the English colonies at the beginning of the European colonization of this country and since have repeatedly besmirched the Southern scene.

Evolution is still resisted in the South, but Social Darwinism (sans this label) is the prevailing everyday reality. Just as water seeks its level, the redneck reportedly finds his place near the bottom of the socioeconomic ladder in Southern white society. Rednecks are described as a group of low-class, stupid, coarse, uncouth, "tacky" roustabouts who get what they deserve out of life—very little.

Some respectable working-class Southerners may escape the redneck label, providing they act respectably or providing "they come from good people" (usually defined as people who owned property or who did not belong to the working class). Thus a poor white Southerner can escape the label by virtue of present or past family status, but his children must obtain property or occupational status to avoid the category. Only one generation of poor people is immune from the label, and members of this generation must avoid social contacts with rednecks, maintain contacts with necessary kin and acquaintances in the middle or upper class, and act respectably (for example, go to church, dress properly, [middle class], attend school, work hard, pay debts, stay out of trouble, sin discreetly—in short, opt for the middle-class life-style whether one can afford it). In these circumstances, many, if not most, Southerners who lose middle-class status are very likely to become rednecks, and their children after them. The process, of course, sometimes, but not often, operates in the other direction. Some poor whites and even some rednecks help their children to attain middle-class status. It takes less time (one generation) to lose it than it takes to gain it: following two or three generations of hard work, proper behavior, and luck, poor whites can become middle class. It usually takes redneck families at least three generations to produce middle-class Southerners.

It is our view that the class lines in the South are hardening. Prior to World War II, a college degree signaled or virtually gave one middle-class status. According to Southerners, this is no longer the case because of the increase in the number of college graduates, four-year colleges of questionable educational status, and lower-class students in colleges.

Avoidance Patterns

On a class basis, middle- and upper-class Southerners prefer as little interaction with rednecks and blacks as possible, especially within social contexts involving women and children—for example, the exchange of family visits, dating relationships, parties, and other intimate gatherings, club memberships and activities, and fraternization in public places.

The desire of this class to worship in separate churches is facilitated by the proliferation and distribution of a varied group of Protestant churches throughout the region. Middle- and upper-class Southerners generally belong to the Episcopalian, Presbyterian, and Methodist churches, whereas rednecks more frequently attend the Pentecostal, Baptist, Church of God, and Church of Christ churches. Although there is significant overlap in class attendance in the Baptist and Methodist churches, a large variety of churches abound within a single denomination, expediting class-linked church membership and attendance. In the exceptional cases where middle- and upper-class Southerners and rednecks attend the same church, the former maintain all the aloofness possible (separate seating arrangements) but pretend to treat the latter as Christian equals. Condescension and noblesse oblige actually characterize any religious encounters that might occur. Even Holy Communion is marked by differences, that is, the upper classes come first. It is clearly understood by both parties that a limited fellowship begins and ends at the church door.

Middle- and upper-class Southerners avoid social contacts with rednecks and blacks by their infrequent use of public facilities such as parks, playgrounds, swimming pools, buses, and certain hotels, bars, cocktail lounges, theaters, and restaurants. When interaction does occur in these behavior settings, the vehicle of conversation, though pitched in a phoney egalitarian mold, is stilted, stylized, and stereotyped. In short, the two parties play at a sociability form wherein conversational content deals with trivial, impersonal, inane subjects such as the weather, sports, newspaper stories, and the movies.

Middle- and upper-class Southerners generally send their children to segregated private schools at the elementary and high school levels. When middle- and upper-class children do attend public schools, social interaction with rednecks and blacks is typically restricted to formalized classroom and sports participation. Clique memberships for play, sociability, and camaraderie follow class and race lines. The school cafeteria primarily serves blacks and rednecks. Middle- and upper-class students drive to restaurants for lunch in their own cars.

Middle- and upper-class residential segregation in affluent neighborhoods, in and of itself, enhances the overall pattern of social segregation. Middle- and upper-class males do interact with rednecks and blacks at work sites such as farms, lumberyards, warehouses, theaters, restaurants, factories, and hardware stores. However, these work-site behavior settings are characterized by secondary group relationships predominately within a superordinate-subordinate context. A dearth of labor union membership throughout the South weakens the redneck wage earner's negotiating power and dignity at the work site.

Frequently, middle- and upper-class bosses deal with the redneck in an indirect fashion via a buffer group of redneck foremen. This work mechanism diminishes bosses' interaction with redneck employees and obviates negotiations between owners or bosses and wage earners on either an individual or group basis. The boss has only to exert economic control and power over the redneck's supervisor, whom he can reward or replace at will. When owners and bosses do interact with redneck employees at the work site, interaction occurs within a paternalistic frame—that is, the boss is always called "Mr." and deferred to, whereas the redneck is called by his first name and treated with patronizing familiarity. The boss, in near impunity, may chide the redneck about his idiosyncracies and personal life, even about members of his family. The redneck, on the other hand, is never permitted such latitude and during personal encounters must stick to work-related or inane, impersonal subjects.

In spite of the social distance between them, middle- and upper-class Southerners never deny the humanity of the redneck or the fact that certain similarities obtain between them. Some even go so far as to suggest playfully (to one another and to rednecks) that their necks, too, are a little pink in spots. After all, both rednecks and middle- and upper-class Southerners are whites in a racist society, whereas blacks are at the bottom of the heap. The redneck must never be allowed to forget the importance of being white. Otherwise, a lack of race consciousness might generate a class alignment with the black, which could be dangerous for the middle and upper classes. Variations of the following story are frequently related among middle- and upper-class Southerners. It is intended to illustrate both the similarities and differences between rednecks and themselves:

> The differences between the redneck and the good 'ol boy is that the redneck drives around in his pickup truck on a Sunday afternoon goofing off and nursing a six pack of beer. He indiscriminately tosses each empty can out the window. The good 'ol boy [a middle- or upper-class Southerner] drinks a six pack of beer on a Sunday while using his pickup to make inspection trips to his property sites. He retains all his empty cans until he finds a suitable disposal site.

Some highly educated Southerners (posing as liberals) contrast rednecks negatively to blacks. Rednecks wolf down coarse, greasy food (greens, pork, and black-eyed peas), whereas blacks consume "soul food." Rednecks guzzle booze, fight, and engage in cheap sex; blacks who behave in a similar fashion are simply demonstrating a unique life-style. Any poor white driving a big, new automobile is a redneck spendthrift; a poor black doing likewise is an innocent victim of our consumer culture. Intellectually, rednecks are hopelessly backward; blacks are educationally deprived.

Views of Blacks

Middle- and upper-class Southerners prefer a sort of long-distance living arrangement with blacks, that is, across town. They reluctantly acquiesce to integration in the public schools, where many of their children do not go but where redneck and black children must go. They condone black cultural nationalism (as opposed to revolutionary nationalism) in the name of "democratic pluralism." The rhetoric of ethnic pluralism appeals to the middle- and upper-class whites as a means to enjoy "democratically" what they have always had in the South: differential life-styles within a segregated society—white neighborhoods, churches, and social clubs, and white occupational and professional organizations, and so on. These patterns persist despite civil rights laws and such governmental organizations as Health, Education and Welfare (HEW) and Housing and Urban Development (HUD) because of local patterns of residential segregation and white political power. De facto segregation exists everywhere but in the public schools. Whites no longer go to city parks and swimming pools, and many avoid the use of public transportation and other public facilities. Rednecks and blacks must use such facilities because they do not possess private facilities.

Most interaction between white middle- and upper-class Southerners and blacks ensues on a racial caste basis within work site situations. Unlike interactions with rednecks, there is not even the pretense of equality during most encounters between whites and blacks. Whites of this class usually know blacks as servants and subservient employees.

Views of Outsiders

This class membership tolerates outsiders so long as they do not, by expressed thought or action, disrupt the Southern way of life. The longer the outsider lives in the South and the more he conforms to the Southern race, class and political modes, the more approvable he becomes. However, complete acceptance is unlikely. One and one's ancestors have to be born and bred in the South before one can really know, appreciate, and belong to the region and its concomitant way of life. The outsider remains a stranger. Outside working-class whites are frowned upon because of class differences in and of themselves, and because of their possibly contaminating the Southern working-class with democratic ideas—for example, promoting labor unions. Black outsiders of all classes are unwanted because of race per se and because of the fear of imported black militancy.

BLACKS

Blacks and rednecks have lived out an intertwined, rough, and precarious social and economic existence in the South. The cultures of the two are similar in many respects, that is, in diet, language, religion, folk knowledge, recreation, and customs. Working-class wage earners, both are exploited at the bottom of a class-bound, racist, capitalist society. Both enjoy "soul food" (pork, collards and turnip greens, fried chicken, grits, cornbread, molasses, black-eyed peas, and chitlins), practice a fundamentalist Protestant religion, share similar superstitions, resort to deviant health care practices, and hunt and fish as a means of recreation. Blacks, however, unlike rednecks, have always occupied a rigid caste status based on race and have suffered more intense discrimination relating to housing, occupations, education, and social participation throughout the social, economic, and political structure.

The Lack of Class Consciousness

Generalized white racism and the successful efforts of the white power structure to drive a wedge between lower-class blacks and whites have militated against the unification of these two groups (Lawrence

1975; McLaurin 1978; Marshall 1967). The weakness of labor unions in the South has also enhanced this divisiveness. Blacks view themselves as a racial minority within the Southern region and seek economic, political, and educational equality within a frame of cultural pluralism. But the overwhelming majority are not separatists and desire acceptance by, and parallel entrance into, the dominant culture. They place little faith in white political machines, political parties, churches, or labor unions (Holloway 1969). For most, black power is seen as a means to an end and not as an end in itself—a means to gain a sense of identity and self-confidence enabling them to compete successfully with other Americans in a biracial society. They accept the capitalistic system and, like whites, stress racial rather than class differences. All they want is a piece of the capitalist "pie in the sky." In short, no less than rednecks, Southern blacks suffer from a lack of class consciousness. Neither group can see that cultural pluralism frequently touted by pseudoliberals and reactionaries for different reasons will continue to separate the population along ethnic, racial, and religious lines, thereby blocking the necessary unification along class lines—that is, the unification and solidarity of the working class.

The liberals believe that the frills of race, ethnic, and religious differences must be preserved in the name of "democracy." The more perceptive reactionary knows that these frills must be preserved in order that the capitalist class might divide and rule. In short, ethnic, racial, or religious allegiances block the development of class consciousness. Ergo, there is little real socialism in the United States today.

Definitions of Rednecks

Southern blacks define rednecks as the most biased, racially pre-judiced, cruel, and violent group in the United States. Moreover, they attribute these characteristics to the redneck's intrinsic stupidity and meanness. That is, not unlike the redneck who views black character traits as biologically determined, the Southern black views the bigotry and the violent disposition of rednecks as intrinsic to them, rather than attributing these phenomena to the redneck's location in the society or to an ideological process originating at the top of the Southern hierarchy.

Blacks are also quick to note that cultural differences obtain between themselves and rednecks: an African versus a European heritage; jazz and rhythm and blues versus hillbilly and country and Western music; expressive and emotional dancing styles versus macho, mechanical dance styles; colorful and modish manner of dress versus drab and cowboyish dress style; black English speech patterns versus hick language; soft, meaningful, and egalitarian courtship and conjugal relations versus hard-nosed, chauvinistic, and exploitative relations; loving, joyful, and emotional religious experiences versus fearful, vindictive, and retributive experiences; and humanitarian, egalitarian, easygoing, sensual, and forgiving everyday philosophy versus cynical, self-serving, guilt-ridden, punitive, fearful, aggressive, paranoid, racist, and misanthropic positions.

Blacks hate rednecks and think rednecks hate them. Blacks tend to view these differences as "in the nature of things" and immutable. Blacks must come to see the falsity of this position before class consciousness can develop. Again we see the persistence of the Southern folk culture: rednecks and blacks as separate groups complement each other, share in part each others' stereotypes, and thereby remain apart.

Contacts with Whites

Avoidance patterns characterize the relationships between most blacks and rednecks. Blacks live in segregated neighborhoods apart from middle- and upper-class whites and rednecks, attend separate churches, patronize separate clubs and restaurants, and occupy separate social spaces in everyday activities. Occasionally, rural blacks and rednecks hunt, fish, and trap together, though much less frequently than before the Civil Rights movement of the 1960s. During such excursions, blacks must accept an inferior role. Blacks ignore unacquainted rednecks in public places and pass them in the street without extending any salutations. Blacks speak or nod quickly to redneck acquaintances in public places but evade protracted conversation. Civil inattention is the rule. Older blacks (over 60) engage some rednecks in public conversation. However, the dialogue in such cases is confined to trivia or workshop topics. Younger blacks tend to shun any encounters with rednecks except in the school and work situtations.

Blacks work alongside rednecks at all sorts of menial and blue-collar occupations, including factory employment. Conversation and interaction at the work site, however, is limited to "shop talk" and negotiations necessary to completing the task at hand. The two groups segregate themselves during rest periods and lunch breaks, and when the work day is over, each goes its separate way. Black professionals, such as morticians, ministers, doctors, dentists, and lawyers, serve a black clientele. Black teachers do teach both black and white students, but black barbers and hairdressers service black clients exclusively. Black professionals have very limited contact with rednecks and employ only black labor and service workers as needed.

The black middle class (with the exceptions of schoolteachers in the school and lawyers in the courtroom) has very few contacts with whites and, in fact, has traditionally eluded such encounters to escape de-nigration as an inferior caste. Most members of this class are residentially segregated from whites and in turn segregate themselves from lower-class blacks. Middle-class blacks associate with other blacks along traditional class lines; however, there is more intraclass association and marriage among blacks than among whites. Blacks say that there are four interrelated reasons for this differential: blacks are not as class conscious as whites; demarcation along class lines among blacks is relatively new; the small numerical base of the black middle class, existing in a sea of lower-class blacks, generates a necessity for intraclass communication, mutual aid, and dependence; and many middle-class blacks are tied to lower-class blacks through kinship, family, and friendship connections.

Most personal associations between blacks and white Southerners occur between lower-class blacks and middle- and upper-class whites in the domestic service situation, a post that is now largely limited to black females because of increased work opportunities for black males elsewhere. Black cooks, maids, nurses, babysitters, gardeners, chauffeurs, and handymen interact with white families as employees in a domestic behavior setting where primary and secondary group relations are mixed. This makes for a situation that is potentially threatening because primary and secondary group relations are mixed. The servant is not only an employee but also a member of the family because she works in close personal relationships with family members, particularly with children. Personal attachments are formed, which many times clash with employee relationships. Hence, a paternalistic superordinate-subordinate definition is explicitly maintained no matter how close the affectional ties. For example, regardless of age, blacks are always called by their first names, whereas all whites from adolescence on are called "Mr.," "Miss," or "Mrs." Through the years lower-class blacks have received firsthand knowledge of the middle- and upper-class white Southern family life via these service employments. On the other hand, the latter's knowledge of the black has been limited to affairs of the work site and principally to lower-class service workers. Blacks of all classes would rather come in contact with middle- and uppr-class Southerners than with rednecks.

A few black and white intellectuals and professionals interact on a professional basis, and a few of these few interact socially and intimately behind closed doors on a very limited individual or group basis. Whites and blacks who do associate usually keep these associations a secret from relatives and other group members "who would not understand or accept" such social contacts.

This is not to deny the occasional black or white who does flaunt convention in this area, but in such cases, the white or black party is excluded from his or her respective group. The rare white woman who marries a black male (of any class) becomes black, and she and her children become part of the black community. The rarer black female who marries a white male remains black and so do the children of such a marriage. White families cast out whites who intermarry with blacks as does the white community. The black community is more likely to accept such marriages reluctantly. In most cases interracial couples move out of the South before marriage. Even blacks who pass for whites and marry whites move from the South, because family backgrounds are frequently known.

Some blacks hold contacts with all whites to a minimum and see all of them as being alike. Rarely do white men talk to black women in public, and rarely do black men converse with white women in the open. When such rare encounters occur, a group of disapproving whites and blacks gather around the two deviants who get the negative message and move on.

In general, blacks distrust outside whites and stay clear of them because they are white and because they are strangers. Exceptions inhere in fairly close ties with white civil rights workers, ministers, and some schoolteachers and professors. Some outsiders in these categories are received as "enlightened" whites, though complete acceptance is rare. All whites remain somewhat strange. Southern blacks welcome association with outside blacks because they are black and because many of them belong to Southern family and friendship networks. Also, some outside blacks are seen as successful role models to upward mobility.

REDNECKS

Self-Concept and World View

Throughout the South many working-class Southerners refer to themselves as "rednecks" among themselves but consider the term an epithet when applied to them by outsiders. To insiders, the term *redneck* designates an honest, hard-working Southern white man distinguishable from "trash" (a good-for-nothing, lazy white man) and big shots (middle- and upper-class Southerners) who really do not work for a living. Most rednecks, like their parents before them, are resigned to their lower-class status and marginality. Aspirations and respectability center on a steady job, an honest living, putting meat and bread on the table, and getting by. Status is sought within, rather than beyond, redneck social groups. A plumber's helper reports:

> I know I'm nobody to the big wheels. I ain't educated neither and all that shit. But I'm a hard workin' man. I take care a my family. They love me.

My work buddies know I'm a man who holds up my end. What else I need?

Things they wish for are wished for in the near future, the only future they are concerned with, and complement a lower-class life-style—for example, guns, fishing equipment, hunting dogs, boats, trailers, and work tools. Most see their children as following in their footsteps, growing up to be hard-working, proud men like themselves. Therefore, books, school, art, music, and things intellectual are not stressed. The concrete physical world, especially the work-tool world, is stressed. Boys must know about starters, wrenches, gears, engines, and hunting, fishing, and fighting. Girls must know about cooking and sewing and taking care of "chillen" and men. Of course to them, females are born knowing a lot about the latter. Those few who show some educational aspirations for their children are confused. They want them (children) to be somebody, but they are not sure what kind of somebody, for example, perhaps an engineering man or a businessman. Few think of their children as ever becoming professionals.

Rednecks identify themselves as poor working men; residents of a particular county, town, or city; Southerners; rebels; and members of a particular family. They voice a strong sense of place, family, and continuity. Loyalty is frequently professed for the Southern region and its customs. One redneck carpenter relates:

> You know I went up to Dayton, Ohio, a few years back to work. Got good wages, too. But I spent most of my wages driving back to Alabama. I couldn't stay up there at holiday time. Then seems like a bunch of my kinfolks passed on. I just had to come back then. I got sick up there, too, and no one to take care of me was around. Them people up there are different.
> They don't believe in nothin but money and 'bout themselves. Kinfolks don't mean nothin to them people. They talk funny and 'niggers' git treated as good as I did on the job. You know, I feared to die up there. Them bastards prob'bly would a put me in that Yankee dirt. Not even called my people. I got the hell outta there one day. Jes packed my bag and took off ta home. T'hell with all the money and union dues. I'll stay right here in Dixie. Be buried here with my kind of people. If yer heart ain't in Dixie, git yer ass out.

Loyalty toward the South and things Southern is juxtaposed to a hate for Yankees and the thinking, feeling, and doing of Yankees. Yankees comprise all non-Southerners but designate, particularly, Northerners from the Northeast and Midwest and, still even more particularly,

Northern big city people. Yankeeism connotes not only people from a Northern geographical region but also a disdain for people assumed to suffer from modernity, liberalism, unionism, the "liberal"press, urbanism, industrialism, big business, big government, "socialism," the theater and the arts, any social gospel religion, the "liberal" clergy, and all things intellectual or foreign.

Rednecks are much more open, blunt, physical, and aboveboard with their peers than are middle- and upper-class Southerners. One usually knows where he stands or lies with the redneck. Subtlety and hidden agendas are rare. As the redneck says, "What you sees is what you gits with me. Take me or leave me alone. It don't make no difference to me."

Though the redneck resorts to the personal and physical redress of wrongs more frequently than other white Southerners, violence is generally intra- rather than intergroup directed. Even when pressured and derogated by upper-class people they know, they are deferential, polite, and respectful, especially to southern "bosses," managers, owners, employers, professionals, technologists, and bureaucrats—the people who exploit them and really control their lives. Consequently, higher-class Southerners are not unduly concerned about redneck violence. As one upper-class Southerner explains:

> Rednecks are just like animals. It's natural for them to beat up on one another. Who gives a damn. Let them kill one another off. We have too many around anyway. Just so long as they keep their violence to themselves, my kind of people could care less. They don't bother us if they know us, but you have to be careful with the necks you don't know.

Rednecks are keenly aware that latitudes of behavior for them relating to drinking, fighting, and emotional expression are wider than those for the upper classes.

Rednecks' Views toward and Interaction Patterns with Outsiders

Rednecks view outsiders, regardless of class affiliation, as foreigners who do not understand the South and as exploiters of its people and its physical resources. Outsiders are uppity, socialistically inclined, nigger-lovers; skilled workers who are taking their jobs; union organizers, civil rights leaders, and meddling government men; and unwanted tourists and representatives of big business—all out to change the honest, God-fearing, easygoing Southern way of life. The outsider's dress and manners are too fancy; his speech is too rapid; he expects quick service and generally acts like a "smart ass." White immigrant working men are socialist sympathizers who are in favor of labor unions. (Actually, they know nothing about socialism and would not know a socialist from Santa Claus.) Outside foremen and supervisors go too much by the book and expect workers to produce like machines. Outside white owners and businessmen do not appreciate the redneck's human qualities and way of life and are only interested in "working the hell out of him." Except in secondary relationships on the job, rednecks shun contacts with white outsiders. All outside blacks are "uppity niggers" who don't know their place; therefore, contacts with them are minimized. Services performed for outside blacks (and many outside whites) are often slow, shoddy, and contemptuously performed.

Outside skilled workers are shunned at the work site during rest and lunch breaks until they begin to talk and act like Southern rednecks, and even then they are suspect as spies and never quite fully accepted. Should these outside workers join redneck churches and go out of their way to assimilate, they might eventually be taken in. Union organizers are placed in the same radical boat as former white Civil Rights leaders and communists—all wish to make us like the Soviet Union. Some few labor leaders are listened to and followed in cases where a union shop has already been established. Even then, rednecks are likely to join and drop union membership continually on the basis of personal whim and perceived self-interest. Although very few are concerned with the welfare of other redneck working groups, they are very concerned with other rednecks as individuals.

Anybody who works for the federal government in any capacity is feared and looked down upon, even those who represent the Occupatonal Safety and Health Administration. They tend to put "government men" in the same class as their fathers and grandfathers before them put revenue officers. Outside work foremen are despised, hoodwinked in every way possible, and avoided. Rednecks prefer Southern bosses whom they are not too fond of either. Any boss man, by definition, is a son of a bitch, but "inside bastards are preferred to outside asses." Tourists and visitors are foreigners to be exploited in every conceivable way—for example, short change, slow and sloppy service, overcharge, discourteous treatment, false arrest for "speeding," and even physical abuse.

Rednecks' Views toward and Interaction Patterns with the Middle and Upper Classes

The Savage Ideal

Rednecks express ambivalent feelings toward middle- and upper-class white Southerners, whom they simultaneously admire, envy, and resent. As fellow Southerners, all white classes share many Southern traditions, customs, and cultural views: much of their diet; reactionary politics and economic positions; an etiquette of race relations; a sense of place, time, and continuity; and a history of resistance to Northern interventions. They also share a series of characteristics, some of which Cash (1941) referred to as the "savage ideal." The savage ideal is expressed by hostility to new ideas, concreteness rather than abstractness of thought, antiintellectualism, militant Protestantism, sensuality, romanticism, the duality of Calvinism and hedonism, clannishness, narrow totalitarian view, exaggerated regional pride, exaggerated national militaristic patriotism (stemming from the pronounced and glorified Southern military tradition), individualism and the lack of feelings related to social responsibility, a penchant for hierarchical arrangements, paternalism, noblesse oblige, *violence*, cruelty, and a fantastic, unrealistic, mythological past.

The South bristles with a large number of privately run military schools to which middle- and upper-class families have traditionally sent one of their sons. A disproportionate number of Southerners have always served in the armed services—middle- and upper-class men as officers, poor whites and blacks as enlisted men. Southerners of all classes, including politicians, have always been hawkish, militaristic, pro-national defense, and superpatriotic during wartime. The South supported the Vietnam War more firmly than any other region, and fewer Southerners were draft dodgers during this conflict than were men from other regions (Roebuck and Weeber 1978, pp. 190-200). To most Southerners the officer role is honorable and glamorous. Many poor whites and rednecks consider 20 years in the service as an enlisted man with retirement at the noncommissioned officer level a very good deal. The ultimate for a middle- or upper-class Southern family is to have a son graduate from Annapolis, West Point, or the Air Force Academy. Southern belles fall all over themselves in pursuing these "annointed knights." But then as the Southern belle says, "The man chases the woman until she catches him."

Southern belles usually have "big daddies," and the two roles (belle and big daddy) are complementary. The belle learns much about life and men from big daddy to whom she is usually more attached than to mamma. Big daddy is invariably a very successful upper-class Southern male with a very strong personality who is very discriminating about his daughter's suitors. Thus, in the courtship situation the Southern male faces a formidable female who usually has no difficulty in manipulating him as long as she is attractive, sensual, and mentally strong. By definition, the belle must be attractive.. Plain Southern girls of upper-class status frequently become old maids.

Frequently, the females in Southern middle- and upper-class families are stronger in mental makeup and character than men. Southern women in the upper classes exert strong and, in many cases, dominant parental influences over male children. It may be that to some degree the savage ideal offers the Southern male a masculine alternative to, or an escape from, things cultural and mamma. Daddy, poppa, or big daddy is usually stern, aloof, and preoccupied with business and professional activity. Redneck fathers spend more time with their sons than do middle- and upper-class males, and neither neck parent stresses "things cultural" to their children.

The Extension of the Savage Ideal

Numerous white and black inmates residing in several prisons located in different areas of the United States told the authors in formal and informal interview situations that the Southern white man of whatever class was the meanest man in the world in any type of situation. Both authors agree on the basis of personal experiences. For example, we have found in the study of bars and bar life and behavior (Roebuck and Frese 1978) that an unknown white middle- or upper-class Southerner is safer in a black bar than in a redneck bar within or without the South. No matter how you dress, rednecks will find you out and let you know you are not wanted. And if you are not known to them, your body is in danger. On the other hand, black bar patrons and employees may not welcome your presence, but they will generally accept the middle- or upper-class Southerner but, rarely, the redneck. This acceptance is not based on any fear they might have of whites but on a more tolerant and softer disposition toward whites than whites express toward blacks.

The point is not that the "savage ideal," as used herein a mixture of Cash's and the authors' definitions, is expressed exclusively by Southerners or by all Southerners. We are saying that the white Southerner is more likely to think and act in terms of this syndrome than other Americans. The redneck, of course, is more direct and primitive in the expression of this ideal than in the Southern middle- or upper-class person. For example, the redneck more frequently belongs to the Ku Klux Klan and is more likely to resort to violence and rant and rave about the "niggers," outsiders, and all sorts of foreign liberal and radical people and ideas. The source of the rednecks' savage ideal inheres in a studied and informed ignorance embedded in the poor white folk Southern culture that has been handed down from generation to generation since the antebellum period. The middle- and upper-class white's savage ideal is also in part based on this culture but, additionally, on a received, self-serving Southern history obtained from schools, colleges, and kinfolk.

History is not founded so much on informed and studied ignorance as with the neck but rather on a genteel transformation and justification of Southern history. Southern teachers and some professors help their student with this task. This inexcusable failure to face Southern history and to give up faulty traditions either emotionally or intellectually has emasculated, monumentalized, and mummified the ideas of the Southern upper classes and the views they pass down to the rednecks who look up to them as leaders. Therefore, leadership is weak and corrupt.

Excuses and rationalizations exist in many forms—for example:

We Southerners unlike you Yankees have always had the Negro problem.

We didn't bring them over, you did.

The War between the States was not fought over slavery but because the South was an economic colony of the North.

You Yankees treat Negroes worse than we do.

You Yankees have poisoned the South with all of your foreign ways and ideas.

The North started the War between the States.

The South is the most American region in the United States.

We are more individualistic and Christian and moral than you people.

We hang on to the traditional American values more than you people.

Yes, we are violent, but then some things are worth fighting for like your family's honor.

You people live too fast, while we enjoy our easy pace.

Yes, we have poor people, but most of them are happy, proud, and not contaminated with your outsider unionism, atheism, and foolish do-good-ism.

We've always had the poor—that's in the nature of things.

Don't meddle around with what God has ordered.

All men are evil and some are just smarter than others.

So don't try to change things you can't change.

Most people get what they deserve to get.

Life is a dog-eat-dog proposition.

You have to work hard and take care of yourself.

You don't have time to worry about taking care of others.

Many of the poor are worthless.

People get what's coming to them.

The preceding excuses and/or justifications are held and expressed throughout the Southern class structure, though most, if not all, are spurious in terms of incontrovertible historical knowledge. Man is always revising history from the perspective of the present, but historical transformation in the name of a pernicious lost cause serves no worthy purpose and keeps the South tied to a dangerous mythology. The authors know no rednecks and a very few Southern intellectuals who do not subscribe to and express in one form or another most of these fallacious platitudes. Some few intellectuals try hard, with little success, to overcome this insidious constituent of the Southern culture, especially should they remain in the South. And even those who migrate are tarred with the brush. The Southerner is a feeling rather than a thinking animal and therefore has difficulty in accepting with pride part of his culture while rejecting other elements. This is difficult for any people because cultures are made from whole pieces of cloth, and when one attempts to cut them up, the whole pattern tends to fall apart without a contextual base. Perhaps the redneck has a point, "You sees what you gits. Take me whole like I is, or forget it." This tragedy is that Southern intellectuals suffer from the same analytical problem, though some—in similar vein to John C. Calhoun—are brilliant (though not as brilliant as the South Carolinian exponent of nullification) in defending false causes.

We Southerners need to reverse the process—think first and feel later —but is this possible? And if so, would we still be Southerners? If so, upon what identity base? It is very difficult to fashion a new ethnic identity. The answer, of course, is class rather than regional or racial identity.

Communication and Racial Etiquette

Southerners of all classes have no problem in communicating with one another because their background expectations are similar and because they have worked out tried and true mechanisms for thinking and acting among themselves and outsiders—for example, on the etiquette of race relations, an etiquette for the proper behavior of middle- and upper-class whites when they are in the presence of rednecks and the proper subjects to discuss in the open. When they talk together, blacks and whites, including rednecks, speak of inane subjects such as the weather, gardening, and sports. Rednecks rarely speak to black women in the open but frequently joke about them in a fantasy fashion among themselves. For example, "God made only one big mistake. He put the best 'lovin' on a black women"; "I'm going to find me a red-headed Negro to change my luck"; "If you once go black, you never come back."

Actually, any kind of social relationship between rednecks and black females is very rare. Black women hate them and in fact are increasingly standoffish in their relationships with all white men. This, of course, is understood in terms of history (the sexual exploitation of black women by white men in the South)—but again, a history that has been mythologized by blacks and whites within and without the South. The point is that the prevailing sexual pattern in the plantation South and since has been that of marital and extramarital sex between black men and black women. Miscegenation certainly occurred and occurs but probably less frequently now than before and during the depression, a miscegenation practiced in secrecy on a consensual basis. Certainly men in the South, as well as elsewhere, with power and wealth (and before 1865, ownership) enjoy certain advantages in the sexual sphere. Black men also exchange all kinds of sexual stories and experiences about the white woman, referred to as "Miss Ann."

The Rednecks' Perceptions of Class Differences and Class Contacts

Though the redneck as a Southerner shares a similar heritage in some ways to white Southerners of all classes, he differs from middle- and upper-class Southerners along important dimensions. Higher-class Southerners enjoy a standard of living, a life-style, and status rewards that are out of reach of the working man. Rednecks perceive the upper and middle classes as pompous bosses who manipulate them excessively and deserve to be told off for acting so high and mighty; and yet, most rednecks also believe that these same elites are biologically their superiors. Rednecks distrust the middle and upper classes as guileful softies who are adept at avoiding real work.

Interaction between these elites and rednecks is held to a minimum because both groups, for different reasons, attempt to avoid each other. Rednecks feel uncomfortable, out of place, and inferior in the presence of superiors and fear being placed in compromising situations, for example, being obliged to display an exaggerated deference. Rednecks and their wives and children act deferentially toward middle- and upper-class men, women, and children. Male bosses occasionally stop by rednecks' homes on business (for example, seeking employees, delivering work instructions, and the like). Men and women always refer to them as "Mr." Women compliment them on their looks, families, cars, houses, clothes, et cetera, and offer generous hospitality in the form of drink and food invariably refused.

The Southerner abhors drinking and eating with unequals, but he is quick to have sexual intercourse with women in any class or race. White and black women are much more discriminatory in their choice of sexual partners. Whites and blacks possess all sorts of fallacious sexual views about one another. White males tend to perceive black women, referred to as "brown sugar," as sexual pristine creatures. Black males are viewed as superstuds. Blacks, in turn, believe whites are carnal and too much concerned with sex, particularly white males.

When in the presence of social superiors, redneck children are sternly commanded to say hello to Mr. Big Shot and then to "get out of the way." Women and children are nervous, flustered, overawed, and fearful in the presence of middle- and upper-class members. They squirm, avoid eye contact, look down at the floor, stutter, and talk in high-pitched agitated voices. Children shrink away, look downward and away, and shuffle their feet. By age six they know when they are in the presence of "somebody," and they become frightened when their mothers insist that they say something nice to the boss.

Redneck men, women, and children never exchange family visits with middle- and upper-class Southerners. They do not play, work, or worship together. Redneck children are ignored by upper-class children at school even in the classroom. When passing upper-class members on the street or when coming in contact with them (males, females) in public places, rednecks speak or nod and move on quickly. The redneck and his family's contacts with the upper classes are generally within work contexts. The redneck and all members of his family are painfully aware of the social discrimination they face. Public service employees (post office, courthouse, and school workers, police, utility workers) as well as private sector workers (clerks, mechanics, pharmacists, doctors, and the like) treat rednecks with much less respect than they treat middle- and upper-class Southerners. "First come first served" frequently does not hold. Many times rednecks lose their turns, which they do not resist.

Frequently, in interactions among themselves, rednecks put down big shots as being phony and effeminate and having "no grit in their trough." However, references to biologically based superiority color even these put-downs. A short-haul trucker states: "The line ran out with ole man Jones. His son ain't got it. Weak seed."

Sometimes opportunities arise that permit rednecks to get back at the elites in a more direct manner. A handyman-plumber tells the following story:

> I called my doctor at his house one night. Needed him to come see my wife. She was terrible sick. The doc he jes ask me 'bout if she had a real

high fever, and tole me to git her two aspirins and call him in the mornin. Week or so later he done call me middle the night to come fix his john what was running over fer him. I tole him to drop in two aspirins and call me in the mornin.

Views of and Contacts with Blacks

Rednecks realize that the economic differences between themselves and blacks are not very great, but there is a feudalistic dimension to the Southern sense of one's rank in the stratification system. That is, it is not economics, per se, but coming from good "blood" that, to them, is the principal basis of one's social standing. Being white is not sufficient for being somebody, but it is a necessary first attribute to such a status. Fearful, insecure, narrow-minded, dependent, hostile, rigid, and envious, the redneck adopts the racial dimension as a master identity in his self-concept, that is, he is a white man.

In line with the Southern emphasis on blood ("good seed," "bad seed," "weak seed," "good stock"), the redneck perceives the cultural differences between himself and blacks (in music, dancing preferences, speech patterns, body language, body tonus, style of walking, sexual and marital patterns, and alleged black indifference to achievement goals) as biologically based.

As noted earlier, rednecks feel that their entire way of life is not only threatened but actively in the process of being replaced by "foreign" ways. Thus rednecks hate. They vent much of this hatred toward blacks, a familiar, weak, and highly visible "competitive" group that is safely and firmly at the bottom of the Southern pecking order. So far, rednecks have focused little of their hostility toward their real enemies: the social system and the middle (managers, professionals, technocrats) and upper classes it serves at their expense.

Rednecks are aware that they have much in common with the Southern black. They realize that both groups are working class, virtually propertyless, economically insecure, marginal, powerless, disvalued, and undereducated. However, it is always groups who are the most similar to a culturally stigmatized population who hate them the most. Whereas similarity ordinarily leads to attraction, when the similarity is threatening, the opposite occurs (Coles 1971; Rubin 1973). Likewise, to minimize the threat rednecks shy away from all associations with blacks other than the few (and increasingly exceptional) who will still accept condescending treatment and otherwise acknowledge "their place" as inferiors.

SIX

THE WORLD OF WORK

The redneck's life is work centered, and without the work milieu the typification of the *redneck* would be meaningless to those who identify themselves with the term as well as to those who identify as rednecks. Hard, physical work is a central component of the redneck's folk culture, ubiquitous to his life-style and essential to his sense of manliness and stock of knowledge. Therefore, pride in physical work is the major focus of redneck life. There is little else for him to be proud of other than being a Southerner and a male, two roles that encompass physical work as far as he in concerned. Several themes characterize the reality of the redneck's work setting: physical orientation, pride in work accomplishments, a common stock of knowledge placing one on the "edge of things," male domination, and informal work relations (Dotter and Moore 1979).

PHYSICALLY ORIENTED WORK

Rednecks define *work* as physical activity directed toward making a living without the orbit of play, and people who do not work with their hands do not "really" work. Sports and recreational activity (hunting, fishing, golfing, et. cetera) do not qualify as work. College athletes and professional sports figures (for example, ball players) do not work because they are really playing, nor do lawyers, bankers, preachers, or school-teachers. Some M.D.'s might work to some extent because they use their hands to make a living, but most just make money. Not only are nonmanual tasks exempted from real work, but those who perform them are neither manly nor trustworthy. Yet at the same time, rednecks admire and look up to professionals. They derogate that above their reach in a manner the psychologist would call "reaction formation" or what the man in the street would call "sour grapes." Professional and white-collar Southerners are keenly aware of the rednecks' ambivalence and resentment toward them. The following comments made to one of the authors by an attorney illustrates the typical professional and white-collar reaction as well as some general attitudes toward rednecks.

> People like me, you know, people who are somebody, know that the rednecks envy us. They always have. It's kind of a natural thing. So what. We don't give a damn about how they feel so long as they show us respect and pay us. And they do that in most cases. Who gives a damn about how they really feel anyway? They're a bunch of losers . . . .They know it and everybody else knows it. And they know that we know they are losers. The better class of people has always had to look after them. The way I look at it, and the way most all the people I associate with see it, is very simple. We service them as long as they pay. No pay, no services. Otherwise, to hell with them and their stupid feelings. But they're not like "niggers." Who in hell needs "niggers" anymore? Machines took care of them. We need some neck business and they need us. And we don't have to worry about them disappearing. We will always have rednecks around . . . too many. But somebody has to do the dirty work. Thank God they're white. Otherwise who would do the low class work around here. I pray they never get labor unions or a white Martin Luther King. If they do, my class of people will be in big trouble.

Typical redneck occupations include factory workers, construction workers, mechanics, gas station attendants, policemen, truckers, carpenters, house painters, welders, electricians, and working farmers (not big farmers and planters who do not actually work the farm themselves). Rednecks are, generally speaking, wage earners who do not own the work establishment where they are employed. *Redneck women* (a new term used by some since the early 1970s) work as waitresses, sales clerks, cashiers, typists, bookkeepers, cooks, factory and mill workers, and babysitters. All of these lower-working-class jobs (with the exception of farming) are typifications of the redneck's view of work as a physically oriented, body-centered activity pursued in the interest of a livelihood.

Rednecks take pride in varied manual work skills, physical endurance and strength, seniority on the job, and a sense of personal satisfaction and indispensability at the work site. Many brag about their ability to fix things: clocks, cars, tractors, machinery, plumbing, irons, tools, tires, et. cetera. They also boast about how much weight they can lift, how long and hard they can work, and how far they can drive a truck without rest or sleep. Most are proud of being good handymen (for example, house painters, fence-post setters, trappers, timber and sawmill workers, hog and cattle workers, truck drivers, welders, and farm workers). All profess a certain uncommon know-how about the performance of one work task or line of work and emphasize length of job experience. Very few can claim job skills learned in formal trade school settings.

The following exchange (reported by Dotter and Moore [1979, p. 10]) illustrates the physical aspects of work:

College Student (talking to a gas station attendant): Well, even if you don't get paid much, this is pretty easy work.

Attendant: Hell, I'd just as soon be working my ass off as sitting on it.

Obscene expressions frequently communicate the physical aspects of work, and expressions about body movements often convey rednecks' strength. In the following excerpt from Dotter and Moore (1979, p. 12) the correct way to stack construction materials is a point of disagreement between an older, more experienced redneck and a younger one who has learned procedures in a trade school:

Older Worker: Hey you shithead, don't stack those beams behind me like that. It's easier for me if you stack them next to me.

Younger Worker: But this is the way they taught me in welding school.

Older Worker: I don't give a fuck what those paper-pushin' pussies told you. I have been weldin' those cross-beams for 25 years and I know how to do it. Do it like I told you, son.

This quote also shows the rednecks' disdain for and/or jealousy of formal schooling, even trades training. The designation "son" conveys two things: the younger worker is less experienced on the job than the older worker, and the younger worker must respect the older worker for being his senior. Respect for age is found throughout the Southern social structure, but more emphasis is placed on maturity among working-class men than among professionals where skill, family background, and wealth count more. Frequently, age or lengthy work experience is the only thing the redneck has going for him.

PRIDE IN WORK AND INDIVIDUALISM

The redneck's expressed positive attitudes toward work are individualistic rather than work organization directed. He stresses the high quality he puts in work tasks and devalues the worth of supervision involved. The redneck approaches the work situation in an egocentric fashion and stresses the application of work skills in concrete rather than in abstract modes. Emphasis is placed on "learning by doing" on the job. Trade school knowledge and book learning is scorned. Poor white Southerners have historically worked more or less on their own without gang or group supervision as small farmers, herders, and tenant farmers and have escaped the close group supervision common with blacks. A tradition of freedom on semifrontier or rural or small-town scene has permitted them free time to goof off, hunt, fish, trap, and work on a seasonal and self-determined basis without disciplined direction or management. Raw individualism and a loose definition of time schedules, rather than laziness and sloppiness as the media would have it, are characteristic of the redneck's attitude toward work. Work pride is expressed in various ways, depending upon specific tasks. Mechanics frequently tell stories about how they spent all day or night to "finish that sucker" car. The redneck works at his own pace on whatever he is "fixing" until it works. Should he not be able to make do with the tools at hand or should the job prove impossible (to him) because of the poor quality of the product or object he is working with, he will refuse to work further on the project.

The traditional lack of supervision and quality control becomes at times a point of contention between rednecks and their bosses. The following comments overheard by one of the authors illustrate the point. A carpenter states:

Nobody needs to tell me how to do my job. If he thinks he can do it better, he can do it himself.

A sawmill worker comments about a disagreement with his "educated' foreman:

I don't want no goddamned foreman or college boy telling me how to do my job. I been at it for fifteen years. And I don't like to be rushed neither. I told that jackass to get off my back . . . .that I'd git around to it when I could.

A cotton mill worker takes a somewhat softer line on supervision but still maintains the traditional view:

I told that damned foreman the story he didn't want to hear. Hell with all that trade school shit. You gotta learn how to run those goddamned machines in the mill yourself. Course somebody's got to git you started along. You know, when you start out. After that it's every man for his self.

A mechanic spouts off about his boss, the owner of an automobile dealership and garage:

> I worked on that lemon the boss sold that old man every week for two months. I finally told the boss, "it twant no use fer me to work on that sucker no more ... it want no good and can't be fixed even by Jesus Christ." He said to me, "John, you go on out there and fix that car. I know you can do it. Don't give me no more lip. I'm the boss and you do what I say, do you understand?" I tole him, "O.K., Mr. Bossman, you go fix that sucker. You can shove it and your fuckin' job up your ass. I quit. Do you understan?"

Though pride is taken in individual work performance, an explicit unconcern ("fuck 'em") is expressed about employers, factory output, and achievement of organizational goals. Close supervision by supervisors and foremen is resented and avoided if possible. Rednecks prefer to work at their own pace and to negotiate work tasks among fellow workers on an egalitarian, simple, direct, and informal basis. A tobacco warehouse floor worker complains about his foreman, close supervision, and organizational goals to one of the authors at the work site:

> I told that pissy ass foreman I didn't give a shit if the American Tobacco Company didn't sell another frigging cigarette ... that I didn't smoke the poison shit anyway. I chew. I 'splained to him I didn't care a rat's ass about team work 'tween warehouse work and the factory and all that marketing bullshit. I tried to git over to him that alla what I was interested in was gitting these basket fulls of tobacco off the floor and ready for the drying plants ... thass all me and the other fellers give a shit about cause thass all we git paid fer. And we do a good job when left alone. If that smart ass foreman who's buckin' for a buyer's job would leave us floor men be, we'd do the job better. We work things out fine mongst us selves. You know one pulls, one sweeps, two of us load and one drives. We all unload at the drying plant. We shift up. If he keeps on a'messing with me, he can take the whole ball of wax and shove it. I mean the whole shit-a-roo cousin, you know what I mean? You been there, too, right?

Note in the above quote that the warehouse worker personalizes the work situation to his boss and to the author interviewer. (I had told him that I had worked as a floor man in a tobacco warehouse.)

Southerners, particularly rednecks, have a tendency to personalize their relationships with others, whereas outsiders more frequently reserve intimate topics for relatives or close friends. Some outsiders are actually embarrassed by Southerners' revelations. (And who wants to hear them?) The redneck tries to personalize the work situation for three reasons. First, he is telling the boss, other employees, and himself that he counts, that he is a human being worthy of consideration just because he is human. Second, he thinks that the more he personalized a situation, the more equal he becomes to all the other actors. In the first instance, he appears to be successful in the South, but he usually fails with regard to the second point. Third, he thinks that personalization gives him a hold over others; that is, according to rednecks (and to a lesser degree, other Southerners), when people get to know you and listen to your personal experiences and tales, they become involved with and obligated to you. This ruse works sometimes. Generally, the higher the social class of the Southerner and the greater his or her competence, the less personalization in the work situation. Class and competence, unfortunately, do not always coincide. In any event, to personalize among strangers and work acquaintances "shows no class," according to middle- and upper-class Southerners.

The individualistic attitude of the redneck toward the work situation explains in part his antipathy for labor unions and government inter-ference with job activities (even that "interference" that obviously benefits him such as OSHA, the Office of Safety and Health Admi-nistration). The redneck is suspicious of any "progressive" government program that has been played up in popular culture. In reality the redneck is a marginal man straddling the fence betwen the economics and social benefits of work and potentially threatening calls for equal rights, that is, from his narrow point of view. Actually, he might have a point in the short run—for example, if all blacks were immediately given equal job opportunity with rednecks, perhaps some rednecks would lose their jobs. In the long run both groups would be better off with equal job opportunities. The redneck, unfortunately, is only concerned with the here and now, and from his position job discrimination against blacks helps him. As the redneck says, "I'll take mine now." This immediate need for gratification hurts him in many ways. For example, he is too quick to settle with insurance companies following personal injury cases. Many rednecks frequently make hasty, insufficient settlements with insurance companies without the aid of an attorney, whereas middle- and upper-class Southerners always consult attorneys in insurance cases.

Work Activity and Living on the Edge of Things

Ray Raphael (1976) claims that certain groups in the United States are caught on the edge of things, torn between traditional and more liberated contemporary life-styles. Such groups' common stock of know-ledge, according to him, is contradicted by much of the information they receive from the popular media. The redneck's common stock of knowledge comes from the poor white's folk culture and conflicts with many ideas he encounters in the media. The authors know several rednecks who do not allow their children to own or listen to "nigger music," jazz records. A redneck father dictates to his adolescent son: "Hey boy, cut off that 'nigger' music. Put on some white soul. You know, a country record fer me and my guest. You hear me boy." Rednecks only watch soap operas, westerns, some news, country and Western productions, sporting events, and fundamentalist religious programs on television. We have seen many turn off the set when problack, prounion, or proliberal positions of any kind appear during any program. Few take any newspaper or magazine. Nevertheless, the media gets through to them primarily through their children with whom many are in conflict.

The redneck is occupationally marginal in a changing society, and his work attitudes are increasingly opposed by other Americans at the work site who are joining unions and trying to get ahead. Rednecks are neither concerned with the same type of respectability as middle-class people nor (in most cases) preoccupied with attaining middle-class status. To them respectability means a steady job, an honest living, and work activity that provides room for individual contributions, all increasingly difficult to find. Additionally, the days of the creative handyman are past. The redneck's position toward work is contrary to widespread notions of future social mobility, increasing professional standing, and getting ahead. To the redneck a custodial services worker is nothing but a janitor, a correctional officer in the prison setting is a guard, sanitary workers are garbage collectors, professional underwriters are insurance salesmen, and foremen by whatever name are bosses. Additionally, absolutely everyone who works in the personnel office is a son of a bitch. He knows what he is and is not concerned with phony or real upward mobility. As one redneck reported:

> I told my boss at the factory he could shove that new title he wanted to give me ....materials inspector or something like that. I told him he could shave the phony promotion, too, that he claimed went with it ....all but the money. I told that phony, "Just give me the money and hold the bullshit."

The redneck needs his job to "get along" or "get by" rather than to increase his social status. He is concerned with personal status among his peers in a marginal subculture, a status that is achieved and preserved through and by taking care of his family, putting the bread on the table, being a man of his word, showing loyalty to his peers and work buddies, being a man who is ready and willing to fight or resort to violence, displaying loyalty to the Southern region, possessing a repertoire of expletives, and manifesting virility and the ability to hold alcohol.

Furthermore, he must take an open stand against "niggers," libbers, welfare programs, big government, big business, socialists and communists, the United Nations, labor unions, heathens, Catholics, Jews, foreigners, Yankees, social workers, big shots, bosses, fancy clothes, fancy food, jazz music, classical music, the opera, the ballet, museums, and all things artistic or intellectual. As one redneck reported, "I'm agin all that cultural bullshit. If I can't eat it, wear it, or use it, piss on it."

Rednecks utilize derogatory stereotypes in defense of their marginal occupational position, as the following quotes from Dotter and Moore (1979, pp. 15-20) demonstrate:

> *Older Mill Worker*: Last night I saw on the news where they let in some more of the damn fur-ners. I guess they'll be trying to take our jobs.

> *Younger Mill Worker*: Well, the government give money to the Chinaman. They give dollars to the poor, grain to Russia, and taxes to us working people. Some justice that is. Those "niggers" just want our jobs. That's why we don't have nothing. We gonna have to ventually stand up and fight them "niggers" fer our jobs. I don't know why people want to hire them. They ain't good but fer one thing. God fixed it so we'd come to keep the niggers from fucking themselves to death.

Note that the last two lines of the quote are racially illogical, but then that is the point. Southerners and especially rednecks are rarely logical about anything—even making love. Rednecks despise phoniness in any form, but they are serious rather than cynical actors. It is very risky for anyone but a boss man to present a false front to the redneck. They attack the perceived faker and respect the honest actor. There is more to the honest actor than how he acts. The status of the actor also makes him honest or dishonest. Most bosses and big shots are dishonest by definition. Bosses, minority group leaders, liberals, politicians, poverty program workers, and do-gooders are perceived to hide behind facades. The redneck sees himself as honest and still marginal—so why should he respect those are marginal and false?

Emotional Display, Male Domination, and Chauvinism

The folk culture of the redneck, like the poor whites folk culture before him (basically the same culture), is dominated by male work values. Traditional male and female relationships have been defined in unequal terms for several reasons: The physical nature of the male's work and the necessity of possessing considerable physical strength to perform most work tasks is one prime reason. The male's role has traditionally been that of the breadwinner. Certainly religion, Southern culture, and a patriarchial background also explain dominant male work values. Moreover, being on the "edges of things" causes rednecks to feel more threatened—hence, defensiveness is frequently found in redneck interactions with "modern women."

Rednecks have always performed physical work and thereby have been the principal providers for women and children. Most prefer that their women not work but rather stay at home with the children. This view has persisted in redneck culture, which is somewhat insulated from the mainstream despite the fact that many of these women do work outside the home because of economic necessity. Like other possessions, rednecks also own their women and children. Women, therefore, have developed manipulative techniques to cope. Currently, these techniques are resented by the male who feels that he is being attacked by the "new woman." Historically though, Southern men owned their women and children. Southern folklore abounds with the ways the Southern belle and the Southern bitch (many times one and the same) have manipulated men by flattery, guile, seduction, coquettishness, glamour, sex, and clothes. The Southern belle is a master at revealing and concealing simultaneously her sexuality, which is frequently more thrilling in contemplation and expectation than in actuality. The price tag emotionally and financially is exorbitant. Nothing comes for free with the Southern belle. One must even pay for worshipping her. The point is that middle- and upper-class white Southern men and women have been more subtle than rednecks at sex games and have enjoyed them more.

Redneck work culture is particularly amenable to male emotional displays. These dramas express masculine attributes such as aggression (for example, knocking a hand through a doorway), loyalty to the boys (for example, going drinking with the boys when they want to, even if a marriage is at stake), courage (for example, never backing down from a good fight), and virility (for example, never turning down a good piece). Rednecks frequently use obscene and profane language in the presence of women in their own social class (but never in the presence of middle- and upper-class females) to show their manliness and dominance. Females often interpret this dirty talk as offensive and demeaning, and should they express such reactions to the redneck offender, he revels in his superiority and talks even dirtier. Dirty talk, then, is one way of defending the masculine position in redneck work culture. For example, one redneck husband orders his wife to perform a masculine task in the presence of one of the authors:

> Woman git out there to my pick-up and bring me those tools in the seat and the six pack in here, too, right away. You hear me, right now bitch and don't give me no shit neither. I told you before. Now you better git off

your big ass and fetch the beer. I might even do you later if you act right.

This quote demonstrates the redneck's direct and crude approach to sex. His black counterparts are more indirect and romantic in sex talk. The redneck says, "I cut the chick"; the black man says, "I balled the fox." The redneck says, "I'll do you later"; the black says, "Later for the happenings, baby."

The following scene reported by Dotter and Moore (1979, p. 20) demonstrates male dramaturgy and the use of dirty talk:

> *Construction worker 1*: Bring me that tool or I'll wrap this pipe upside your head boy.
>
> *Construction Worker 2*: Fuck you you son-of-a-bitch, get it yourself or you'll have to deal with *me*!

The traditional pattern of male dominance and emotional display is being tested now by the increasing influx of female participants in the redneck workplace. In this respect, some rednecks distinguish between the *redneck woman* and the *woman redneck*. These two typifications differ because of their linguistic and dramaturgical strategies. The contemporary redneck woman, a member of a redneck family, conforms to more traditional language and the presentation of self in most situations. However, she does not always submit to the male but rather walks a thin line between partial liberation and traditional submission. She endeavors to state her own opinion and establish some independence, while simultaneously avoiding ridicule and physical abuse. She may drive her own redneck car (a masculine symbol) and still defer to her man when it is necessary. Most redneck women work in discount stores, factories, and mills and as waitresses. Frequently, in the job situation she must give lip service to the notion of male dominance or subject herself to male group sanctions. In the following situation, reported by Dotter and Moore (1979, p. 22), a redneck woman obviates the issue of overt sexual confrontation by manipulating the idiom to her own advantage:

> *Waitress*: Hi, honey, what can I get you this morning?
>
> *Truck Driver*: Hi baby, what will you give me?
>
> *Waitress*: Well, the special is two eggs, sausage, hash browns, muffins, and coffee.
>
> *Truck Driver*: Is that *all* I can have?
>
> *Waitress*: No, but that's all *you* can get.

Had she rejected him at the beginning of their conversation, she might have lost a customer. Instead, she played along just enough to allow him to treat her as a sex object and still stay within the informal rules of the restaurant. Otherwise, she would have committed a residual rules violation and been labeled as "the frigid waitress at the truck stop on Highway 221."

The so-called woman redneck, on the other hand, takes on both the linguistic and dramaturgical strategies of male rednecks. She challenges male rednecks on their own grounds and walks and talks like them. She attempts to prove herself in the workplace to obtain redneck respect. Should she conduct herself like one of the boys in expressed opinions and acts and display strength, courage, and pride in the physical aspects of work, she is likely to be accepted as an equal member of the work team. We are not certain as to how many women rednecks will appear on the scene, and we are not sure how they will be treated outside of the work setting, but we receive frequent reports about more modern and egalitarian relationships between redneck men and women outside the workplace. As long as they both share a common stock of knowledge and the same work site, the door is open for more egalitarian social relationships. Frequently, people of all social classes go out with and marry those with whom they work. At this point redneck women abhore, stay away from, and try to keep their men away from women rednecks whom they see as sexual threats to their households. Most middle- and upper-class Southerners perceive women rednecks as freaks of nature.

Informal Negotiation in Work Experience

These illustrations highlight the informal nature of the work situation among rednecks. Social relationships are regulated by informal norms emerging from the linguistic and dramaturgical strategies of the participants. The use of dirty talk is one way of ensuring informality as well as masculinity. Physical play in the form of pushing and shoving and other physical expressions of "good work" or friendship also ensure informality. Work buddies are frequently drinking and social buddies. Sociability among rednecks includes a large amount of "deviance" (drinking, emotional displays such as anger, time out, and horseplay) on the job, which is tolerated by peers. "Getting along" informally with coworkers is a must for the completion of work tasks. Dotter and Moore (1979, p. 24) report the following typical work scene. Two gas station attendants face a lull in customer traffic and the following dialogue ensues:

> *Bill*: Well, why don't you go down in the back of my pickup and get that six pack of beer. It otta' still be cold enough to drink.

Jack: What if the manager drives in and catches us?

Bill: What the hell does that matter? It's two o'clock in the morning and the front's clear. It ain't gonna' hurt nobody any way.

In this case, acceptable deviance renders the job situation more bearable. The refusal of the invitation to drink beer could have strained the relationship between coequals and made future work activities more difficult. Antiunion sentiment and individualism, both mentioned above, are also products of this traditionally informal work milieu.

CONCLUSION

The redneck work culture represents a blue-collar social world, and the Southern working class is similar in some respects to the working class in other regions but significantly different in others. Like E. E. Le Masters's (1975) subjects, "blue-collar aristocrats," rednecks are conservative on social issues such as women's rights and race, though more so. Unlike many of their outside counterparts, rednecks are antiunion, extremely regionally conscious, narrowly religious, emotionally tied to the open country and a small-town life-style, and above all rooted to a poor white Southern folk culture.

The work world of the redneck is changing, and the rednecks' definition of work and respectability and his insistence on informal authority, personal negotiations in work relations, and male domination at the work site are all under attack. Even in the South the work site is becoming increasingly regulated, impersonal, and competitive. More Southern women are entering the labor force, and some of them insist on an equal work basis with men.

On the other hand, certain aspects of redneckery are being assimilated by some members of the middle class—for example, a laid-back personal life-style, country music, and the precepts of the moral majority. Prior to the 1960s country music was always the folk music of the white Southern working class, "white soul." It has been somewhat jazzed up as "pop-country" music and has now spread across the country as the nation's most popular type of music. The lyrics and central themes remain the same, centering on the personal problems of individuals, and supposedly require simplistic, personalized answers—for example, one sees the light and straightens up, goes to work, changes his life-style, et cetera. The problems posed and their antidotes constitute a false package deal that comes right out of a poor white folk culture. Black music has been much more revolutionary than country music, and though jazz is certainly misery music, its themes do not include simplistic answers. At worst, one continues to suffer.

The seriousness that outsiders place on country music, reactionary politics, a Southern laid-back life-style, racism, square dancing, chauvinism, fundamentalism, and the preachments of the "moral majority" remain to be seen. Americans have eternally tried to change the South while showing no, or little, concern for the South's influence on other regions. The extent of the rednecks' diffused culture without and within the South will determine in great part the development or non-development of class consciousness. The more redneck Southern diffusion, the more weakened class consciousness. On the other hand, rednecks are selecting some attributes from nonredneck life-styles. Long-haired rednecks of the younger generation use unconventional drugs such as marijuana and some cocaine when they can afford it (and get it) yet retain redneck social meanings toward work.

Some people have "left" the traditional redneck culture as a primary reference point and entered the middle class by becoming a part of the bureaucratic milieu and/or obtaining a middle-class position. These newcomers invariably retain selected redneck definitions and relinquish others in an effort to "make it" in a more highly structured and sophisticated environment, while religious views and attitudes toward women remain unchanged. Some of the informal linguistic and dramaturgical strategies learned in the redneck work culture "pass" in the more formalized middle-class work setting if toned down—particularly among Southerners, most of whom have some pink spots on their necks.

The place of the redneck at the edge of things, male domination, and informal work relations contribute to the openness of the redneck world. At best he is honest, open, and straightforward—and a hypocrite he is not. He wishes to get along in an unchanging world, an impossibility that he does not understand. Were he ever to develop a strong working-class consciousness, things could be much better for him and other working-class people and, eventually, for all of us with the exception of the 4 or 5 percent superrich. And, who really cares about preserving the small capitalist upper class? The answer to this rhetorical question is: members of the upper class and fools who want to keep them there to worship or to join eventually (pie-in-the-sky dreamers).

SEVEN

THE LANGUAGE OF
THE REDNECK

Verbal and nonverbal communication typifies the redneck as a part of the Southern blue-collar social class. Communication is essentially a means of entertainment, since the primary medium of interaction for the Southern redneck is oral. In fact, this form of entertainment is a two-way monologue that Flynt (1979) has referred to as "spinning yarns." This "storytelling" takes place when two or more rednecks are gathered together in a socially acceptable place, with one story following another. The stories are not necessarily associated with one another. Acceptable places have included moments sitting around pot-bellied stoves in general stores, fishing and hunting trips, and white blue-collar beer joints.

While academic journals have been somewhat lax in analyzing the conversations of the Southern redneck, reports have been written in popular anecdotal publications, many of them regional in nature. The books indicate that rednecks develop their own vocabularies, and outsiders have trouble identifying the rhetoric since most are Southern and rural expressions. Most of the expressions as well as the stories themselves are experientially based. However, the reporting of events is often exaggerated, colored, expanded, and dramatized. The fishing tale may be used as an analogy for other redneck stories that are built around ignorant blacks—encounters with the law, fast cars or trucks, loose women, drinking sessions, or trips taken elsewhere.

The structure of the redneck language is visible in their descriptions of themselves to us:

Us rednecks are jes nobodys.

We're as good as anybody. Bus we jes never had no chance.

We figer things out different and we're stubborn, too, 'bout niggers and foreigners.

We think like you 'cept we jes got different enemies.

We otta stand together like them big shot whites and them Jews.

I reckon we're better off like God made us: poor.

We don't need no help from nobody.

We're jes po honest working folks who work for an honest day's pay.

Folks like us work for a livin'. The big guys are a bunch of phonies, know what I'ma talkin' bout?—phonies and bullshitters.

I guess the whites who got it got more ejacation an brains than us.

Us rednecks are tween the rock and the hard place, ya know, the big shot whites and the niggers. And don't fergit big business and big gov'ment.

Maybe us rednecks otta git mor politickin' and stand up fer what's ours. Lookie what them niggers git from the gov'ment and everthing.

Hit tain't fair. We gotta pay fer all that welfare.

Us rednecks are jes God-fearing Christians who don't cheat like niggers and the rich white man. Maybe we'll git ours in heaven.

Us rednecks are a holdin' the South together. Without us the rest of the whites and the niggers, too, would git et up.

I might be a redneck, but my chillen won't be. I ain't justa talkin cousin.

There ain't much difference tween us necks and other people hereabouts—'cept maybe money. All us live bout alike. I mean none us is a goin' hungry.

Some big shots is necks, too. All us come outta the same bag. Fact is, it's hard to tell who be and who ain't a redneck.

Shit, anybody can be a redneck; it ain't who you be—but how you think.

While one can see that rednecks do not particularly mind being called "redneck," by other rednecks, they do object to terms such as *cotton mill trash* (Killian 1970, p. 49) or *po' white trash* (Flynt 1979, p. 8).

LANGUAGE STRUCTURE

The structure is notably incorrect according to standard American English. Typical errors include subject-verb disagreement (We is);

incorrect tense usage (We drunk a whole gallon a wine); mispro-
nunciation of words (*figer* for *figure*); the use of words in an incorrect or
awkward context (I'm fixin' to go to the store); the substitution of *d* for a *th*
sound as in *dat* for *that*); leaving the *g* off of "ing" words; and the creation
of a private, redneck vocabulary. As Lewis M. Killian (1970, p. 11) has
noted, the redneck Southerner can "easily be identified by his accent."

As Greet (1935, p. 595) noted, the substitution of the *d* for *th* is found
in *de* for *the* and other substitutions as well. Other substitutions include *sez*
for *says*; *frum* for *from*; *en* for *and*; *instunce* for *instance*; *izn't* for *isn't*; *thar*
for *there*; and *sartin* for *certain*. A most common Southern term *y'all* is
used by rednecks as well as more influential Southerners. Although many
of the substitutions, such as the *d* for *th*, are used by blacks as well as
rednecks, many black terms (such as *ax* for *ask*) are not used by rednecks.
Some Southern drawl expressions are predominately upper class, such as
he-uh for *here*. Others are found primarily in the blue-collar group: *waah-
ah* for *war*; *bee-ah* for *beer*; and *pot likker* for *pot liquor*.

Some other notable words we found in the vocabulary of the
Southern redneck are also found in the work of Mitchell (1976). *Argy* is
one. Mitchell defines *argy* as "to dispute in a contentious manner. Ah told
you to take your bath, boy, and I'm not gonna stand here and argy with you
about it.'" Other interesting expressions are related to Southern cuisine, as
noted by Mitchell. For example, "Fatback: Salt pork—an essential
ingredient in the cooking of collard greens and beans. Ah like fried out
fatback as much as bacon.' " "Griyuts: What no Southern breakfast would
be complete without—grits. 'Ah like griyuts with butter and sawt on 'em,
but I purely love 'em with red-eye gravy.' " Other food of importance
includes *okry* ("okra"); *bobbycue* ("barbeque"); collard, turnip, and
mustard greens (all referred to as *greeuns*; and black-eyed peas as well as
butta beans ("limas").

Generally speaking, however, the redneck has learned his language
and pronunciation as both a Southerner and as a blue-collar person. To
this extent he resents the concept of standard American English as used
by the upper middle and upper classes. Correct pronunciation and
grammar are perceived of as effeminate and something that is of little
importance. People who use correct pronunciation and grammar, and who
do not use such terms as *y'all*, are thought of as "actin' lik they's betterun'
de res' us." A summary of this might be: "Ejacation *don't* make de
man."

One interesting phenomenon has to do with how geographical areas
are located. Cities with "ville" in their titles are pronounced with the
emphasis on the last syllable: Gaines-*ville*, Stark-*ville*, Collins-*ville*, Louis-
ville. In addition, people are more often referred to as being from Pickens
County or Rankin County than from a particular city or town. A person
from Atlanta or Miami may be considered an outsider even though he is a

Southerner and may be a blue-collar worker. These cities have become, for the redneck, full of Yankees, niggers, and Cubans. When explaining directions, a system is usually used to indicate that the redneck is familiar with the history of the area, while the person asking directions is not: "Well, ye go down de highway thar about three-quarters uv a mile to ye git ta de ol' Simmons' place, take a left ta de Johnson farm an' it'll be de third house on de right." When it comes to directions involving states outside the South, the redneck has little expertise. Iowa and Idaho are often confused. Most rednecks have not been outside the South.

VOCABULARY

Ernest J. Bunch (1978), a self-proclaimed redneck, has translated several blue-collar terms into English. Among the phrases that are of significance are the following: *made a killing, lowrate, beat the daylights out'ta him, reck-o-lect, got the big head*, and *passel*.

> *Made a killing*; An expression used to denote that someone had been engaged in a profitable venture, usually of a monetary nature. *e.g.* I think old man Woodard's boys have *made a killing* with that 'air sawmill. [Bunch 1978, p. 1]

> *Lowrate*; To degrade someone by voice or action. To make an offensive or disparaging remark about someone. To belittle. *e.g.* Since Sarah Jane and Ralph busted up, she never misses a change to *lowrate* him something awful. [Bunch 1978, p. 3]

> *Beat the daylights out'ta him*; Give someone a severe physical beating, Bested someone in a contest, or got the best of someone in a trade or barter. *e.g.* I knowed if he tangled with Horace, that he would *beat the daylights out'ta him.* [Bunch 1978, p. 3]

> *Reck-o-lect*; To recall or remember. *e.g.* I *reck-o-lect*, when I was a boy, my dad put up this here lowest post for the lot gate to hang on. Well sir, that post was so sound it stayed there long enough that it rotted four holes out. [Bunch 1978, p. 137]

> *Got the big head*; Descriptive expression used to denote, infer or imply that the person, or persons, under discussion has recently enjoyed, either real or imaginary, some good fortune that has had the unfortunate results of influencing the person to assume a status of great import. Especially so in his own mind. Such an obnoxious person attempted to "live above his means" when favorable occasions presented themselves. *e.g.* Old Lady Jones has shore *got the big head* since her husband got that spank fired new Tennessee wagon. [Bunch 1978, pp. 15-16]

> *Passel*; a large but undetermined amount. It could easily be used to

describe time or material, and often was. *e.g.* Lee Ellis and two or three of his boys went to the creek yesterday. They took a bunch of hoes and muddied some of the ponds down ther and came back with a whole *passel* of fish. [Bunch 1978, p. 1]

AMBIGUITY AND SPECIFICITY

When the terms are created, they are often more ambiguous in the redneck language than they are in standard American English. This quality of ambiguity allows for flexibility when speaking of size, speed, age, et cetera. As one can easily see, a *passel* may be almost any number. The concept of numbers and statistics being ambiguous among blue-collars has been pointed out in other research (Sacks 1979, p. 7):

Ken: In that Bonneville of mine I c'd take the thing out, an' if I've gotta *tie*, an' a-a sweater on, an' I look clean? . . . ninedy nine percent a' the time a guy c'd pull up to me, and the *same* car, same color, same year the whole bit, . . . roar up his pipes, . . . and he's inna dirty grubby tee shirt an' the guy'll pick the guy up in the dirty grubby *tee* shirt before un he'll pick *me* up.

( ): hheh

Ken: J'st-Just for //, uh-

Al: (Bu') not many people get picked up in a Pontiac station wagon.

Sacks's example is from a study of hot-rodders, but we found the language could have been used by rednecks as well. The "99 percent" is a figure that loosely interpreted means most of the time. The ambiguity of the language is also demonstrated in the use of the term *guy* to refer to both the hot-rodder and the policeman. The specificity of the language dominates the conversation of the redneck only when discussing referents of importance. An example in the above quotation is the explicit terminology used in referring to automobiles: the Bonneville and the Pontiac station wagon.

Rednecks told us that automobiles and pickup trucks are their most prized possessions. As Sylvia Wilkinson (1980, p. 130) has pointed out: "Stock car racing had an image problem from the start, a hard hat, blue-collar association that made it a one-class attraction." She continued, quoting Bledsoe: "'Respectable' people didn't think much of stock car racing at the time, 1950. Stock car races were looked down on as much as motorcycle gang members are today. Roughnecks. A wild bunch banging around on those dirt tracks, drinking, gambling, fighting—always fighting" (pp. 130-31).

Although rednecks keep up with the results of stock car racing today, the National Association for Stock Car Racing (NASCAR), nationally sanctioned races, appear to be too expensive for their tastes. Wilkinson's (1980, p. 132) conclusion still has merit, however: "Stock car racing is without a doubt a sport for rednecks, not the southern gentility." The fact is, though, that the language and the spirit of the stock car race has now become a sports spectacle of the local variety, similar in scope to the local political picnic or the Sunday afternoon softball game. Bobby Allison and Richard Petty are still names in the trivia of redneckery, but it may be just as important to know the names of the local boys who build their cars from scratch and race them in Louisville, Mississippi, or Byron, Georgia. These local races, which Wilkinson (1980, p. 134) calls "illegal," were defined to us by rednecks as "outlaw races," not sanctioned by NASCAR. But if the national heroes are not in the experience of the contemporary redneck, they are in the dreams and aspirations of the redneck. A redneck may purchase books, magazines, and manuals to read about the men and their cars in the hope that one day they themselves will win in Atlanta, Darlington, or Talladega.

Cars and trucks are important possessions for the redneck. Today a number of rednecks also get into motorcycles and dirt bike racing. They often "live" out their vehicles. Their vehicles are topics of conversation. If an outsider does not know about motored vehicles, he will have a difficult time communicating with some rednecks, especially mechanics.

The late 1970s brought with them a new tool for redneck rhetoric: the citizens' band (CB) radio. While the CB has been around for sometime, the Federal Communications Commission had not made its use as free and open as it now is. The redneck can now communicate directly with one of his hero professionals, the truck driver, while they are both on the road. "Hey, good buddy" is only the beginning of a conversation filled with "10-4's" and "Where's Smokey?"

According to the *Complete CB Slang Dictionary* (1981), there are currently more than 6 million CB enthusiasts throughout the country. With the relaxed restrictions for obtaining licenses and with the cost of equipment going down, the redneck joined the group. There are a number of terms that are called "CB'ers 10-codes," which includes *10-4*, which means, "OK, message received." The term *10-100* was used extensively in the movie *Smokey and the Bandit*, and afterward it became a more prominent code in the redneck vocabulary; *10-100* means "rest room pause." There are other codes used by both civilians and the police to refer to specific situations; all begin with "10."

Some terminology has also been generated to refer to specific cities. In some cases, the terms are complimentary to the city and reflect a "Chamber of Commerce" orientation. In other cases, they are more negative in nature. Atlanta, for example, is sometimes referred to as the Big "A," Hot Lanta, or Hot Town; Birmingham is B Town, Magic City, or Steel City; Chattanooga is Choo Choo Town or Rock City; Forest City, Arkansas, is Bar City; Hot Springs, Arkansas, is Hotwater City; Jackson, Mississippi, is Capital J.; Montgomery, Alabama, is Monkey Town; and Arkansas (as a state) is Hog Country.

Below are a few terms with their English translations from the *Complete CB Slang Dictionary* (1981).

Accidentally on purpose	Drunk driver
Alky	Liquor
Ape	Rough trucker
Babe	A woman
Bang up	Accident
Battery acid	Coffee
Bear poem	Traffic ticket
Beaver hunt	Cruising for women
Benny	Benzedrine
Bone box	Ambulance
Camera	Radar
Clip joint	Barber shop
Fat daddy	Overloaded truck
Garbage	Interference
Jock	Young man
Nazi wheelbarrow	Volkswagen
Nipper	Child

The terms tend to reflect the general orientation of having a CB in a vehicle: alcoholic beverage, police, women, types of drivers, uppers, and references to traffic itself. Individuals develop their own names for use on the CB—their *handle*.

In everyday conversation, persons are referred to in specifics only in cases where the credibility of the source is important. That is, usually one will say: "m'ole brother", "m'ole cousin", "th' ole lady", "m'ole man." However, if the information is important and the speaker wants to be believed, he will say: "Uncle Bob said . . . ." In the redneck culture double names, such as Bobby Joe and Tommy Lee, are just as common for males as they are for females (Nancy Faye, Joyce Ann, Betty Jane). A woman who purchased a beer joint in Mississippi while she was pregnant named the establishment for her daughter a few months later. Apparently, the reasoning was that this action would increase the credibility of the daughter in the redneck community.

In addition to the general lack of specificity, the redneck language is often filled with profanity and obscenity. Common terms we found are "damn," "hell," "son-bitch" and "shit." Bunch (1978, p. 97) notes a common expression:

> *Like a bat out'ta hell*; Expression used to denote someone or something made a very quick start and then continued to move with great speed. *e.g.* I don't know what's wrong at the Jenkins house. That biggest boy of his'n has been by here two or three times in the last hour. He was in that red pick-up truck and running *like a bat out'ta hell.*

Profanity is dominant in almost every sentence in beer joints. The following encounter took place between a customer and a barmaid in a Mississippi beer joint in our presence:

> *Customer*: When the hell you gonna' pay off this damn machine?
>
> *Barmaid*: When the hell da ya want me to pay off tha damned machine?
>
> *Customer*: Right the hell now.

Thus, females who work in redneck bars and women who frequent these bars feel the obligation to return as many profanities as they receive. This mode of argumentation allows the woman to be "one of the boys" (woman redneck), which makes everyone more comfortable and prevents the woman's becoming an object of sexual ridicule. Throwing in a "hell" or a "damn" provides a sense of machismo, an essential aspect of the redneck language (Eakins and Eakins 1978).

The body is often used as an analogy, as in Bunch's example of "sucking the back [or hind] tit":

> *Sucking the back tit*; A term used to denote someone is having a hard time, suffering setbacks or otherwise encountering bad luck. In other words, he is having a hard time of it, like the little pig that gets shoved aside by his brother pigs and has to root around and find a back tit to get his dinner. The back tit is difficult to gain access to and he is considered to be handicapped in his gastronomic efforts. [Bunch 1978, p. 137]

At times the rhetoric becomes much more graphic and gross. Two terms that are of particular interest have to do with eating. One redneck, for example, told us that he was so hungry he could "eat the ass end outta' ragdoll." Another, desiring a meal, said he needed "a gut stretcher." Food "to go," and especially a drink "to go," is referred to as a *roadie*.

In terms of structure, then, the redneck language has the following qualities. First, it contains profanities, particularly *hell, damn,* and *shit.*

Second, words are mispronounced, particularly by leaving the g off of "ing" words. Third, incorrect grammar is acceptable, while correct grammar is not. It is here, in fact, that the redneck often distinguishes his "good ole boy" socioeconomic superior from himself. The good old boy can be detected as easily by his language as by his dress or shaving lotion.

The language of the redneck is often included in the good old boy's language but not vice versa. Flynt (1979, p. 115) has described the good old boy:

> Part redneck, part practical genius, the good old boy belonged to a world of moonshining, modified cars, country music, and Saturday night wrestling. For him, professional baseball or a college football scholarship was a ticket from poverty to the good life.

Later topics of conversation for the good old boy have included stock car racing, evangelical religion, and blatant racism. We noted a difference between rednecks and good old boys regarding conversation in that the good old boy has experience conversing with the upper middle and upper classes. The good old boy is much more likely to have served in the military where he had to communicate with officers who were, presumably, in the middle or upper classes. The military experience provides the good old boy with another topic of conversation—"the war story."

NONVERBAL COMMUNICATION

While researchers differ in the specific percentages, nonverbal communication is generally considered at least as important as the words one uses (Birdwhistell 1970; Burgoon and Saine 1978; Hickson 1980; Knapp 1978). The areas of nonverbal communication that impinge upon the verbal interaction include vocalics, physical appearance, proxemics, and kinesics. Vocalics deals with the way that one says a word, that is, the intonation; in addition, vocalics includes loudness, silence, pauses, moans, groans, sneezes, coughs, et. cetera (Hickson 1980). Physical appearance takes into account factors such as body shape, height, weight, skin pigmentation, clothing, and accessories. Proxemics is the study of distance betwen people and often considers environmental factors such as room temperature, color of walls, and lighting. Kinesics studies gestures, posture, eye behavior, and facial expressions. Chronemics involves the study of the use of time. For the redneck, as with other human beings, each of these nonverbal factors contributes to the communication process.

Vocalics

How something is said is as important, if not more important, than what is said. According to Judy K. Burgoon and Thomas Saine (1978, pp. 80-81), "*Vocalics* includes all stimuli produced by the human voice [other than words themselves] that affect the auditory sense. Everything from sniffs and sneezes to rapid speech, nasality, and singing fall into this category. So do silences and pauses during speech." Probably the most notable vocalic factor of the redneck is the intensity or loudness of his talk. Killian (1970, p. 111) reports that a Chicago tavern owner made the following comment about redneck communication: "And they holler at everybody—holler at the bartender, holler at the orchestra, holler at each other." We found the same obtaining in the South.

Obviously, one of the reasons for the loud talk is the loud jukebox music in the beer joints. Often even intimate coversations are conducted in intense voices, so that the partners can hear one another. This is an attempt to overcome what Erving Goffman (1971, p. 51) refers to as "acoustic space violations." These space violations take place when some type of noise prevents conversation from occurring at a normal level of intensity. Even without noise, rednecks usually holler.

Other vocalic differences are incorporated into the redneck culture as promachismo factors. Intensity remains one of these factors. The redneck laughs in very loud tones, and he often laughs longer than a middle-class person. Laughing is particularly common in redneck beer joints where yarns and stories are the primary medium for entertainment, supported by the often depressing country and Western music being played on the jukebox and the undercover preoccupation with a pool game or the pinball machines.

Silence becomes a dominant factor primarily in playing the pinball machines, where many joints will pay off in cash. Here the communication is similar to that one might find on a golf course—even the caddy is to keep his mouth shut. One redneck, philosophizing about the nature of life, claimed, "It's jes a mattuh spendin' quarters."

Sometimes, when the redneck is attempting to get something from an outsider from the role of the good old boy. Here diplomacy surfaces and language improves. The outsider is often asked where he is from—however, the redneck is simply asking what county one is from. The ensuing conversation is a name game of: "Oh, I know ole so-and-so from Crawford County."

When communicating with one another, however, it is very important to maintain the Southern drawl, to use incorrect grammatical structure, to be loud, and to be macho. The macho image is tied up with a deep voice. As Barbara Westbrook Eakins and R. Gene Eakins (1978, p. 98) indicated,

"Male virility is associated with vocal depth." Rednecks who do have a higher-pitched voice are often not accepted by other members of the group, because there appears to be an implication that these men are, at best, latent homosexuals. The deep voice appears to be a masculinity factor throughout American society. Eakins and Eakins (1978, p. 113) point out that "one factor may be our culture's encouragement and pressure on males to live up to, or at least appear to live up to, the masculine morality of machismo, or female conquest."

Rednecks wolf down coarse, greasy food (greens, pork, and black-eyed peas), which tends to produce intestinal gas. It is acceptable among rednecks to release gas in public, in the form of vocalic burps and belches or passing gas. Belching or farting "contests" are not uncommon.

Physical Appearance

The clothing of the redneck is stereotypical of most blue-collar workers. Bluejeans are prominent; tee shirts make up the other half of the uniform. Rednecks rarely wear eyeglasses, contact lenses, or hearing aids since they cannot afford these "luxuries" and since wearing aids would lower the machismo image. The same rationale may be used to explain why most rednecks do not take care of their teeth. The result is numerous cavities, chips, and tobacco stains. Cigarettes are often carried rolled up in the left sleeve of a tee shirt. To say the least, rednecks do not "dress for business success" (Thourlby 1978). Dressing for business success has become quite popular recently; and according to Molloy (1975), it is a scientific process. The types of clothing recommended for a successful businessman are upper middle socioeconomic level garments. John T. Molloy (1975, pp. 40-41) suggests that a suit would range in price from $275 to $600. Most rednecks would not own even one suit in this category. Most rednecks wear double-knit leisure suits when they wear suits. Of course, since most rednecks have blue-collar jobs, this type of dress would be inappropriate. However, rednecks' dress is almost the epitome of not dressing for success, from the top of the head to the tips of the toes.

Although many people think that rednecks wear boots, this mode of dress is more typical of the cowboy. Instead the redneck wears tennis or jogging shoes purchased at outlet stores. As Nina Savin (1981) suggests, they also wear workshoes. Most of the clothing is the same everyday. The variability in the redneck's clothing is often found in what is written on the tee shirt and what kind of cap he wears.

Tee shirts may be "walking advertisements" for some type of business. In addition, they are purchased when the redneck goes on vacation (usually to the coast of Florida), so that "Panama City Beach" and "Myrtle Beach" (South Carolina) tee shirts are common. Beer advertisements are also popular. However, one of the most popular is a country and Western singer's picture on the front with the sentence "If you ain't cowboy, you ain't shit" on the back.

The most important piece of clothing to the redneck is his cap. The authors know one redneck that owns more than 40 different caps, who wears one at all times, even inside. In almost every case, the cap was a giveaway from a parts store, a fertilizer company, or a construction firm. The caps represent the redneck image in its entirety, and they should be worn on almost every occasion. One of the originals of this mode of advertisement, the Caterpillar Corp (CAT) hat, is not often found anymore.

The redneck seldom looks "clean," except on Saturday night, which is the time for "going out." The dirty tee shirt is discarded, and he wears a shirt with buttons, usually bought at an outlet store or, at best, from Sears or Penneys. Usually, the shirt does not match the slacks, so that two types of plaid may be worn, or two checks, or a combination of a plaid and a check. The "dress-up" outfit may include some type of plain, black, inexpensive shoes. The shoes do not have buckles and the like, as only an effeminate person would wear them. The working white socks may be accessories to the dress-up outfit. Belts are used solely to hold one's pants "up"—but beneath the beer belly; there is no attempt to match the color of the shoes and belts. The importance of the belt is found in a status item, the belt buckle. Buckles with beer brand names are popular, as well as anything that is popular in the Texas cowboy culture. Little or no jewelry is worn; when jewelry is worn, it is usually gaudy. Even the watch, usually worn by the white-collar person, is absent—time is not that important to the redneck. However, his knife usually accompanies him.

The redneck's hair is often longer than that of other Southerners. In fact, in recent years the redneck's hair length has approached that of his number-one enemy of the 1960s, the hippie. Many rednecks wear beards and even more wear moustaches.

In terms of accessories, rednecks usually smoke cigarettes (and some, marijuana), but it is rare to find a redneck smoking a cigar or a pipe. While researchers have found that the pipe is of higher credibility among white-collar students, the cigarette may be more credible among rednecks (Hickson 1979). The pipe is effeminate and represents education and middle-class values. Dipping snuff and chewing tobacco are frequently found in the redneck culture. Some rednecks sip whisky with a chew of tobacco in their mouth and spit only now and then. Smoking marijuana outside a beer joint is a mode of entertainment for the younger redneck. Most of the rednecks who engage in this behavior are less than 25 years old. Generally speaking, no redneck complains to the participants, the management, or the law about pot. Rather, they just let "them young uns do they own thing."

Proxemics

Rednecks have a tendency to increase the amount of space between themselves, even more so than average American males. The only time that male closeness occurs is during physical violence. When two rednecks are seated in a beer joint at a booth, they sit across from each other. They would not sit next to each other because this would be interpreted by others as homosexual behavior. When interacting at drinking places, the seats around the bar are generally reserved for regular customers. This particular behavior makes the barmaid's job easier when there are few customers in the house.

In the home the "man of the house" has his space reserved— like"Archie Bunker." Other space in the house is not reserved by anyone, except space for the redneck's few significant possessions (such as his truck, his tools, or his shotgun). Generally speaking, the woman in the house has no rights to social space and the children have few.

Rednecks prefer to live in the country where they have more space (Scheflen and Ashcraft 1976, pp. 161-65). Thus, the need for space is ever present. He needs space to function at work, space at home, and space in his interpersonal relations. Because he perceives the need for space, privacy, and home territory, the redneck touches very little, even members of the opposite sex, especially in public when sober.

Kinesics

Although the redneck is in an inferior position at work and in the general social order, he is "in charge" of his own house, in his own truck, and in those social places where the redneck is usually found. For this reason, his gestures are expansive. Just as his language is exaggerated and intensive, so are his gestures. Handshakes are made with fanfare. Waving as a greeting is also made with a flourish and intensity. In fact, if one travels in rural areas of the South, he will find that rednecks wave to almost every white person that drives by, regardless of social class or county of residence. The wave represents the friendliness of the redneck, which is rarely found in other types of interaction. The type of gesture found in many other social classes is "the finger." Rednecks will "shoot the bird" anytime they "get pissed off wid somebody." They do not look to see to whom they are transmitting the gesture. Most redneck gestures result as reactions, not as responses or as well thought out messages. Middle- and upper-class Southerners rarely "shoot the bird"—only when extremely agitated.

Middle- and upper-class Southerners have learned how to qualify, moderate, simulate, and neutralize verbal as well as facial expressions, thereby controlling the emotions of happiness, surprise, fear, anger, disgust, sadness, et cetera. Those same emotions, which Ekman and Friesen (1975) characterize as "universal," are present in the facial expressions of rednecks. For the redneck, however, emotions are a natural part of life. While some emotions, such as fear, would appear more neutralized in the redneck, others, such as happiness, are much more obvious than among the upper and middle classes. The educational system has not been very successful at "thwarting the emotions" of the redneck, and to a large extent, he "lets it all hang out."

Kinesic game playing occurs at various points in his life, however. Two of the most notable are when he is dealing with a boss and during what Albert E. Scheflen (1965) refers to as "quasi-courtship behavior." Rednecks feel they are at the mercy of the middle- and upper-class Southern white. Their reactions to some of their bosses are similar to a career naval enlisted man's reactions to a new ensign who graduated from a reserve officer's training corps at some university. As working men, rednecks resent being told how to do something that they have been doing for 10 to 15 years. Most of the time, they hold back their emotions. But the resentment has a cumulative effect, and at times they will make an obscene gesture to a superior or more often, simulate a physical conflict behind his back. Richard Sennett and Jonathan Cobb (1973, p. 34) relate the feelings of blue-collar workers in such a position, "'I . . . .I feel like I'm taking shit even when, actually, even when there's nothing wrong.'" Thus, "work talk" is important for the redneck. His references, usually only in conversation with other males, may be about his boss, how difficult his job is, how simple his job is, or some comment about a fellow worker. It is important to note, however, that the redneck takes pride in his work. As Sennett and Cobb (1973, p. 58) have suggested when discussing the working class, it is as if "ability is the badge of an individual." When the boss corrects the redneck, the boss is essentially "spitting on his badge of individuality."

If the job situation provides the redneck a conflict-oriented type of game playing, his recreation provides a challenge. According to Scheflen (1965, pp. 245-57), quasi courting takes several forms. Some of the characteristics include high muscle tonus, brightened eyes, preening, direct body orientation, soft speech quality, flirtatious glances, gaze holding, et cetera. Except for the soft speech quality, these nonverbal cues are used when the redneck attempts to "pick up" a member of the opposite sex in a bar. While there is some game playing in these interactions, there is probably much less than would be the case if both partners were from the middle or upper socioeconomic groups.

Chronemics

While vocalics, physical appearance, proxemics, and kinesics are important nonverbal factors for the redneck, another important element is chronemics. *Chronemics* may be defined as the study of the human use of time. Rednecks are obsessive-compulsive in their use of time. For example, when a mechanic is working on an engine that he cannot fix, he stays with it, regardless of time extenuations. When he is working for someone else, he is extremely conscious of the time, since he is a wage earner. During recreation, he does not want to be bothered by time. In many ways, then, the redneck is like all of us, but in many ways, he is different. Most important, his verbal and nonverbal communication reflects a life-style.

NONSTANDARD REDNECK RHETORIC

Rednecks speak in a rough, ungrammatical, obscene, and profane vernacular embroidered with regional colloquialisms. Vocabulary is concrete rather than abstract and parochial with the exception of religious allegorical content. Words and sentences run together, tenses are mixed, sentences are not completed, syllables are left out, words are slurred, and *r*'s and "ings" are not pronounced. Voice quality is flat, drawling, and characterized by relaxed articulation, jerky rhythm control, thin resonance and amplitude, slow tempo, and latency of response. Vocal characterizers include frequent loud laughing, whispering, yelling, moaning, groaning, whining, coughing, clearing of the throat, spitting, sneezing, swallowing, and sighing. Vocal segregates (fill-ins) such as "uh", "um", "huh", and "uh-huh" and pauses are often present.

Along with paralanguage (vocal styles) and vocabulary, these phenomena offer the most important set of criteria for identifying social class in the South. Rednecks can identify one another via telephone conversation and, in turn, are identified as rednecks by other Southerners. The redneck's verbal and nonverbal communication is reflective of his socioeconomic class. As Aron Wolfe Siegman (1978, p. 189) has noted, "In the U.S. today, social background is a significant source of variance in a variety of speech dimensions, independently of the speakers' education and intelligence level."

Studs Terkel (1974, p. 237) interviewed a Southerner who had moved to Chicago. Terkel asked him what he talked about most of the time when he was at work:

> Somebody's old lady. I'll be real honest about it, they're teasin' this guy about his old lady. All of a sudden, they're on you about your old lady. And the routine. Nothing serious. We make jokes with different black people. Like Jesse Jackson this, Jesse Jackson that. The black man makes jokes about George Wallace. But any other time, there's baseball, it's hockey. it's football.

When asked what he wanted to do, the utility worker answered: "I would just like to farm. You set your own pace, you're your own boss" (p. 239). He continued about his goals: "Thirteen more years with the company, it'll be thirty and out. When I retire, I'm gonna have me a little garden. A place down South. Do a little fishin', huntin', sit back, watch the sun come up, the sun go down. Keep my mind occupied" (p. 239).

In general, the redneck's verbal and nonverbal communication portrays a man in charge. Communication is a vital element in the macho image. The redneck is loud, verbose, frank, profane, obscene, and vulgar. He varies his language patterns very little. He is a blue-collar, working-class man at all times.

EIGHT

ASSOCIATIONS, RECREATION, AND LIFE-STYLE

Rednecks are generally antiestablishment—or at least, apathetic—when it comes to politics. For this reason, most are antisocial groups in general. However, certain situations provoke group formation; other groups evolve as a result of peer pressure; still others result from family responsibility.

FORMAL GROUPS

The Church

The most common formal group is the church. Most rednecks are members of a Protestant denomination of a conservative lean. The Church of Christ, the Primitive Baptist Church, Jehovah's Witnesses, the Assembly of God, and some of the more conservative Methodist churches are those most attended by rednecks. Often the wife and children attend without the husband. For the first half of the twentieth century "leisure time was irregular and leisure activity unplanned; Sunday was literally a day of rest" (Newby 1978, p. 406). For all practical purposes, this remains the case. While his family goes to church, it is generally not the habitual behavior of the "man of the family."

Those that do attend church believe in a religion characterized with "emotionalism, simplistic theology, and sectarianism" (Flynt 1979, p. 27). The purpose of the church experience is to have religion "for hope, purpose and sense of community" (Flynt 1979, p. 32). As is true of the rednecks themselves, their religion may be described as resistant to change. For this reason, the fundamentalist concept emphasizes individualism, antiintellectualism, and legalism (Flynt 1979, p. 30).

Individualism is a trait given high value in the redneck culture. Most rednecks consider themselves individuals, not members of organized groups. The redneck experience teaches one to "do things for himself"— that "you can't count on nobody else." This concept is consistent with a religion that holds the individual responsible for his own actions and fate and requires that one "believe in Jesus" and "be saved" to go to heaven.

Antiintellectualism is another trait that dominates the redneck. Education is viewed as a nicety of the middle and upper classes. While a fundamentalist religion is often seen as one's holding to a literal interpretation of the Bible, the fact is that many rednecks have traditionally been illiterate and many still are. Instead of the Bible, their comments on religion surface from everyday experience (Hudson 1972, p. 123). Their faith is characterized by fate and supernatural justice, both of which are "contradictory by ordinary logical standards" (p. 123). The contradiction may be described in the following manner. The fundamentalist religion claims that "on the one hand that virtuous people will be rewarded and evil people punished through supernatural justice, and on the other hand that virtuous people may suffer and evil people prosper through the workings of fate" (pp. 124-25).

The belief system is comprised of three elements: the mind, God, and the Devil. The mind is the link to both God and the Devil (Hudson 1972, p. 125). God is viewed as a "personalized spiritual being" who is believed to be the ultimate cause of everything, while the Devil is "a personalized agency who is believed to work from the inside only" (p. 125). Metaphysical concerns such as "Where did God come from?" are silly and irrelevant to the redneck because of the general negative feelings about intellectualism. If anything, the preacher determines the meaning of the Bible, which at times is a literal interpretation and at other times is supportive of the social and economic aspects of redneckery. As James W. Silver (1964, p. 54) has written, "Mississippians torture the Scriptures into sacred sanction for inequality and inhumanity."

While antiintellectualism is particularly important to the metaphysics of fundamentalism, legalism is the ethical-moral base. The Ten Commandments are accepted as law by members of the fundamentalist religions. However, as with the American judicial system, there are exceptions. Killing, for example, in self-defense or for military purposes is acceptable. Horse racing, theater going, gambling, and dancing are often considered "fancies of the elite" and religion says they are "wrong" (Flynt

1979, p. 29). Divorce, extramarital sex (adultery), and excessive drinking are probably the sins committed most often by rednecks.

Many of the males who practice fundamentalism seriously are former sinners, that is, big drinkers and/or woman chasers. Once they are "saved," however, their habits immediately change. They no longer appear in beer joints, and they now associate with other male members of the church; many times they become leaders in the church—and sin secretly like members of the upper classes. Even backsliders are accepted because once saved, always saved.

In a study undertaken by Andrew M. Greeley (1972, p. 89) the following statistics were presented representing the Baptist religion nationwide. Only 10 percent of its members were college educated (lowest of those denominations represented). Only 33 percent lived in the East and the Midwest, and only 19 percent lived in cities over 500,000. In 1972 Greeley claimed that there was a strain toward fundamentalism. The main-stream Baptists may be among the more liberal of the fundamentalists, so that uneducated, rural, blue-collar individual members seek other fundamentalist churches. These more sectarian churches are the religious homes of the rednecks.

Once a "born-again" Christian, Christian conduct is of little significance. Religious concerns focus on hazy Old Testament stories, "orthodoxy," individual sin, redemption, and salvation. Salvation depends on a personal relationship with the Savior and on baptism, correct religious beliefs, and church attendance rather than on good deeds. Religion, therefore, becomes a belief system and a sometime-Sunday thing removed from the individual and social problems encountered in everyday life. The redneck receives his limited biblical knowledge from unlettered preachers, folk culture Bible stories, and lay ministers—a truncated fare relating to vengeance, crude justice, piety, violence, sin, and hate. His formative years are suffused with religious stories, myths, legends, and enhortations mixed in with secular tales involving masculinity, adventure, and violence.

Rednecks usually belong to Baptist, Pentecostal, and Church of Christ "sects" that maintain individual church autonomy and practice a studied separatism from modern "nonfundamentalist" Protestant churches. These churches stress the "call to preach"; they accept lay clergymen and distrust church hierarchy.

The redneck's fundamentalist religious education is reflected in his everyday language and in the structure of his thinking. Speech patterns contain fragments of Old Testament stories, allegories, and metaphors, combined with expletives and sexual jokes. Frequently, preachers are the protagonists in the latter. Conversational form frequently takes on the quality of a morality play where a real or imaginary, present or absent, social actor, or cast of actors, plays out a real or allegorical scene and finally gets his just desserts (or will certainly get such desserts in the hereafter). The redneck thinks and speaks in a dichotomous, self-righteous vein: one is right or wrong, good or bad, strong or weak, with you or against you.

One redneck reports:

In the South, I know where I'm at. People go to Baptist churches. Course a few big shots go to other kinds of places on Sunday, but they ain't really worshippin' like you do in real churches. They jes got 'em a social club. Now up North, you run into a bunch of foreigners who believe in the Pope and a bunch of junk. Them people don't know who God is, or what religion is all about.

John Wilson (1978, pp. 62-63) has described fundamentalism this way:

Fundamentalism is an attempt to cleanse and purify the churches by reasserting the indispensability of certain "Fundamentals" of Christian teaching: Virgin Birth, Satisfaction Theory of Atonement, Resurrection of Jesus, and Inerrancy of the Bible . . . .Its ideas have been kept alive by small groups (often acting covertly), by periodicals, and later, by loose associations of assemblies and ministers. All Protestant Churches are virtually segregated in the South. Fundamentalist Churches (preachers, and congregation members) are the most strictly segregated. Church doctrine, interpreted from the Old Testament, supports racial separation between blacks and whites.

Political and Racial Groups

If the Church represents the formal organization for family responsibility, the political party is the center of citizen responsibility. But Southern blue-collar workers have traditionally avoided political patterns. Part of the reason is that in recent years the Republican party has been associated with the middle and upper social classes and the Democratic party has been associated with blacks. Given the choice, as during Reconstruction, Southern poor whites have joined the antiblack group instead of asserting the common class interest with the blacks—in other words, race before class (Flynt 1979, p. 36). But in the last 30 years, the redneck has asserted the little political power available to him by following "independent" politicians such as Lester Maddox and George Wallace.

The redneck's interest in politics has never been high. After Reconstruction the lower-class whites were disenfranchised through the levy of a poll tax and qualification by literacy examination (Flynt 1979, p.

38). Although these methods were initiated primarily to disenfranchise blacks, they also affected the redneck. The redneck, for good reason, does not trust politicians or political parties.

The Ku Klux Klan

Only two political issues have affected the redneck significantly enough to involve him in politics within the past 120 years: racism and gun control. The most prominent political organization for the white supremacist in the South has been the Ku Klux Klan. Although the Klan began its existence in 1865, the organization has since had its ups and downs (Chalmers 1965). As Juanita H. Williams (1961) has pointed out, Stone Mountain, Georgia, once the mecca of the Klan, was revived in 1915 and met its downfall again in the 1920s. "A new spirit of life for the Klan was proclaimed at Stone Mountain in the fall of 1956, after the implications of the 1954 Supreme Court decision again enforced segregation of races in public schools had become apparent" (p. 43).

In 1960 the Klan announced a recruiting drive for 10 million members in 30 states. Though the Klan had been split into several different segments throughout the country, the 1960 drive was, in part, a unifying force. Newspaper reaction to the Klan, even in the South, had become negative. The Klan was associated with night riding, cross burning, and violence in general. Although the newspapers and the vocal public indicated disapproval of the organization, the Klan moved onward. The avowed purpose was to keep the South white, and a large number of Southerners from all social classes secretly approve of the Klan—and some covertly support it. It is an extreme expression of racism, and racism shows no real signs of abatement in the South. The public school is the only social institution that has been partially integrated.

Segregation Policies since Integration

Keeping the South white meant several things to the Klan and to *most* Southerners. For one, the public schools were not to be integrated. The Kluxers were particularly concerned about their little girls' going to school with "nigger boys." Some school systems (such as Macon, Georgia) had planned ahead for the potential problem by having sexually segregated schools for the whites. Second, the restaurants in the South were to remain segregated. Historically, blacks could buy food from white restaurants only by going to the back door. Many restaurants maintained a sign: "We Reserve the Right to Refuse Service to Anyone." Particularly in small towns, the town café was the center of local political and economic activity, as well as a place to talk about "the nigger situation." Third, medical offices and medical services were to remain segregated. Some blacks went to black physicians, "eye doctors," and dentists, but many others were distrustful of professionals from their own race. While these blacks went to white doctors, they entered through separate doors and maintained separate waiting rooms. Fourth, housing patterns were to remain segregated; they still do. The segregation signs have been taken down, but two separate waiting rooms still persist in many doctors' offices. In many small towns, in some cases, black and white families lived immediately across the street from one another, but there was always a predominately "black section" of town and the "white section" of town. Cemeteries were to remain segregated (they still are). Blacks would have their cemeteries, and whites would have theirs. Separate funeral directors handled the ceremonies for the two races, which is still the case.

With each of these segregation priorities, different solutions emerged in the South in the wake of federal enforcement in the middle 1960s. While the public schools became integrated, separate white racist private academies emerged. The result was a segregation by socioeconomic class as well as by race. The middle- and upper-class whites began attending private schools, while the rednecks and the blacks were forced to attend school together. The restaurants were legally integrated, and while the local town cafés lost some of their importance, for the most part blacks continued to go to their restaurants and whites to theirs. Local banks started their own "coffee rooms" inside the bank. Blacks were not excluded per se, but certainly a black would "stick out like a sore thumb" in such a context—and few attend. Mostly middle- and upper-class whites sit around drinking coffee and talking economics and politics. In most cases, they are served by blacks. Some medical waiting rooms were integrated (only the white and colored signs were removed), but many were not. However, there was a significant increase in "specialists." These doctors generally were more exclusive in their diagnostic areas and in their clienteles. These doctors charged more for their services than the "family physician." In essence, medical services became segregated by socioeconomic class. The redneck was again forced to integrate with the blacks. In local hospitals, wards became integrated. For the middle- and upper-class Southerner, however, potential problems were avoided by staying in private rooms. Thus, some hospitals were now segregated by having private rooms for the upper classes and semiprivate and ward rooms for the lower classes, both black and white.

Housing patterns were also integrated. For the real estate agencies in the South, the "block-busting" syndrome was a gold mine. Once a house was sold to a black in a white neighborhood, the values decreased. Homeowners were quick to sell. The turnover brought quick profits to some real estate brokers, but most adhered to the segregated pattern. Eventually, formal class segregated housing patterns developed, but they veil the underlying racial pattern.

For the most part, cemeteries have remained segregated by race. One white "plot salesperson" sold plots by telephone. She was instructed to listen to the person's voice carefully, lest she sell a plot to a black. Most insisted the potential customer appear in the office in person.

Thus, the Klan's as well as most Southerners' missions were clear. Secondary considerations, such as the anti-Semitic and anti-Catholic themes, took a back seat. Quotations from the Bible and other sources were used by Klan leaders to support their purposes. Here the Klan could add another dimension: the maintenance of segregated churches.

While some of the Klansmen were of the middle and upper classes, many of the leaders, such as Robert Shelton, had "made it" from the redneck group. Shelton had been a rubber worker in Tuscaloosa, Alabama (Chalmers 1965). The leaders renewed the call for violence, which predominated Southern racist politics through the late 1960s.

According to P. Sims (1978, p. 240), Jewish homes were bombed by the White Knights of Mississippi as late as 1968. One of the terrorists, Thomas A. Tarrants III, related his story in an autobiography. He had been a member of the John Birch Society, the National States' Rights party, and the Minutemen as well as the Klan. He and Kathy Ainsworth discussed the bombing of a Jewish businessman's home in Meridian while in a restaurant near the Ross Barnett Reservoir in Mississippi. Tarrants (1979, p. 42) later claimed: "But I was ignorant of the facts, I knew only the distorted 'facts' of the radical right." For most rednecks, however, the level of commitment needed for acceptance in the Klan was too much.

The National Rifle Association

The other political issue that was important to the redneck was the issue of gun control. The issue reached its pinnacle following the assassination of John F. Kennedy in 1963. Rednecks were sincerely concerned that their rifles and shotguns would be confiscated by "liberals and communists." Membership in the association also brought the additional benefits of purchasing weapons at discounts. Many rednecks still have bumper stickers on their pickup trucks that read: "If guns are outlawed, only outlaws will have guns." The possession of good guns, especially hunting guns (shotguns and rifles), tender status to the redneck.

Other Formal Groups

The other groups that rednecks might member include veterans' organizations such as the American Legion, the Disabled American Veterans, and the Veterans of Foreign Wars. However, the number of members has decreased tremendously—since the Vietnam era would have contributed few members.

The final group that has made numerous attempts at gaining inroads to the redneck is the labor union. Success rates have been minimal. The trials and tribulations of labor unions in the South are well epitomized in the recent movie *Norma Rae*, which exposes some of the problems that a young, white textile worker encounters in a small Southern mill town.

Whereas unions have had their successes in other parts of the country, the South has been a different situation. Carolyn Ashbaugh and Dan McCurry (1980, p. 205) found that there was some success in Andrews, South Carolina, in 1964 when the Textile Workers Union of America for one company tried to hire black workers.

In one case an equipment company did, however, put up several barriers before unionization. According to Don Stillman (1980, p. 217), company officials "quietly passed the word to hand out half pints and beer to the workers in the second shift." Union attempts to distribute handbills had failed twice the preceding year. Some of the foremen and employees, armed with billy clubs and crowbars, ran the union people off, as the local police looked on. The auto equipment workers smashed the unionists' car tires. Finally, the unionists had to call a tow truck from a service in nearby South Carolina.

The company portrayed the United Auto Workers (UAW) as communists. The company used the churches and local radio stations to tell its story. After quite a bit of conflict, the union won out. One worker indicated that he finally realized that the company was in the wrong as well as some of the union people. He said, "We're country, but that don't mean we ain't smart." Some other places in the South eventually became unionized, but unionization generally occurred in textile areas such as Greenville, South Carolina; Opelika, Alabama, and West Point, Georgia—primarily among low-paid and unskilled female textile workers and telephone operators.

Rednecks do not like unions, and because of the open shops in the South (as a result of Section 14-B of the Taft-Hartley Act), Southerners do not have to join unions even in companies that have them. Southerners in general are suspicious of unions, as they are usually run by people from the North—Yankees. Rednecks are generally pleased to have some job where they can make just enough money to buy their own farms eventually. They view factory work as temporary—until retirement on a farm—and they do not want Yankee unionists to destroy their dreams. Therefore, the development of class consciousness is difficult. "It just ain't Southern to be fer unions," as one redneck put it.

INFORMAL GROUPS

While formal groups are relatively unimportant to the redneck, informal groups are essential to his life-style. The most dominant feature here is a partner, a male, drinking, fishing, and hunting companion. Sometimes this other person is referred to as an "asshole buddy." In many cases, these buddies met at school, grew up together, and just kept on doing what they had always done together. The activities usually include drinking, fighting, working, fishing, hunting, honky-tonking, courting, and hanging around together.

Fishing

Most redneck fishing is freshwater fishing in a local public or private pond or lake. The usual catches include bass, trout, and catfish. Botkin (1977, p. 582) characterizes the fishing experience for the redneck thusly: "If you were a poor white, you didn't have to work, or assiduously avoided it, you did a lotta fishing." Fishing is a mode of recreation for the redneck as well as a way of escaping the reality of everyday life, which includes a buddy, beer, fishing paraphernalia, a pickup truck, and a boat.

Because fishing is a relatively inexpensive sport, the paraphernalia is quite diverse. Rods and reels, fishing poles, lures, and live bait are used by rednecks as well as by other members of Southern society. Numerous lures are included in a metal "fishing box," which also contains fishing line, other reels, hooks, et cetera. The lures are often quite colorful and are sometimes handmade. Fishing poles are still used by rednecks and their womenfolk but are generally not used by the expert. Small pails of earthworms and crickets are also used for bait.

The pickup truck is usually used to transport the boat to the fishing site, though sometimes a trailer is used. Boats are usually made of aluminum or wood (aluminum is preferred), and expensive boats are one of the consumer items that many rednecks would like to have but often cannot afford.

The most important items are the buddy and the beer. Two rednecks might spend an entire afternoon without catching a single fish, but all is not lost if beer is consumed and tall tales are exchanged. Thus, the fishing trip is an inexpensive, functional, profitable form of recreation for the redneck and his buddy.

Hunting

Hunting is a much more expensive sport than fishing, although its rewards outnumber those of fishing. Game for hunting include large animals (primarily deer), small animals (rabbits, squirrels, coons, possums), and fowl (primarily dove, quail, and ducks). Large game require much more time and effort and are generally more boring to hunt than small game and fowl. Tom Sterling (1981, p. F) writes: "Every fall, Southern hunters spend untold hours sitting high in tree stands, sneaking quietly along game paths, or carefully watching wide-open grain-fields for whitetail bucks. Yet one of the most overlooked places to hunt December's bucks is a spot deer come to everyday: water." Hunting and fishing, now primarily engaged in for sport, inhere in the redneck's poor white Southern folk culture where these activities were once necessary for survival.

Deer

Hunting large game becomes a significant problem because the hunter must camouflage himself (even in water hole areas) and because the hunter must refrain from noise, smoking, and drinking. All of these factors might frighten away the deer. Thus, deer hunting is not a very sociable means of recreation for the redneck.

The quiet boredom is somewhat accentuated when the hunter selects to use a tree stand. A stand is a mechanism attached to the tree, which the hunter uses as an observation post. Hours and hours may be spent observing from such a device, and the selection of a pivotal tree is important to success. As Jerry Meyer (1981, p. 20) has noted:

> Hunting deer from a tree stand is a lot like playing chess—success is directly proportionate to how you anticipate the moves of your opponent. Just climbing up into a tree does not insure success, even when it is the right tree. Deer are pretty much creatures of habit with predictable patterns of movement. Determining which routes they are using and when they are moving is the first step toward securing the makings of venison chili.

Deer, as well as the other animals hunted by rednecks, are used for food. States forbid the wanton destruction of game animals. In addition, Southern state legislatures spend an enormous amount of time and energy writing laws on dates and other regulations for hunting various game. Game meat may not be sold commercially. As with fishing tales, one of the rewards of hunting is spinning yarns about what happened. B. A. Botkin (1977, pp. 69-70) relates the following tale. A man boasted that he had a few days before killed a large buck by shooting him through one of his hindfeet, the ball passing out at his forehead. Of course some doubts as to the possibility of performing such a feat arose in the minds of the hearers; whereupon the Colonel called upon his old body-servant, "Bob," to verify his statement. This Bob did, by saying that, "as the deer raise he foot to scratch he head massa's bullet pass through bofe." A short time after, when the company had dispersed, Bob turned to the Colonel, and exclaimed, "For Hebben's sake, massa, wheneber you tell anuder sich a big lie prease to not scatter dem so; for I tell you what, Sir, I had mighty hard work to bring um together."

The idiom continues in a more updated version.

In addition to the venison and the folktales, deer bring the deerskin and the head for mounting as trophies to the redneck. Many rednecks claim all of the deer as some kind of reward. The mounted deer head is a machismo symbol, and it is very significant in the redneck subculture. Skins and pelts are also part of the machismo glamour. The authors visited one redneck home where a huge stuffed white deer stood in the center of a very small den. What a conversation piece it was!

Small Game

Rabbits and squirrels are also hunted by rednecks, but these animals provide little meat and are not as attractive game as a deer. Charley Dickey (1981b, p. D) writes:

> Cottontails are not a glamour game species such as bobwhite quail, turkey, or deer. Farmers frequently will give you access to hunt bunnies when they might refuse your request to hunt premium game. Chances are, rabbits do a little damage to garden and shrubbery, and the farmer probably is glad to have their numbers temporarily reduced.

In most Southern states, there are few, if any, legal restrictions on hunting rabbits. They are far from being an endangered species. Although these small animals are not hunted for their attractiveness, they are often brought home at the conclusion of a hunting trip and make delicious eating.

Fowl

According to Dickey (1981b), dove hunting may take two forms, in which either 5 to 50 hunters surrounding an open field shoot at the birds or one hunts with a single partner, known as "puttering." In the second case, decoys are used and are placed on small trees. The other common nonwater fowl is the quail, which is flushed in conveys by trained bird dogs and shot in flight. No self-respecting hunter shoots a bird on the ground. Rednecks haul their hunting dogs around in trailers—and pen them up at home.

Ducks are also hunted by rednecks. They may be hunted from boats on the water, or the hunter may wear rubber walkers and shoot from a standing position. As well as decoys, many duck hunters use duck calls, often homemade. Fowl restrictions, including those on ducks, require that the hunter kill only a limited number of birds on a given day.

Information

Fishermen and hunters get their information about their prey from several primary sources. The most significant one is word of mouth. However, television and magazines also provide useful information. Fishermen watch the local nightly news to get the fishing calendar, which tells them the best times for fishing. Nature-type television programs provide information on hunting and fishing. Magazines also provide useful information, particularly *Field and Stream*, *Sports Afield*, *Outdoor Life*, and *Gun Times*. While these magazines have useful articles, they are filled with advertisements for trucks, liquor, cigarettes, jeeps, guns, and knives.

The female of the family usually enters the hunting and fishing sport when the "food" is brought home. Her function is to pick or skin the birds or to scale the fish. Depending on how often and how many, some wives may resent performing these tasks.

Hunting Dogs

Rednecks also favor owning dogs for hunting. The most common are bird dogs, used to retrieve, to point, or to run birds out of a covey. But there are squirrel dogs and even deer dogs. Some rednecks make a significant amount of money by raising hunting dogs.

While hunting and fishing are recreational sports for the redneck during certain times of the year, many everyday activities are built around country music, drinking, and sitting around in honky-tonks.

RECREATION

Country Music

While rock singer Bette Middler proclaimed in the film *The Rose*, "Drugs, sex, and rock 'n' roll," the redneck's life is from a different perspective. "Beer, sex, and country 'n' Western" might provide a more accurate representation. There can be little doubt that country and Western music provides the backdrop of the redneck set.

The "old" country musicians are generally from the southeastern part of the United States. Roy Acuff, Eddie Arnold, Chet Atkins, Floyd Cramer, Lester Flatt, Tennessee Ernie Ford, Homer and Jethro, and Carl Perkins all come from Tennessee or Louisiana (Stambler and Landon 1969). The two classicists Hank Williams (Georgianna, Alabama) and Jimmie Rodgers (Meridian, Mississippi) were from small towns. Even the more recent stars are from states in the traditional South: Bill Anderson, South Carolina; Jim Ed Brown, Arkansas; Glen Campbell, Arkansas; the Carter family, Virginia; Johnny Cash, Arkansas; Roy Clark, Virginia; Sonny James, Alabama; and Conway Twitty, Mississippi.

The interesting facet of their backgrounds continues with the specific places that they are from. Earl Scruggs was from Cleveland County, North Carolina; Mel Tillis is from Pahokee, Florida; and Hank Locklin hails from McLellan, Florida. Only in recent years has the "Western" form blended with the traditional "country." Primarily responsible for this change are two Texans who moved to Nashville, Waylon Jennings and Willie Nelson (Stambler and Landon 1969). These local "heroes" became a source of pride in small Southern towns for generations.

Country music is usually sung by individuals, rarely groups, who provide a brief life's story in their music, which is demonstrated by Loretta Lynn's autobiographical "Coal Miner's Daughter" (Offen 1977, pp. 6-7). While the autobiographical song is often used to express one's background and roots, it is also used to convey a momentary feeling of sadness, desire, or loneliness, as expressed by Hank William's "I'm So Lonesome I Could Cry" (p. 28). Country songs are generally focused inwardly, but on occasion they focus on the object of the singer's problems, as in Hank William's "Your Cheatin' Heart" (p. 46).

Although country music has become very popular in the late 1980s, it has traditionally been viewed as "monotonous, sentimental, obvious, musically inferior, and lyrically substandard" (Lyle 1980, p. 140). As described by Lyle, "The lyrics and tunes of country songs portray an aspect of the American scene that appears to be fairly constant in a world where few things endure unchanged for life" (p. 141). From a 1977 study of the *Billboard* top 100 country songs, Lyle has reported that the dominant theme involves love of some form or fashion.

One of the love themes prominent in country music is the "good woman-bad woman-wayward husband triangle" (B. Sims 1974, p. 27). In these songs, the man is portrayed as leading a wicked life "mostly in bars— boozing it up, throwing away the money he needs to support his family, associating with the 'wrong kind' of woman, and generally behaving as no responsible family man would" (p. 24). Of the "love theme" 100 records mentioned by Lyle (1980, p. 143), "about 43 percent were about marital infidelity." The wife, in these songs, "waits patiently for him night after night, suffering and crying but offering no reproof other than her own misery" (B. Sims 1974, p. 24). According to Sims, the men in these songs know the "errors of their ways," ask for forgiveness each night, and "carry on" again the next night. Historically, Sims believes that "the masochistic role portrayed by the good woman in country music was conditioned, in the fundamentalist South and in the lower and middle classes particularly, by the image of the 'two kinds of women'" (pp. 26-27). The "good woman," as described by Waylon Jennings and Willie Nelson in "Good-Hearted Woman," did not "drink, smoke, curse, go out at night, wear red dresses, paint her face, or lose her emotional control" (p. 27).

While Barbara B. Sims suggests that Protestant fundamentalism is largely responsible for females in the South abiding by the saintly role, it is her contention that the stigma of divorce was the most rigid compliance factor. Divorce was seen as a social disgrace, a religious sin, and an economic disaster for the uneducated woman. Therefore, the saintly woman simply decided to "make the best of it'" (p. 29). Sims contends that this is changing today but is generally upheld in country music, if not in social reality.

Recently, some country songs portray the male as the saint and the woman as sinner, such as "Ruby, Don't Take Your Love to Town" and "Lucille." One revealing song that demonstrates Sims's point, however, is Tammy Wynette's "Your Good Girl's Gonna' Go Bad," and it may reflect the growing number of women rednecks.

Whether the music reflects the current redneck subculture, it is certain that rednecks buy the records and listen to them. As noted by Patricia Averill (1973), however, the redneck behavior demonstrated in the music is often exoteric instead of esoteric. In other words, the music reflects the middle-class view of the redneck, not the redneck's view. Some rednecks ape the musical idiom that claims to represent them.

Alienation is another theme in country music that reflects redneck culture. According to Larry Powell (1975), Hank Williams may have been the most characteristic of the country loneliness/alienation songwriters. Powell indicates that Williams's music fits into an alienation model because of four factors: it "(a) originates in a social relationship, (b) results from disillusionment with the quality of the relationship, (c) is maintained by spatial or psychological proximity, and (d) is based upon the perceived powerlessness of the individual to restore the situation to a positive state (p. 131). The social relationships described in Williams's songs were "deeply emotional and romantic" (p. 132). The disillusionment took two forms: either losing a romantic, positive relationship or never gaining a desired one. Proximity enters as a factor when, for example, the object of the emotion is seen walking down the street. The powerlessness, as indicated by Powell had two aspects: "as an internal psychological element" and "because the situation is controlled by an external source" (p. 133). The powerlessness theme tends to dominate both the music and the redneck, leaving open only alternatives that might appear irrational to the outside observer.

In long-range terms, only chance may decide for the redneck, as indicated in Kenny Rodgers's "The Gambler." The redneck is certainly alienated from the upper classes, as always in the South, yet his individualism, religion, and fatalistic approach to life render him what he is—or the stars are responsible for his plight. They are the simplistic themes in redneck music.

Drinking and Drugs

Country music provides the entrée to an even more fundamental portion of the redneck backdrop: alcohol. Katie Letcher Lyle (1980, p. 153) writes: "In country songs drinking is condemned as a recreation but it is accepted as a solace for grief." In this sense, drinking is all right if one is lonely, depressed, or alienated; however, drinking is unacceptable if it makes the redneck happy. Utter misery is the only motive for drinking; this misery can be brought on by being away from home, losing a lover, losing a friend (often to a lover), losing a job, and losing at life in general.

It is important to remember here that rednecks think of themselves as "losers." Sometimes a redneck may go to a beer joint to get drunk after he has gotten a new job—not to celebrate but to consider the new misery of having to work eight hours a day. While the middle and upper classes tend to do almost all of their drinking at lunch or after work, there is generally no time schedule for the redneck. Because the work situation often provides for freedom, it is not unusual to see four to ten redneck workers at a beer joint any time in the afternoon. This behavior is particularly true of construction workers. Painters and mechanics more often take the "booze" to work with them and are notorious heavy drinkers who migrate from one job to another.

For many rednecks, drinking is an everyday activity. For others, abstention is the only answer. But Friday and Saturday nights are generally accepted as times to "go out on the town," to "get wiped out," or to "get shit-faced." Most rednecks drink beer of the domestic vintage. Ordinarily, Budweiser, Schlitz, Miller, and Pabst Blue Ribbon are the norm, but in recent years, it has become more acceptable to drink light beers, particularly Natural Light and Miller Lite. While imported beers are often advertised in redneck joints (particularly Heincken and Moosehead), rarely does a redneck drink them. Anything imported is considered effeminate and foreign—even imported beers.

Beer is the everyday drink of the redneck. On a daily basis, the redneck may drink four to six beers, usually in a beer joint between work and home. Frequently, the last of these four to six is a "roadie." It is important to note here that drinking and driving is a common occurrence with rednecks, and many are arrested on driving while intoxicated (DWI) charges—and some lose their driving licenses.

The two most common weekend drinks are beer and bourbon. The redneck may bring a fifth of bourbon into the beer joint and ask for "setups." The bottle is usually brought into the joint in a paper bag, either by law or by convention. "Setups" are usually ice and Coca-Cola or ice and Seven-Up. Bourbon is the Southern drink; it is the redneck drink. Wine, gin, vodka, and rum are seen in rare instances and are more frequently consumed by blacks. Scotch is almost never seen in a redneck beer joint. As one redneck stated: "How can anybody drink dat shit?" Rednecks have never heard of liqueurs. Many are problem drinkers, and most cannot afford the cost of alcohol and its consequences, so their families suffer consequently. Many wind up in jail frequently. Many lose their jobs and get involved in conduct associated with booze (for example, drunk driving, fighting, and disturbing the peace).

Beer and bourbon are the primary means of escape from reality. Drugs play a very minor role in redneckery. Marijuana is consumed by young rednecks. "Uppers" are used by some rednecks, usually when job related. Mostly truck drivers use uppers, such as various forms of caffeine, bought across the counter. Sometimes more potent uppers such as "black mollies" are consumed. Generally, however, "downers," such as Valium, are not used by rednecks. Neither are cocaine, heroin, LSD, or other hallucinogens. Uppers are used only for working situations—until they become habitual. Alcohol is used as a relaxant. Except for marijuana, rednecks do not have contact with pushers, and most do not go to physicians for legal drugs because they do not trust doctors of any sort. (They have to go to lawyers because they get in trouble frequently, but not doctors.) They are not in the best of health.

The Honky-Tonk Set

Country music and beer do not account for the overall scene where the redneck finds himself. As an outsider enters the typical honky-tonk or beer joint, he sees a few people outside near the parking lot drinking beer, smoking marijuana, and often trying to pick up a member of the opposite sex. When he opens the door (if it isn't already open), the stench of beer and sweat is phenomenal. In most cases the building is made of concrete block. The walls are painted on occasions, but usually not. The floors may have had tiles at some point in time, but about every tenth one is missing. The walls and the bar area are covered with beer advertisements. Bumper stickers are often stuck on bars and on the walls. Almost everything that has ever been broken (glass, doorknobs, pool tables, mirrors) stays broken. The mirror behind the bar may have a quotation that reads: "We Reserve the Right to Refuse Service to Anyone." Other reminiscences of the pre-Civil Rights' days may be present, including George Wallace bumper stickers, autographed photographs of Lester Maddox, and blantantly racist signs.

In one redneck bar in Dallas, Texas, the ceiling is "decorated" with spitballs. This particular aspect of decoration personalizes the joint. A customer might be able to go in and claim his own spitball. When I asked one of the waitresses if the spitballs fell on customers on occasion, she answered in a quick and matter-of-fact, "Oh, year." In general, glasses are not used in honky-tonks. Most people drink out of the bottle or the can. On rare occasions, beer on tap is drunk in plastic cups. This particularly "effeminate" behavior, however, is rarely practiced by rednecks.

In addition to beer, most honky-tonks sell soft drinks, peanuts, candy, beer nuts, cigarettes, cigars, beef jerky, pickled eggs, and chewing tobacco. In those honky-tonks where there are cooking facilities, the honky usually serves hamburgers (HB's) and cheeseburgers (CB's), usually of a somewhat greasy, inferior quality. In addition, it is quite important for a honky-tonk to sell barbeque pork sandwiches (referred to as *bobby-que poke*).

Many honky-tonks do not sell cooked fish, however, because this brings in the Health Department and, in addition, is not very profitable. Profits are made on beer and on pinball machines and pool. Pinball machines are especially profitable since the upkeep is done by the leasing agency. Pool tables are easy to keep up since usually they are easily fixed. The primary problems of the pool table for outsiders are that they are not level and there is dried-in beer all over the green felt on top, often forming a distasteful-looking map of the world. A few pool balls may be missing (or there may be two with the same number), and the cue sticks are usually not straight.

The sequence of events at the honky-tonk include walking into the place, walking up to the bar, and ordering a "Schlitz in a can." It is important to state "can" or "bottle." Then one takes his beer with him and proceeds to shoot a game of pool or play a pinball game. After the beginning sequence, all other actions are repetitions of putting money in the game machine and playing the game, putting money in the jukebox and making a selection, buying and drinking another beer, and going to the restroom.

The honky-tonk restroom may be the epitome of its typification. Crickets and/or roaches are usually crawling around in the urinals. The plumbing in the toilets and in the lavatories often does not work. However, most people would not use them anyway because they are filled with yesterday's leftover vomit. Soap is rarely found in the lavatory, and there is seldom anything to dry one's hands on except very thin toilet paper and a rolling cloth towel that does not roll anymore and appears as if hundreds of people have wiped their hands there. Usually, there are some graffiti on the walls of a very elementary and sexual nature, no poetry, and no creativity. Some of the graffiti is homosexual in content. The honky-tonk restrooms almost always contain vending machines that sell prophylactics ("rubber machines"), "French ticklers," and other sex items. The prophylactic machines are often found in the women's restroom as well as the men's as if to ask, "Who do you trust?"

Other Hangouts

As one can see, the redneck does not ask for much in the way of entertainment. Listening to country music, drinking beer, playing a machine, and having sex pretty much cover the waterfront. Other places where rednecks interact with one another, however, include: restaurants, discount stores, service stations, barber shops, carnivals, jails, and truck stops.

Restaurants are often the home of rednecks at two times during the day: early in the morning for breakfast and late at night after leaving the honky-tonk. The early morning breakfast, which often includes only coffee, is a place for discussing the athletic events of the preceding day, including national sports such as the Atlanta International Raceway races and the World Series. It is also a time to discuss local sports such as the local all-white high school academy football team and the Sunday afternoon softball game played out in the cow pasture. In addition, fishing and hunting stories abound.

After getting "high" or drunk at the local honky-tonk, the redneck may frequent an all-night restaurant such as a "pancake house" or an "omelet shoppe." Coffee, cigarettes, and perhaps greasy food make up the menu. This is the time for complaining about one's boss and the overall work one has to do. Sometimes it is a time for complaining about the wife and kids and home life in general. Primarily, it is a time to "sober up" before going home. If the occasion arises, the redneck may try to pick up a girl, particularly if he has been unsuccessful in this line of endeavor at the honky-tonk.

Discount stores are ordinarily family oriented. The husband, the wife, and all the kids go to "look around." In part, going to the discount store is a social event. One goes to find out who else is there, and this sets up an upcoming weekend for watching baseball or football together or for going hunting or fishing together. Usually, few items are purchased; often the items include a small number of quarts of oil and "a little somethin'" for the kids. The wife can use this time for "wishin'" for Christmas, birthday, or anniversary (although the latter is often forgotten).

Service stations are also "hang-outs" for many rednecks, particularly those interested in automobiles. The conversation here is quite technical, dealing with how automobiles work, intuitive guesses about what is wrong with a car, and trial-and-error attempts at "fixin'" or "helpin' fix" a car. In addition, conversations may include memorabilia (that is, about cars and people). "I 'member when I had that '57 Chevy Impala: it was so-oo-oo fast." "Was Jim Bob Luke Jenny Lynn's brother?" "Whate'er happened to ole Travis Johnson?" These are the kinds of statements and questions one might hear. Knowledge of automobiles, kindred relationships, and obituaries are quite important. Many service stations also carry fishing supplies, which opens up a "whole new can of worms." Fishing tales become prolific. One tale is used to top another. On each occasion the fisherman attempts to be specific about what kind of gear was used, including the specific lure used. A homemade lure is highest in respectability, especially if it was used to catch an extraordinarily large bass. Earthworms and crickets are much lower in status. Women do not hang around service stations.

The barber shop is another place where women are not welcomed, if not prohibited. This is a place for "catching up" on gossip and for telling "off-color" stories and jokes. Jokes about a particular college football team may be told.

Carnivals provide another family place for the redneck family. Here the children can meet other children from the same socioeconomic mold. The "little woman" can have her own conversations. The redneck can continue to have his typical conversation with his "in group." Even when middle- and upper-class families go to these events, they dissociate themselves from the blue-collar people. The upper classes pointedly ignore the rednecks as if they do not exist. Great pains are taken not to touch or get too close to them.

Rednecks do go to jail, but they are often "good buddies" with the members of the police force. Indeed, many rural policemen and deputies as well as some of the police chiefs and sheriffs are rednecks themselves.

When a redneck has been drinking, he may be picked up by the police and brought down to the station. If he "sobers up" enough in a limited amount of time, he may not have to stay overnight. Drunk driving and other more serious charges are not overlooked. The policeman says, "I'm sorry Johnny, but you got to go."

Rednecks are frequently arrested for minor traffic violations, driving under the influence, public drunkenness, disturbing the peace, and domestic conflict. When one was arrested in a small Georgia town, the arresting officer was somewhat puzzled about the charge. When the dispatcher asked what the charges were, the officer replied, "Jes put down, 'throwin' wife's stuff in the yard."

The disturbing-the-peace charges usually stem from getting drunk in a honky-tonk and becoming involved in a brawl. The legal consequences for such behavior are usually minimal. The most apparent consequence is showing up for work on Monday morning with both a hangover and a black eye.

While in jail, rednecks are fairly quiet, providing to others only the story of their charges and the circumstances of their arrest. They are usually well-behaved and do whatever is necessary to get out as soon as possible. They usually do not want to stay in there with "them nigger preverts [sic]." They also do not want to stay in any longer than necessary because they must then "face the music" from the wife at home. Bond is usually provided by a bondsman or, more often, from the redneck's boss, who wants to ensure that the worker will be back on the job on Monday.

Truck stops are used by the redneck for a variety of purposes. The primary factor that determines the purpose is whether the truck stop sells beer. If beer is sold, the redneck may go in for a conversation with his buddies and have a few "brews," usually no more than four. However, if beer is not sold, the truck stop replaces the all-night restaurant. It is a place for drinking coffee, sobering up, flirting with waitresses, and meeting with friends.

LIFE-STYLE

The life-style of the redneck is characterized by his workaday habits, his formal and informal associations, his recreational activities, and his home life. While there are differences in the way the redneck functions in these varied contexts, one seed of commonality prevails: his concept of machismo and violence.

Machismo and Violence

The Southern bully has traditionally been described as a "swearing, tobacco-chewing, brandy-drinking bully, whose chief delight is to hang about the doors of village groggeries and tavern taprooms, to fight chicken cocks, to play Old Sledge, or pitch-and-toss, chuck-a-luck, and the like, as well as to encourage dog-fights, and occasionally to get up a little raw-head-and-bloody-bones affair of his own account" (Hundley 1979, pp. 223-24). As Robert Brent Toplin (1975, p. 171) has described it, "violent reprisals are quite common."

Rednecks who habitually attend honky-tonks "exercise without let or hindrance the glorious privilege of getting beastly, senselessly, and rip-roariously drunk at their own royal will and pleasure" (Hundley 1979, p. 225). Upon getting drunk, machismo is the value that becomes dominant. As Toplin (1975, p. 167) has described it, "manly spirit or style." The values that surface are sexual prowess, virility, and power. Toplin explains the concept of sexual prowess:

> Statistics suggest that the cult of sexual prowess figures in America's strikingly high homicide rate. For example, cases involving "Domestic Triangle and Lovers' Quarrel" and "Spouse Killing Spouse" accounted for almost one-fifth of homicides officially recorded for the 1960-1970 period—situtations in which, in many cases, a machismo complex can violently emerge. [P. 171]

The second element of the machismo, or macho, image is that of virility. Toplin claims that "the virility cult emphasizes toughness of character and a fighting spirit" (p. 172). Here there is an emphasis on bravery and courage. One of the more typical versions is the "chicken complex" used by teenagers. However, rednecks maintain the virility complex, which may be related to such diverse actions as "holding one's liquor [or beer]," the use of drugs, or the use of handguns, fists, or knives, et cetera. According to Toplin, this "violence arises from powerlessness or impotence rather than from great power and confidence" (p. 178). Certainly the redneck has no economic, social, or political power and knows it.

The lack of power has been stressed thus far, and it is a very important factor in the redneck's need for violence. Only in fights does the redneck feel he has control of the situation. For the brief time that he is engaged in pugilism, the redneck can forget his social and economic dead ends. As Cash (1941, p. 44) has pointed out, violence is inevitable where men are "simple, direct, and immensely personal." He states that "conflict with them could only mean immediate physical clashing, could only mean fisticuffs, the gouging ring, and knife and gun play."

The third element of the machismo image involves what Toplin (1975) has referred to as the cult of power. "This attitude stresses the importance of holding *complete* power, at least for a man concerned with his macho image" (p. 178). In a sense the machismo complex is an extension and a reflection of American male chauvinism, as Susan Griffin (1971, p. 35) has pointed out about forcible rape:

> The same men and power structure who victimize women are engaged in the act of raping Viet Nam, raping Black people and the very earth we live upon. Rape is a classic act of domination where, in the words of Kate Millett, "the emotions of hatred, contempt, and the desire to break or violate personality" take place.
>
> As the symbolic expression of the white male hierarchy, rape is the quintessential act of our civilization, one which, Valerie Solanis warns, is in danger of "humping itself to death."

In many cases the machismo, dominating male syndrome has been supported by females who "give in to it"—or actually admire it. One of the most obvious cases is a book Marabel Morgan wrote in 1973 entitled *The Total Woman*. Although Morgan was married to a Southern attorney, her audience became the wives of rednecks. Many different "groups" sprang up, all over the South, not in educational institutions or psychiatrists' offices but in very conservative churches. Morgan's book contained an acknowledgment to Anita Bryant and referenced the Bible no less than 39 times. *The Total Woman* was published in the middle of the women's liberation movement, and leading activists in that group detested the book, its author, and her ideas.

The redneck wife, however, has never been in favor of liberation, and the book came to her as a godsend, something that might save her marriage. The cover of the book advertised her method as "guaranteed to work." The book also provided a plan for saving the marriage, including the following ideas. Chapter 2 emphasized that the total woman was to be organized. In Chapter 4 she was instructed to accept her husband as "he is" and to stop nagging. She was to "admire him," to "make him feel special," not to interrupt him, to "tell him you love his body," "adapt to him," and "appreciate him." Morgan recommended meeting the husband in pink baby doll pajamas and white boots. The experiment may or may not have worked well for the redneck wives, but it was apparently unsuccessful for Bryant (an alumna), who subsequently was divorced. It is interesting and significant that the book provided a mixture of sex and the Bible. Most fundamentalist religions demand or suggest that females and wives be submissive to males.

Middle- and upper-class Southern males are much more egalitarian in their relationships with women, though certainly they prefer ultimate dominance in a fictive if not actual sense, that is, for appearances. These males grow up in a less male-dominated family than the redneck. They tend to be actually closer to their mothers than to their fathers and to their sisters than to their brothers. Males in the upper classes leave the educational function to their wives. Wives belong to book clubs, not men, and any instruction in art, music, and things intellectual comes from the mother, not the father, who is too preoccupied with practical affairs. Therefore, the male from the upper classes is much more androgynous in makeup and in his relationship with women than is the redneck. Unfortunately, when he gets married, he follows his father's "savage ideal" and leaves education and things intellectual to his wife. It has been said— with, probably, some justification—that middle- and upper-class males make better lovers than husbands and fathers. They find it easy to teach other people's children but not their own—and they do much better with females than with other men.

Herb Goldberg (1979) has provided the macho man's general social rules, which are often epitomized in the redneck character:

1. Emotional expression is feminine.
2. Giving into pain is feminine.
3. Asking for help is feminine.
4. Paying too much attention to diet, especially when you're not sick, is feminine.
5. Alcohol abstinence is feminine.
6. Self-care is feminine.
7. Dependency is feminine.
8. Touching is feminine (pp. 35-38).

Emotional expression involves both verbal and nonverbal factors. As with many males in the United States, rednecks seldom use words such as *sweet, nice, pretty, love, hurt,* and *I'm sorry.* To use such terminology is effeminate and portrays the neck as vulnerable and sensitive, which he does not wish to be. Nonverbally, the redneck does not generally perform those kinds of gestures that are positive and affectionate in nature, such as sitting close to another person and touching another person. On the other hand, rednecks are not particularly reluctant to perform negative (violent) types of nonverbal communication. While love is an unacceptable emotion to display, hate is perfectly acceptable. The macho enjoys sex with many women (who are emotionally committed to him) without emotional commitment.

Giving in to pain is something that the "weaker sex" might do. Rednecks do not like to be sick. They avoid physicians, dentists, and hospitals like the plague. Being sick or hurt is an admission of physical disability, which the redneck can ill afford. Rednecks may go weeks or even months with an illness to avoid the admission that something is physically wrong with them. Once in a hospital, the priority is to get out as soon as possible. Problems such as arthritis are likely to be channeled to a chiropractor rather than to a licensed physician. It appears that going to a physician is a true admission. While rednecks rarely engage in planned physical activity, such as jogging or tennis, they like to believe that they are in good physical condition simply as a result of the work that they do.

Asking for help is also considered a nonmacho means of dealing with life. The types of help that a redneck might need run the gamut, and their problems are similar to those of other Americans. A redneck may not know how to read a driver's manual to take a chauffeur's test—even so, he avoids asking more educated people for assistance. In addition, he will not stop and ask for directions when driving. He may be in an economic bind at a particular point in time but be unwilling to admit that he cannot be the family provider. Thus, he often obtains economic assistance from loan sharks instead of going through the more legitimate channels at a bank or other financial institution. When he has emotional problems, he avoids going to a professional counselor or psychiatrist. As one redneck told us, "I'm not crazy; I've never been crazy." That statement followed his relating a story about shooting up a bar in east Texas. The redneck is often even unwilling to ask for help when the task is virtually physically impossible. When rednecks move from one house to another, they like to move everything themselves; they do not like to ask friends or even relatives for aid.

Dieting is something that females do. Rarely does a redneck become concerned about his beer belly, for example. He *knows* he is in good shape. He will not hear of restraint in his consumption of food or alcohol, particularly since alcohol abstinence is also feminine. There is hedonism among the rednecks when it comes to food. He likes fried chicken and "bobby-que poke." He figures that he will die someday of something and generally is not particularly concerned about when it will be or of what development. This attitude supports his life-style.

Self-care is also feminine. The redneck is generally not concerned about physical appearance, and to a large extent, he devalues personal hygiene. He cannot see spending a lot of time and money on toothpaste, deodorant, aftershave, et cetera. He feels that people can accept him as is, or they can forget it.

Finally, dependency is feminine. He wants little or no help in a temporary fashion (asking for directions, et cetera), and he absolutely does not want to be dependent permanently. He dislikes it when his wife receives presents or money from her family. He detests the welfare system, and he does not like handouts from anyone or any group. He does not want to be dependent on his job: the ideal of most rednecks is to own their own little farm—to be independent.

While these factors make the redneck macho, there are several demographic and attitudinal factors that contribute to the degree of the redneck's machismo. To some extent, then, violence is a repercussion of the machismo image that rednecks wish to maintain. Toplin (1975, p. 179) writes: "Among the lower classes in the South, these 'indignities' to one another's macho image were settled more spontaneously. Bar room brawls and street fights were common." We found that physical violence is the means used by rednecks for handling their defensiveness. Violence might take place in a simplistic, loud, verbal argument, or it may result in the redneck's killing someone. Usually, he does not understand symbolic power. He cannot argue logically. He blurts out. He demands. He fights. While he responds against other males who challenge his masculinity, he is even more defensive when a female does so, particularly his wife.

According to Roger Langley and Richard C. Levy (1977, pp. 19-20), between 50 and 60 percent of all American families engage in husband-wife physical violence. These events range from slaps to torture to murder. They may occur as few as twice a year to as frequently as daily. The actual incidence is difficult to determine because many cases are not reported and police sometimes distort the charges. Langley and Levy provide the following account from the New Orleans Crisis Center: "'When we do get a call from a battered wife, it is never the first time she has been beaten. By the time she gets around to calling us, she's desperate and searching for a way out'" (pp. 26-27).

Historically, the South has maintained a legal "hands off" in domestic quarrels. However some significant changes have occurred over the past 150 years. In 1824 the courts in the state of Mississippi ruled in the case of *Bradley* v. *State* that it was all right for the husband to "moderately chastise his wife." Assault and battery, however, were forbidden. In 1864, in North Carolina (*State* v. *Black*) wife beating was viewed as "a matter best left out of the courts." Dissent for the North Carolina decision was gained in the 1871 Alabama case (*Fulgham* v. *State*) in which the court ruled that wife beating was not acceptable under the law. In 1961 a Mississippi court (*Austin* v. *Austin*) ruled that it was unacceptable to chastise or restrain physically.

According to Langley and Levy (1977, pp. 58-60), wife beating spans all income levels. In fact, they suggest that wife assault is more common in the middle class. We found otherwise, in the South particularly. There appear to be four categories of husbands who engage in wife abuse: alcoholics, psychotics, psychopaths, and plain bullies. We found most rednecks who beat their wives to fall in categories one and four. Although some rednecks do engage in wife and child abuse, most do not. There is no hard evidence that such abuses occur any more often in the redneck subculture than elsewhere in American society. When domestic violence occurs in redneck families, it is usually triggered by alcohol, it is not physically significant, and it is often forgotten the next day. Honky-tonks are places for violence; for the redneck the home is the place for pacification. The redneck likes to entertain in his home and enjoys his time spent there. He brags about the likelihood of beating up his old lady and the children if they get out of line, but he seldom follows through.

Entertainment in the Home

The redneck does not spend a significant amount of time in the home. Weekday nights and weekend afternoons are the times usually spent around the house. Regardless of the physical appearance of the home, the redneck's "home is his castle." It is a place "to rest." The home is a place to do several activities that "bother" his wife. One of them is the initial stage of what Florence King (1975, p. 58) has referred to as "the Deliverance Syndrome." The first step of the hunting trip is to clean the guns. Rednecks take care of their guns, as they do their trucks. King has indicated that cleaning a rifle or shotgun may become almost sexual: "It is hard to miss the symbolic rejection exuded by a man cleaning out a gun barrel—an activity invariably followed by rubbing and caressing the gun's stock, on which he manifests a tenderness that is both endearing and maddening. Often the entire Smith and Wesson petting party gets on a woman's nerves so badly that she slams out of the room" (pp. 58-59). Part of the entire activity, however, is exactly to get her out of the room.

One sees the same womanly complaints about the redneck's interest in football:

> He is devoted to the big game—in the stadium, drives to one game while listening to another, filled with regret that he cannot be in more than one stadium at once. As he drives on, he drowns his sorrows in the beer can that he holds between his legs. He cannot seem to navigate without this aluminum truss and is able to drink one crotch-warmed beer after another with no apparent ill effects. [p. 110]

The redneck loves his television almost as much as his truck or his gun. If there is one thing he likes to watch, it it football. Rednecks will often tolerate women's being in the house while the game is on, but they will not tolerate their being in the same room. There are certain "side issues" about watching the game that are just as important as the game itself. First, rednecks do not want to be concerned about external factors—any external factors—during the game. They do not want to "set the table," "wash their hands," "go get li'l Ronny," "pick up a gallon of milk," or "take Thanksgiving dinner to Aunt Maude at the hospital." They want to be left alone. Second, they do not want any rules about smoking and drinking. Two of the really *fine* aspects of watching a football game are drinking beer and smoking cheap cigars. No one wants a wife around waving the smoke and proclaiming, "Pew!" Third, rednecks do not want to be concerned about cleaning out the ashtrays or throwing away the beer bottles during the game. Fourth, they do not want to be asked questions (about football, logic, or anything else) during the game. They detest questions such as, "How much longer is it gonna last?" Even more so, they do not like questions such as, "Why do you watch Howard Cosell every Monday night if you hate him so much?" We understand that in Mexico, where machos abound, Howard Cosell is seen on the television screen but not heard. He is bleeped out. Any mention of Cosell drives a redneck up the wall for obvious reasons—and many nonredneck Southerners as well.

So most redneck couples have devised a scheme to remedy this problem: the guys go to one redneck home and watch the game; the girls go to another to talk about "women's things"—which often are other women. This scheme, strangely enough, lasts for years. In fact, it eventually becomes such a ritual that the women make plans early in the week as to which house the girls will go to that weekend.

The sexual differentiation is almost always present in the redneck home. For the redneck, the sexual separation is his equivalent to the "drawing-room society" (F. King 1975, p. 60) of the middle and upper classes. The neck has no "liberry" to take his male guest into for "a smoke and a glass of sherry." Instead, his options are one or more of the following: "Less go in here and watch th' game" or "Lemme sho' ya' my new rifle" or "Less go in the shop" or "Lemme show ya' what I done to my truck." Since the homes are usually rather small, it is much easier for the womenfolk to go to one house and the menfolk to another.

Staying home alone with the wife, after supper, causes some difficulty. This particular disaster is often avoided by the redneck's watching television, *usually something with sex, violence, or country music.* The larger the number of those variables, the greater the chance that he will watch the program. If there is nothing on that might interest him, the husband and the wife may get into a conversation, or more often, the wife listens to one of his monologues. The monologues often begin with, "Ya' know what Jim Bob done today?" Some 10 or 15 minutes later one may have found out that Jim Bob left a metric wrench on the carburetor of Mr. Richardson's car. The "funny thing" about it was that, "Ya ain't sposed to use a metric wrench on that kind uv car." And on and on about work colleagues and the boss. On the other hand, he may get into a diatribe using what F. King (1975) has called "field and stream vocabulary."

> It included something about a thirty-oh-six rifle, whatever that is, a rambling analysis of firing pins, whatever they are, and several verbal sorties into things like coveys; what he had "treed" and what he had "bagged" plus a who-struck-John involving a lost Bowie knife, a drunken farmer with a broken arm, a fish, and a setter bitch [pp. 57-58].

These long, involved stories are often interesting only "if you'd been there." Once the wife tries to change topics, or to enter the conversation in any way other than listening, she is interrupted with, "I don't wanna hear 'bout dat." Some minor exchanges may occur about obituaries, someone's losing his job, sicknesses around town, et cetera. Conversations rarely, however, are personal.

Southern Cooking and Eating

The home is also the place for enjoying Southern cooking. In this sense there are two homes for the redneck: his mama's home and his home. While the redneck's wife is capable of performing some tasks as well as his mother, she can never cook like his mother. Redneck's expect good, country food wherever they eat. James L. Townsend (1980, p. 78) relates a story of having breakfast at a restaurant in Georgia known as the Country Kitchen: "The meal was country and classically Southern— scrambled eggs, grits with butter melting, homemade biscuits with homemade preserves, hot coffee, and what the menu referred to as 'country bacon.' It was fatback, of course, or streak o'lean to some folks, and if you have to ask what it is, you probably won't like it. My wife didn't, and neither did the kids, but it took me back in time to Momma's kitchen, and it was delicious beyond description."

Southern delicacies include the following types of food for the breakfast meal: grits, eggs, bacon, fatback, ham, beef steak, pork sausage, pork chops, biscuits, cereal, toast, French toast, pancakes, waffles, tomato juice, orange juice, grapefruit, watermelon, cantaloupe, milk, coffee, hot cocoa, hot tea, et cetera. Although the breakfast meal contains a wide diversity of choice, the breakfast does, however, vary depending upon the socioeconomic status of those being served.

For Southerners food is an important part of Southern hospitality, and even among poor people, there is often a variety of food to choose from at the dinner (lunch) meal or the supper (dinner) meal. What constitutes "dinner" does vary some in the South, but, generally speaking, lunch is referred to as "dinner." Southerners in general, and rednecks in particular, like to have their supper. *Lunch* is a term used by Yankees and some middle- and upper-class Southerners, usually those who live in urban areas.

There are a number of delicacies in the South that are particularly unique. Certainly eating fatback by itself is one. Grits is another that has received significant press in the past few years. One Southern dish that has not received the popularity (or notoriety) is "potlikker" and "corn pone." Botkin (1977, pp. 293-94) describes it this way:

> Potlikker is the juice that remains in a pot after greens or other vegetables are boiled with proper seasoning. The best seasoning is a piece of salt fat pork, commonly referred to as "dry salt meat" or "side meat." If a pot be partly filled with well-cleaned turnip greens and turnips (the turnips should be cut up), with a half-pound piece of the salt pork, and then with water, then boiled until the greens and turnips are cooked reasonably tender, then the juice remaining in the pot is the delicious, invigorating, soul-and-body-sustaining potlikker. The turnips and greens, or whatever other vegetable is used, should be separated from the juice; that is, the potlikker should be taken as any other soup and the greens eaten as any other food.
>
> Corn pone is made simply of meal, mixed with a little salt and water, made into a pattie and baked until it is hard. It has always been the custom to eat corn pone with potlikker. Most people crumble the corn pone into the potlikker. The blend is an even tasting food.

While the "dish" may not sound very appetizing to non-Southerners, many Southerners like it. For the redneck, potlikker and corn pone has an additional quality: it is inexpensive.

Southerners spend an enormous amount of time, energy, and money on food. Middle- and upper-class women contribute to and buy many different Southern cookbooks. Almost every town of over a thousand has its own recipe book or cookbook. The Junior Auxiliary produces them; the Garden Club produces them; the Women's Club produces them. Southern cookbooks are all over the place.

The basics for any one of them are meat and chicken. Usually, the meat is pork or beef. The middle- and upper-class "ladies" also use the cookbooks to create new salads (particularly those with gelatin and food coloring) and new casseroles. Rednecks, on the other hand, like their food simple and greasy.

Rednecks do not like sautéed foods, nor do they like Italian or French-type sauces. Beef and potatoes. Pork, rice, and field peas. Those are the essentials. The essentials are supported by vegetables. However, rednecks do not like "foreign vegetables" such as snow peas, broccoli, zucchini, olives, or any other that may sound or taste foreign.

Rednecks do not like to have a lot of herbs and spices in their food. Salt and black pepper are basic. They may use cinnamon on their toast in the morning, but they do not like parsley, sage, rosemary, or thyme.

Vegetables that are acceptable are okra, butter beans, snap beans, black-eyed peas, greens, cabbage, carrots, et cetera. Again, these vegetables are prepared in simple fashion—casseroles are not popular. A redneck wants to be able to eat the food and know what is in it. Sliced tomatoes are present at almost every dinner and supper.

The redneck himself generally does not cook. He makes coffee in the morning, and he grills food outside. Apparently, it is macho to cook on a grill because it flames up. Occasionally, he cooks game meat and fish, macho foods. Wives do not like the gamey smell.

Most of the time, however, the redneck wants to sit down, take his shoes off, and eat, without being disturbed by his wife or children. He wants to eat his porkchops, and butterbeans, and sliced tomatoes, and French fries without having to ask for the salt and pepper or the catsup. He allows the dinner prayer ("grace," the "blessing") to be said. From then on, it is time to gulp down his food and wash it down with iced tea— then, it is to the television set. Table manners are not part of the redneck environment. He uses his fingers to push food onto the fork, bends over close to the plate, smacks loudly, and licks his fingers.

REDNECK RELAXATION

The redneck gains some enjoyment from life. He takes part in some formal organization and many informal groups. He likes to listen to country music, to go to honky-tonks, to go hunting and fishing, and to stay at home. His life-style is "laid back" away from work. Home life and pastimes enable him to escape from work and from his lower-class existence and the accompanying hidden injuries of class.

NINE

SEX AND FAMILY LIFE

According to Eakins and Eakins (1978, p. 136): "Research supports the notion that most of the terms our culture has available to label women as sexual beings are negative and tend to demean or trivialize them." Some of the words used to describe females are *hooker, tramp, piece, bitch, slut, whore,* and *pig*. Eakins and Eakins state that the male corresponding terms are more positive than negative. Words such as *Cassanova, stud,* and *gigolo* are used. Other terms for women include *easy lay, pick-up,* and *put-out*. These language terms often reflect the male chauvinistic, double standard of American society in general and the redneck subculture in particular, as we and others have noted. J. A. Newby (1978, p. 407) has written:

> The double standard of social and sexual conduct that men insisted upon may have been a manifestation of... the concern for self-worth. Hunting, loafing, drinking and extramarital sex were activities largely denied women, and partly for that reason especially prized by men.

American women see the role of the man of the family in the following order of precedence: provider for the family, father, and husband (J. Williams 1977, p. 294). The redneck's general concern with self-worth is directly tied to his ability to be the provider. Therefore, the woman's labor is only secondary to that of a man. As Thorstein Veblen (1902) indicated, the lower classes have little pretense of leisure. The wife's duties are to take care of the house and of the children. The wife should not work in the labor force since the wife's staying home is one of

151

the redneck's few opportunities at "conspicuous consumption." The redneck gains a sense of pride from the fact that his wife does not have to work.

Whereas the liberation movement has given the impetus for many women in America to develop the "ESE" factor (O'Neill and O'Neill 1972), redneck wives remain dependent on their husbands. The ESE factor relates to their educational, sexual, and economic freedom. Even in those cases where the redneck *allows* his wife to work, it is understood by both parties to be a "temporary" condition. Increasingly, she has to go to work.

Rednecks do not like for their spouses to enter the work force or to go back to school because the husband has a sense of insecurity. This insecurity is similar to that discussed by Gail Sheehy (1976, p. 190) wherein a male mentor (producer-star, professor-graduate student, doctor-nurse) provides the role of teacher and the female protégée provides the role of student. The redneck husband wants his wife to feel that she needs him, and one of the few vehicles he has available to him is to keep her economically dependent upon him. Thus, he treasures the role of provider.

The husband's role as provider-teacher is developed through a relationship socialization process. Most rednecks marry before finishing high school or, at the very latest, immediately upon graduation or reaching graduation age (18 to 19). Many never graduate. In many cases the individuals have dated few other people before their dating began.

Knowledge and experience in sexual relationships are developed primarily between the two novice partners. Thus, the husband has the fear that if the wife goes back to school or to work, she will begin comparing her husband with the other men around her, and he will lose. And he is absolutely correct on this point. Although the underlying threat of the wife's having an extramarital affair is ever present, sex is only one of the husband's greatest fears. In addition, the husband does not want the wife to have experience or knowledge that are alien to him, especially elevating experiences.

The general orientation toward one's wife is demonstrated in the following quotation from a redneck:

> I love my wife and family and all that good shit, but I wear the breeches. My ole lady does her thing. She cooks and keeps me and the kids happy. She works too. She's gotta if we want to live good. I treat her good too, but she knows I'm the boss. I'm like the other boys. I got to go out and raise hell once or twice a week. You know chew the fat with the boys, drink a few beers and jes raise a little hell. I ain't looking for nothing but if a strange piece turns up I take care of it too. I ain't no chaser but ... .And

when I come home I don't wont to hear no shit from the ole lady or nobody else. They don't mess 'round with me. I ain't no animal but they all know not to git outta line with me. I'll knock em on their ass if they need it—and they know it. I may not be nobody out there but I'm the big stick at home. They know I come first. The ole lady ain't goin' no where. And if I catch her wrong I'll knock her on her ass. She knows it too. If she was ta screw 'round on me the undertaker would soon wipe her ass. I'm the star of the show. [Roebuck and Neff 1980, p. 252]

The redneck's attitude toward his wife is that she is to do what he says. In an economic necessity, she may go out and work, but *he* makes that decision. She should not bring up the idea nor should she press it ("nag about it"). The husband's attitude toward the wife and the children is usually amenable unless his authority or masculinity is questioned.

When masculinity or authority is suspect, the redneck turns into a different person, almost characteristic of Dr. Jekyll-Mr. Hyde without the antidote but often with the potion. Newby (1978, p. 408) has written that "wife beating, child abuse, and alcoholism" are the resultant social problems that have developed from the need for a positive, male self-concept and particularly from the need to be the provider. As Silver (1964, p. xvi) has pointed out about Mississippians in general, "When they are not riled Mississippians in general are a demonstrably hospitable and friendly people."

What, then, riles the typical redneck? Generally speaking, those situations where he finds himself frustrated and powerless and when someone points that reality out. He can be riled by other males at the beer joint, but he is much more vulnerable at home. Statements or questions by the wife that intimate he is not working hard enough as a provider are typical examples of riling. Comparisons and contrasts with other males that make him appear less masculine have a similar effect. Inquisitiveness about what he did last night or who he was with last night also provoke violent behavior. The violent behavior occurs more often when the husband has been drinking. The provoking stimulus is an implication that the man cannot hold his liquor. One example might be: "I think you've had too much to drink." The wife and child beating may eventually end up in legal hands, but ordinarily this behavior is forgiven.

As with many other American males, then, the redneck is chauvinistic, machismo oriented, defensive, insecure, domineering, and authoritarian—just more so than most! At the same time, he owes an obligation to his family. As Flynt (1979, p. 149) has indicated about mountain people: "Familism assumed that an individual's obligations to his kin held priority over duties to other groups." Rednecks feel these same obligations, but they have developed little, if any, social responsibility.

Others can probably shift for themselves without government help. The process of familization, as with sex, involves factors similar to those of all Americans: dating, mating, marriage, extramarital affairs, homosexuality, and divorce.

DATING

Most rednecks live in rural or small-town areas and have contact with members of the opposite sex, through geographic proximity from grade school through puberty to marriage. Few travel far from home. Direct contact with members of the opposite sex, then, is usually within the same socioeconomic class. Mab Segrest (1981, p. 82) describes a view from a second grader's perspective:

> I am at a senior high football game, at the ball field a few blocks away from my house is a small Alabama town. I am not watching the game but playing with my brother and his friends, since I always play with them. I can go anywhere if I do; otherwise, I have to stay at home. We are throwing rocks at some of the girls in my brother John's room at school. The girls are on the bleachers; we are underneath, looking up at their underpants. I have a crush on one of them—Rebecca, dark eyes and hair, small and full bosomed already, in the fourth grade. I like her a lot, so I am throwing rocks at her.

As with the lower socioeconomic class in general, the redneck learns about sexual intercourse at an early age. Segrest describes sex this way: "The man sticks his peter in the woman's pee-pee and they have a baby" (p. 83). These peer group conversations are complemented by pictures from magazines and "dirty comic books" called "fuck books" whose content is only slightly explained in the schools and rarely at home.

As they grow older, redneck boys attempt to gain recognition from girls with their cars (or trucks), by smoking cigarettes (or marijuana), by drinking beer, and by being the "tough guy," which is the case because the socialization process has not provided rednecks a distinction between gaining attention from boys (who support these actions), or from girls (who don't). Chris Mayfield (1981, p. ix) has characterized some differences between Southern children of the past and the present that we have also noted:

> Today's Southern children get their biscuits as often from Hardee's as from Mama. On Saturday afternoons they're as likely to cool off in the local shopping mall as in a shady spring-fed swimming hole. But Grandma and Grandpa and Uncle Joe and Cudn Elaine loom large in the lives of today's Southern kids, just as they did in those of earlier generations.

The teenager may go out to a movie, a high school football game, a drive-in theater, a computerized arcade, a country and western concert, or a shopping mall. Dates typically occur on weekend nights but many occur on a Saturday afternoon (for a local auto race). Dating is the prerequisite (or sometimes corequisite) of mating.

MATING

Sexual intercourse, in the abstract, often is well understood by most rednecks and their female partners. While a few female partners are concerned that their mates only want to marry a virgin, most realize those days are over. However, as opposed to lower-class people in other areas, most rednecks have few sexual relationships before marriage, and most find that they were the "first" for the women who later became the "ole lady." They marry young.

Most rednecks take their girl friends out to a limited number of places. These include movies such as *Smokey and the Bandit* and others that require little thought and are generally more entertaining than intellectually stimulating. The drive-in theater is more suited to the redneck for three reasons: generally, the drive-in is less expensive than the walk-in; alcohol can be taken to the drive-in and usually is not acceptable for the walk-in; and sexual conduct is more permissible at a drive-in theater.

Kissing and "petting" (everything except overt sexual intercourse) are performed in the mating stage. Only after the relationship is accepted by both parties does sexual intercourse begin to be a significant factor in the relationship. Birth control often becomes an issue at this stage. As one redneck stated, "Wearin' a rubber is like taking a shower with a raincoat on," or "going wading with your socks on." This attitude is well accepted by most rednecks within the all-male "morning-after sessions." However, as has been indicated, not only do most redneck men's restrooms provide the opportunity for purchase of prophylactics, but they are also available in women's restrooms. The opportunity for birth control, then, is ever present. In addition, the redneck does not appear to be as concerned about marriage as is his middle- and upper-class brother. As Billie Sue Sanchez (1978, p. 66) has reported: "For whites, early marriage had a depressant effect on adolescent and early adult aspirations and expectations, both educationally and occupationally." In addition, she has stated that "where there were early marriages there were low aspirations, and, conversely, when men were successful academically they were more likely to defer marriage" (Sanchez 1978, p. 66). Because school is simply a hurdle to jump before getting a job and having a family, birth control is a matter of lesser significance for the redneck. This is particularly the case when the redneck is compared with the middle-class male who wants to finish college before thinking of wedlock. Mating, then, arrives early for most rednecks, and, subsequently, marriage also arrives early.

MARRIAGE

In the United States, marriage is often both a legalistic and a religious ritual. Thus, especially for the redneck, marriage becomes a vow associated with the spouse, the church, the spouse's family, and his own family. The marriage vow is a promise not to be broken. While a few redneck marriages are performed by a justice of the peace, particularly by those previously divorced, most are performed by the family minister of the bride. The bride maintains (or is expected to maintain) her orientation to the church. After marriage, however, her number-one loyalty is to her husband.

Once the marriage is in motion, there are several expectations of the wife in the family. These include, but are not limited to, maintaining the condition of the house; taking care of the children; maintaining family relations with both sides of the family; having meals ready on time; servicing the "master," both physically and sexually, and no one else; and keeping her mouth shut. The last function includes noninterference in the husband's work relations, their social relations', and the husband's outside social affairs.

It is the wife's job to take care of the house, to keep it clean, to make sure that it is just as nice as his mother's house. If his mother questions him about the upkeep of the house, she is, in fact, questioning his virility and authority over his wife. We noted that rednecks do not wash clothes, mop the floors, sweep the floors, wash dishes, et cetera. They do not help around the house, even if needed (Newby 1978). Usually, the wife takes care of the children; it is part of her job description. Only when a male child gets old enough to "play ball" does the redneck begin participating. He does not change diapers, and he does not "rock" the baby to sleep. If one of the partners has to get up late at night or early in the morning, the wife gets the call. After all, the man of the house has to go to work the next morning.

The wife is also in charge of maintaining relationships with her family and with her husband's. "Why don't you cook dinner for Mama and Daddy, Sunday?" is a legitimate request of the redneck husband. Most of the family ties are maintained through a patriarchal system. Family ties are maintained with the extended, as well as the immediate, family. Therefore, "Why don't you cook dinner Sunday for Uncle Bob and Aunt Edna?" is also a legitimate question. These meals, whether guests are present, are to be ready at a given time, usually noon for "dinner" and six o'clock for "supper." The wife is also responsible for getting up to have breakfast ready for the breadwinner.

The wife is to service her husband sexually and physically. She is to make certain that the "kids" do not bother him, which means they should be asleep when he gets ready to watch "Monday Night Football." Her function, then, is to make her husband feel comfortable. In addition, she is to have sex with him whenever he desires it. She is not to be "too tired" nor to "have a headache." While he may have extramarital affairs, she must not. As Toplin (1975, p. 171) quotes Jimmy, a lower-class person, as saying:

> As far as her going out with another guy, I'll tell you one thing and you can believe this or not. If she shacked up with some guy, she'll be dead— even if they give me the chair—that you can believe.

The wife is usually loyal. As has been indicated in the section on country music, the wife is supposed to be an "angel," just like the redneck's mother.

Most important, however, the wife is to keep her mouth shut. She is not to ask questions about his work but must quietly listen to all his complaints. She is not to get involved in the financial conditions of the family, unless an emergency occurs and she is asked to participate. He handles the money, and the wife must ask him for what she needs. If she works, she must turn over her wages to him. She is not to complain about the social acquaintances of her husband (no matter how negative her internal reactions) and must accept them as house guests. She is to stop seeing her own social acquaintances if her spouse so demands. She is never to ask where he was, what he was doing, or who he was with on any given occasion. If he has a telephone conversation or receives mail, it is private until he chooses to make it public. On the other hand, all of her conversations and mail are accessible to the man of the family.

She is not to appear "sexy" to other men and must stay in her place as wife and mother. When she gets to the age of his mother she, too, will be sainted providing she follows the rules.

EXTRAMARITAL AFFAIRS

Southern rednecks demand the rights and privileges common to the double standard. In this sense, many rednecks lead double lives. There is the life at home with wife and family, and there is the nightlife, honky-tonk role, which often leads to extramarital affairs. As Roebuck and Neff

(1980, p. 252) write: "They [rednecks] stress the authority, independence, and masculinity in the domestic situation which insures them deference and attention, and permits them outbursts of expressive feeling." As has been mentioned, the sex role of the redneck is often supported by what he hears in country music. As Flynt (1979, p. 123) surmises, "Ballads . . . .lyrics likely as not spoke of divorce, infedelity, seduction, sung by sleazy peroxided blondes in a thousand honky tonks, became moral lessons." The moral lessons, however, are sometimes not so readily apparent to the redneck. Thus, the double standard allows the redneck to participate in extramarital affairs, while his wife cannot.

HOMOSEXUALITY

Rednecks do not like "queers." Most would never consider having a relationship with one (if they knew it). However, we found some rednecks who had a distorted view of homosexuality. Generally, they perceive the homosexual only as the one who takes the passive role. A few rednecks we talked with indicated that they had had one or two homosexual experiences when they were young. They were quick to point out, however, that the "old queer" made them do it. Generally speaking, rednecks are much more negative about lesbians than they are about male homosexuals.

DIVORCE

Fundamentalist religion sets the stage for the redneck's attitudes toward divorce. "'And I say unto you: whoever divorces his wife, except for unchastity, and marries another, commits adultery'" (Wilson 1978, p. 258). Divorce is considered an act of failure. The redneck did not "keep his ol' lady in line." Thus, while arguments, and even fights, occur, the two stay together. It should be noted, however, that rednecks have divorced more often in recent years, in line with the rest of the country.

DOUBLE-STANDARD

Rednecks usually meet all types of people while in school, but their class awareness occurs before puberty. They date girls in the same socioeconomic class and have sex with few partners before marriage. They seek out a wife who is similar in many ways to their mother. After marriage the double standard takes its toll. The menfolk have affairs with "honky-tonk women," but their wives do not have affairs. The redneck wishes to maintain the security of the wife and family while having his fun away from home. While divorce has increased in the redneck circle over the years, few rednecks divorce even today.

Homosexuality is a "no no" in the redneck subculture.

TEN

REGIONALISM AND DEFENSIVENESS

The South is still dominated by a system with the motto "The South shall rise again." Most Southerners characterize the South as the states of Virginia, Georgia, Alabama, Arkansas, Mississippi, Louisiana, Tennessee, North and South Carolina, and northern Florida, Arkansas, and eastern Texas. For the redneck, particularly, Kentucky, west western Texas, and West Virginia are border states. The South involves those states that were fragmented from the rest of the country by the Civil War in the middle of the nineteenth century and by the civil rights war of the twentieth century. Much of Texas is in the West, and Kentucky is in the North. The redneck's perception is in large measure generated by an economic dimension. No longer are Kentucky and Texas "on the bottom" of the American economic ladder. Through this perspective the redneck can explain why Lyndon Johnson was "a nigger lover" and why their heroes were sectionalists who gained the attention of the rest of the country by supporting the lower-class, blue-collar workers of the southeastern United States.

REDNECK HEROES

While Richard Petty and Johnny Cash receive much more attention than political idols, there have been a few political heroes in redneck history. Names such as George Wallace, Strom Thurmond, Lester Maddox, Huey P. Long, and Theodore G. Bilbo appear in a redneck's Hall of Fame.

Most of these individuals have been cast more by their rhetoric than by their behavior with the exception of Huey P. Long, who did more for poor Southerners than any other Southerner throughout history. But for the Southern redneck the rhetoric has been very important.

George Corley Wallace

Wallace was born in Clio, Alabama, and according to Marshall Frady (1968, p. 13), he will be "the greatest of American demagogues." That reputation he achieved largely through his public speaking (B. Jones 1966). Flynt (1969, pp. 47-48) has provided an account of Wallace as a speaker, as described by Ted Pearson of the Birmingham *News*:

> The man is a prolific speech-maker, and he does practically all of it without benefit of even routine preparation. Watch him just before an after dinner speech and you'll see him scribbling a few words on the back of an old envelope while he's downing roast beef and English peas.
>
> Most anybody else would use his time *en route* to a speaking date whipping the speech in shape. Not Wallace. Aloft, he's a fidgety traveler, never giving the upcoming speech a thought.

Wallace's rhetoric was filled with "his repetition of clichés, the interaction of auditor's response and his own heightened emotionalism, in his rambling and disjointed dialectic" (p. 48). While he stood in the schoolhouse door to "prevent" integration at the University of Alabama, he continued to cooperate with Attorney General Robert Kennedy and the Federal Bureau of Investigation to seek out radical racists, particularly violent members of the Ku Klux Klan (Sorensen 1965, p. 493; Tarrants 1979).

In his later rhetoric, in Wisconsin, Wallace would claim, "I am not a racist! I am not a hate-monger! I am not a bigot!" (Makay 1968, p. 202). His earlier rhetoric, like that of his peers, associated integration with "miscegenation, Communism, immorality, military force, the Kennedy family, and a sinister Washington power structure never fully explained" (Flynt 1969, p. 49). In 1963 Wallace had stated, "'*They* may push us to the wall. But we'll climb up on the wall and jump down in the midst of our *adversaries*. You and I should decide what is best for whites and negroes . . . not let that *crowd in Washington* tell us what is best for us.'" (pp. 50-51). Wallace's subordinates took that to mean that the fight against integration was still on. For the redneck his words in presidential primaries in Maryland (Makay 1970), in Wisconsin (Makay 1968), and in Missouri (Harte 1972) were only catering statements to gain the votes of "closet racists." To put it another way, Wallace was carrying the message of the South to the rest of the country, and according to Michael J. Robinson and Clifford Zukin (1976), Wallace was a very successful television communicator to white conservatives who received their news primarily or exclusively from the television medium.

Wallace's rhetoric may be perceived as accomplishing at least three different purposes: separating stereotypes of Southern working blacks and working whites; separating Washington, D.C., from the rest of the country; and separating blue-collar workers from those in other socioeconomic groups. As Flynt (1969, p. 7) has stated, some people thought that "slavery stigmatized *all* forms of physical labor in the South and produced a lower class of whites who were lazy and shiftless." While rednecks perceive most black physical laborers in that genre, they do not think of themselves that way. The redneck identified with Wallace's rhetoric, which characterized most blacks as looking for something for nothing: welfare programs, Medicare, and other federal "'nigger programs'" (Flynt 1979, p. 35).

As Killian (1970, p. 8) has indicated (quoting the late Ralph McGill of the Atlanta *Constitution*), "'It is the fate of the Southerner to be involved in his region, always to feel himself held by it.'" Those words help the redneck—even in 1982—to see his world separate and apart from Washington, the same place that almost destroyed the Southern culture in the middle of the nineteenth century. In the past 20 years or so, the redneck has seen the federal government as a friend of blacks, as an enemy of the redneck; as a friend of the nonworker, as an enemy of the laborer. For the redneck it appears that Washington has only limited his personal freedom. As Newby (1978, p. 407) has pointed out, "Concern with self-worth and self-expression helps explain some of the less attractive traits of the white poor, such as sexism and racism." To the redneck, this means that he rarely has the freedom to "call a spade a spade." He can no longer use the word *nigger* without being concerned about who might be around to hear him and judge him. Neither can he make his stereotypic jokes about the opposite sex without a possible social (or even legal) reprisal owing to the rise of the women's liberation movement and the Equal Rights Amendment. The redneck has not received any "handouts," and he now feels as if he—not the female—is discriminated against in jobs and in personal freedom.

Although the redneck was relatively unconcerned about blacks attending the University of Mississippi or the University of Alabama, he was concerned about an "outside force" as the stimulator of such actions. As Silver (1964, p. 3) has indicated, the University of Mississippi "was the response of a closed society of Mississippi to a law outside itself."

The separations that Wallace implied were also present in class discriminations. Even though Wallace held a law degree from the

University of Alabama, most rednecks did not think of him as a lawyer. Wallace was a spokesperson for the blue-collar worker, for the redneck. That same view was exemplified by the election of Cliff Finch to governorship in Mississippi. Also a wealthy lawyer, and at least upper middle class, Finch ran as a blue-collar worker, campaigning by driving a bulldozer and taking his lunch in a pail. Most rednecks did not perceive of Finch, the attorney, as being in a similar socioeconomic class with his opponent Gil Carmichael, a Meridian automobile dealer. Both Finch and Wallace have been erroneously perceived by rednecks as honest and hard-working regionalists, as states and individual righters (Killian 1970, p. 6), and as identifying with the poor white.

Strom Thurmond

Not only do rednecks have general, regional heroes, but each state also has its hero. In South Carolina that man is Strom Thurmond. In his lifetime he has been a rebel, the youngest to do this and the youngest to do that (Lachicotte 1967, p. 5). A native of Aiken, South Carolina, he has proved himself to his conservative audience with his association with Bob Jones University, a fundamentalist school, and with his rebellion against the National Democratic party in the early and middle 1950s.

In 1956 Thurmond participated with other Southern senators in drafting the "Southern Manifesto," which voiced opposition to the Supreme Court's desegregation decision (Lachicotte 1967, p. 129). Like Wallace, Thurmond participated in creating his own political party (the States' Right party in 1948). In addition, he maintained a macho position by marrying a woman much younger and later by fathering children by her.

Thurmond had also been famous for his "scathing blast at the world communist movement" (Sherrill 1969, p. 255). In one breath he declared it was

> a power-seeking, God-denying, man and material worshipping, amoral force operating from a base of territories it dominates, by conspiratorial tactics of subversion, infiltration, propaganda, assassination, genocide, espionage, political and economic blackmail, all under the cover of nuclear holocaust, through the apparatus of agents, tools, opportunists, and dupes [p. 255].

Thus, Thurmond performed the kind of political role that redneck's demand. He was anticommunist, antiunion, anti-Negro, and macho. To his credit he is the last U.S. senator to be elected by a write-in vote, often with illiterate votes that only came close to spelling his name correctly (p. 265). Now he is a very conservative Republican who has shown no interest in helping the white lower class; however, many rednecks continue to support him.

Lester Maddox

The former governor of Georgia spoke in rhetoric similar to Thurmond's. He once stated: "So you screwballs, Socialists, Communists, mistaken and misguided who threaten me, let me say you are wasting your time. I just plain don't scare" (Sherrill 1969, p. 277). Maddox's bigot-oriented rhetoric has also been reflected in his views on Lyndon Johnson's antipoverty programs: "'It helps the bums, the criminals, the beatniks, and Communists to wreck and rule this great land'" (p. 281). He continued by saying that the antipoverty program was "'aimed mainly at coddling anarchists, keeping a bunch of whoring negra wenches in food while they turned out more bastards'" (p. 281).

Unlike Thurmond and Wallace, Maddox exemplified his rhetorical statements with his behavior. On numerous occasions he physically assaulted blacks and at other times threatened to do so with ax handles (pp. 277-81). When Martin Luther King's funeral was held in Atlanta, he ordered that if any of the marchers attempted to go up toward the capitol, the police were to "'shoot 'em down and stack 'em up'" (p. 280).

Maddox closed his Pickwick Restaurant when he was given the choice of doing so or integrating it. He openly worked with the Klan and appointed Klan sympathizers to high state Democratic party posts. He combined his "racist philosophy that . . . [appealed] to the wool hats with an economic philosophy that . . . [appealed] to the urban businessman" (p. 297). He burdened the white lower classes with increased sales tax, but even so, he satisfied the rednecks who had "an eye only for the Negro" (p. 297).

Even with this positive trait, he did not appeal to even some of his closest associates. One of them stated that Maddox had had a stroke and it affected him. George Wallace claimed, "'Y'know, Lester ain't got much character'" (p. 282). But he was elected to the top position in Georgia— ultimately decided in the state legislature, he was chosen over Howard ("Bo") Callaway, the son of a textile owner. Although distorted, he felt he was a patriot proclaiming: "When I sing 'God Bless America,' I really mean it. Don't *chew*?" (p. 301).

Huey Long

Huey Pierce Long was born near Winnfield, Lousiana, in Winn Parish on August 30, 1893, and died of an assassin's bullet in Baton Rouge on September 10, 1935. Winn Parish had a long history of lower-class insurgency, which included antiseccessionism, Populism, and socialism. Long followed in the tradition and did more for the poor Southern white man in his short career than anyone else before or since. He started out as a poor door-to-door peddler and used his savings and borrowed money from an older brother to study law for one year (1914) at Tulane University. He passed the Louisiana bar examination in 1915 and quickly won a reputation as a poor man's lawyer by specializing in workmens' compensation cases. As a strong, rhetorical, and vociferous opponent of Standard Oil and other corporate interests, he was elected and reelected to the state Railroad Commission and later to the Public Service Commission (1921-26) where he built a ten-year record of warring againt the utilities and won reductions in telephone, electric, gas, railroad, and streetcar rates. He also won the right of the commission to regulate Standard Oil's interstate pipeline as a common carrier.

In 1928 Long was elected governor and immediately pushed through the legislature a constitutional amendment to tax the oil interests and use the revenues therefrom for highways and education. The legislature, under his pressure, issued a $30 million bond for roads and bridges, free textbooks financed by an increased severance tax, higher appropriations for state charitable institutions and schools, and cheap natural gas for New Orleans. Because of Long, Louisiana was the first state to provide free textbooks, free charity hospitals, and subsidized lunches in the public schools. Long increased services in Louisiana by taxing big oil (Morris, Commager, and Morris 1976, pp. 1088-89).

The opposition, backed by oil, succeeded in having him impeached by the lower house in 1929 for bribery and gross misconduct. The senate voted againt conviction. He was elected to the U.S. Senate in 1930 and dominated Louisiana politics from that time until his death. As a senator he used his influence to broaden Louisiana's highway program, to expand Louisiana State University, and to continue aid for charity hospitals, schools, free textbooks, and other public services. He initiated the Share-Our-Wealth program in 1932, which lasted until his death in 1935. This wide sweeping social program (the closest thing to socialism this country has ever seen) proposed, among other things, to liquidate large personal fortunes, guarantee every American family an allowance of $5,000 and every worker an annual income of $2,500, grant "adequate" pensions to the aged, reduce labor's work hours, pay veterans bonuses, and ensure a college education for all qualified students. For his or any day these were radical proposals, proposals which for the first time centered on *structural* change. In 1933 he published a book entitled *Every Man a King* to publicize his intended program, and in 1934 he organized several Share-Our-Wealth clubs.

Long's more radical policies were never inaugurated, but his influence pushed the country toward a more liberal stance. It is unlikely that Roosevelt would have received the presidential nomination in 1932 without his help. Moreover, he helped Roosevelt implement the New Deal and pushed him left of center. In 1935 Roosevelt began to talk about the need to "steal Long's thunder," which he did with the "soak-the-rich" tax of 1935, a tax that sharply raised the surtax on large incomes and levied a graduated corporation income tax. The Social Security Act of 1935 reflects Long's influence and point of view (Tindall 1967, pp. 236-38, 613-14). We believe that Long was too radical and popular for Roosevelt; however, the prevailing view is that he was too mercurial and ambitious for the president (p. 614).

The King Fish, Long's sobriquet, has been called a demagogue by many, and his dictatorial political tactics have been criticized. Long, however, like Lenin, had to resort to authoritarian tactics to get things done, but he should be judged within the context of the Louisiana politics at his time. We contend that he was a true folk hero of the poor as a class, the greatest hero they have ever had, because he cut through the so-called democratic muck and got at structural change, (that is, he taxed the corporate interests heavily and provided human services, never before afforded). Long dramatized himself as the champion of the people against the "sinister interests"—the corporate interests and the rich and powerful, privilege, paternalism, and monopolism. He received political support (votes) from poor white Anglos, French-Catholic voters, and the *blacks*, who hailed him as their champion (Key 1949, pp. 156-60). To this day the poor people in Louisiana sing the praises of Huey P. Long, a paean justly deserved. He was far ahead of his time and, as a matter of fact, his century.

Other Heroes

Though a few politicians have been redneck heroes, most heroes come from without the area of politics. Silver (1964, p. 47) wrote: "If the [Mississippians] hate Hodding Carter or the Kennedys, or love Elvis Presley, Dizzy Dean, the Mississippi State basketball team or South Africa, or feel that a former Miss America is a fine actress, they are not inhibited from saying so." Both the hero system and the antihero system are based on the general values that have been held in the traditional closed society, a society that assumes "1) biological inferiority of the Negro, 2) the sanction of the Bible and Christianity, 3) the aptitude of the Negro for menial labor only, 4) racial separation as an absolute requirement for social stability, and 5) the necessity of the Negro earning his way to a higher and more responsible citizenship" (p. 22).

Heroes must believe in fundamental, Protestant religious biases, accept the genetic inferiority of blacks, and accept as fact that "outsiders" are trying to "do in" the South as they did in the middle of the nineteenth century. However, there have been some changes. Black football players are acceptable on traditionally all-white college teams. If anyone is a hero to the Georgia redneck in 1982, it is a home-grown Georgia black, Herschel Walker, who is a running back for the University of Georgia Bulldogs. According to the redneck, "That nigger can really run, can't he?" For rednecks black athletes became "our niggers."

At the same time, however, blacks are not generally accepted in other circles. Rednecks do not believe that Walker eats with the white players on the Georgia team. Neither do they believe that Walker goes to classes with young, white girls in Athens, Georgia. Rednecks know little about campus life, because they do not go to college as a rule.

In addition, the rights of the black athlete are limited to certain roles on the field. In the South, black quarterbacks are rare because quarterbacks play leadership roles. Quarterback heroes have evolved over the years with names such as Y. A. Tittle, Charlie Connerly, Fran Tarkenton, Joe Namath, Kenny Stabler, and Archie Manning. They are accepted as *white*, legitimate heroes who all (except Namath) were born and reared in the South and played their college 'ball at Georgia, L.S.U., Ole Miss, or Alabama. Their coaches are also white and legendary among the Southern, blue-collar groups as well as among social class groups. Names such as Wally Butts, Shug Jordan, and Bear Bryant come immediately to mind.

As integration has taken place, some black football players have found their places in the hearts of redneck fans. The same story has not been true of basketball players. Southern college basketball teams have too many blacks for the redneck to make any kind of identification. Some rednecks ask the question, "When are they going to integrate the [black] basketball team?" Perhaps basketball is a sport that is too effeminate in his perception for the redneck to deal with.

While many black professionals have been successful in major league baseball, they are not accepted either. Rednecks associate more often with the beer-drinking, redneck-talking, down-home Dizzy Dean types of the old days than with Southern-born black stars such as Henry Aaron, Willie Mays, or Willie McCovey, who are rarely mentioned.

Other sports such as tennis, golf, and hockey are without a place in their lives. Professional hockey teams have failed financially in Atlanta and Birmingham. Soccer is still considered a foreign sport.

Football and stock car racing remain the macho areas for sports heroes in the eyes of the redneck.

ENEMIES AND OUTSIDERS

The Outsider

The perception that those from outside the South have of those in the South is often influenced by what is presented in the media. That image is one of Burt Reynold's hauling Coors beer from Texas to Georgia; it is an image of the "Dukes of Hazzard" Hogg family; it is an image of rough-looking roustabouts drinking beer and never working. As Robert D. Jacobs (1980) has portrayed the Southerner, he is a "hick" from the *Tobacco Road* tradition. Today, the redneck is viewed by outsiders more as an object of ridicule than as a threat. Jacobs writes:

> Today the name "red-neck," with or without the hyphen, is applied indiscriminately to rural and small town Southerners, and it has gained respectability to the extent that the younger brother of the president of the United States was photographed recently wearing a T-shirt that bore the legend, "Redneck Power." But in the early nineteenth century the poor white, by whatever name, was a despicable comic object [p. 209].

This is still the case. Erskine Caldwell's Jeeter Lester of *Tobacco Road* became the stereotype of the early and middle twentieth century. This stereotype was unfortunate, as Jacobs reports, "because Caldwell's purpose was not to disparage the poor white but to account for his degeneracy on economic grounds and to drive the lesson home through comic exaggeration" (p. 220).

Regardless of Caldwell's intentions, readers of his book were negligent in reading through the facade to see the serious aspects of a person like Lester. Caldwell wrote of the Southern poor whites that they had "'such faith in nature, in the earth, and the plants that grew in the earth, that they could not understand how the earth could fail them'" (p. 221). Caldwell perceived of the redneck as one who lives off the land. As Jacobs suggests, "The fish of the streams, the squirrels, rabbits, and opossums of the woods, the half-wild pigs and chickens that took care of themselves . . . . Jeeter Lester is eager to work the land, but he has been conditioned to raise money crops—tobacco and cotton" (p. 221). On the other hand, "Faulkner succeeded in making the poor white a com-prehensible being, neither an object for comic caricature nor a shabby argument for political and economic reform" (p. 223).

Because of the negative stereotypes that have been portrayed in novels, short stories, film, and television, the redneck is often perceived by outsiders to be a new, white version of "Amos and Andy." Therefore, outsiders try to avoid interaction with rednecks as much as possible.

If these are the outsiders' perceptions of rednecks, the rednecks' perceptions of outsiders are similarly stereotypical. Most people from outside the traditional South are considered "nigger-lovers" and "liberals." In addition, people from outside the South are perceived as foreigners. Out-of-state license plates are considered just as foreign as plates from Belgium. Yankees enjoy sports such as ice hockey and soccer, which are considered foreign sports by redneck enthusiasts of fishing, hunting, and football. Yankees dress differently, talk differently, have different values, and "just ain't no damn good."

Rarely do Northern middle- and upper-class persons compare their notions of rednecks with their Northern lower-class whites because of perceived dichotomies in accent, urban-rural, work. Thus, communication between rednecks and middle- and upper-class Northerners is poor, which has been generated and reinforced by mutual stereotyping. As F. King (1975, p. 16) has pointed out, "Yankees always make the mistake of going home the moment they realize they are going mad, which is why they never understand the South. They do not grasp the fact that losing one's mind is the most important prerequisite for fitting in with Southerners. Sanity has never held any charm for us; in fact, we're against it." The Southerner feels first and then justifies his position on the basis of a received and traditional ideology. When he does think, his convoluted mind mixes up fiction and so-called truth.

The Inside-Outsider and Social Class

Rednecks along with middle- and upper-class males maintain a Southern defensiveness which is largely a remnant of Dixie's loss in the Civil War, the accompanying Reconstruction period, and the civil rights war of the 1960s. The redneck is separated, though, by class demarcation. The upper classes—particularly, the high-class Southern gentleman—has some traits portrayed by Ashley Wilkes in Gone with the Wind. The gentleman has respect for Southern ladies, condemns "trash" of both sexes, and like his redneck counterpart, believes that he must "'keep the Negro in his place'" (Killian 1970, p. 34).

Class differentiation is sometimes dominant, and at other times, insignificant. In both cases, however, the freedom of each group is severely restricted. Sennett and Cobb (1973, p. 28) have written: "Class is a system of limiting freedom: it limits the freedom of the powerful in dealing with other people, because the strong are constricted within the circle of action that maintains their power; class constricts the weak more obviously in that they must obey commands."

The Southern good old boy grows up in a manner similar to the redneck. In elementary school one may have difficulty in differentiating between the two. Both groups "hate girls," they fight among themselves and against one another, and they play together at recess. The class lines are relatively thin since this concept is difficult to understand.

As they grow older, both groups begin detecting what may be called "class cues." The middle- and upper-class boy wears clothes that are "more preppie" than his lower-class friend. Redneck clothes, even at a very young age, are more practical and less "sissy" than those of his richer colleagues. The redneck usually lives in the country or across town and must ride the school bus. Little preppie is driven to school by his parents. As they grow even older, the success rate in academia becomes more and more important for the middle- and upper-class boy. Most rednecks are willing to take whatever grades they receive because they do not intend to go to college anyway. Generally, the only chance for a redneck to go to college is for him to become an outstanding high school athlete.

The extracurricular activities in high school vary between the two groups. The middle- and upper-class male spends time not only with athletics but also with social and service organizations as a prelude to later fraternity membership and roles in the Lion's Club, the Kiwanis, and the Chamber of Commerce. The redneck finds little or no time for such useless endeavors as the school newspaper staff, the yearbook committee, or the glee club. These activities are effeminate in nature. In addition, most rednecks do not get involved in the Key Club, the Wheels, the Beta Club, or the Honor Society because of low high school grades and social class politics practiced by students, teachers, and parents. Rednecks know there is really no place for them in school of any consequence. Who really needs rednecks or blacks except for dirty work! Sometimes the rural redneck kid joins the Future Farmers of America and/or the Four-H Club since these organizations are vocationally oriented and largely membered by males. Middle- and upper-class youngsters are the leaders even in these organizations, big farmers' and planters' sons. Organizations such as the Boy Scouts are seen as middle-class pseudomachismo, membered by city boys who want to learn how to do carpentry work and how to "fix" cars—to "soup 'em up."

As a generalization, one might say that young rednecks learn to use their hands, and the young preppies learn to use their minds. The redneck may take mechanical drawing, shop, physical education, and agriculture. At the same time, the preppie may take courses in chemistry, physics, drama, and foreign languages. By the end of the sophomore year in high school, the socioeconomic lines have become thick. Socially, the redneck "knows" better than to ask a middle- or upper-class young lady out for a date. He generally "dates" only those girls from his neighborhood, the daughters of blue-collar workers. He attends a different (usually more fundamentalist) church than the preppie.

All class groups gather together at high school football games and often at the local high school "hangout." In each case, however, there is little interaction among the various classes. The hangouts often contain different sections for rednecks and preppies, and frequently different hangouts cater to different social classes.

Upon graduation from high school, the middle- and upper-class male continues his socialization process, which separates him from the redneck. By college age he can be easily differentiated from the redneck in most any behavior setting. As F. King (1975, p. 94) describes him:

> The name 'Good Ole Boy,' while very male in a hail-fellow-well-met way, lacks the virile imagery. It suggests a male both fat and fatuous, yet the Good Ole Boy is more than a locker-room jock or a Babbitt with a Southern accent; his Sturm and Drang is much more complex because it is unique, peculiar to him alone and unshared by his fellow country-men.

Good old boys often move in groups, with one of them taking on the role of "Shucks, ma'am." The "Shucks, ma'am" boy often acts as the intermediary between other boys and the comments that are made to ladies. King provides some examples similar to ones we have noted.

> Shucks, ma'am, he didn't mean to insult you. He just thinks yore mighty sweet, thass all.
>
> Don't pay no mind to him, ma'am....He's just foolin!
>
> I just wanted to see if you were aw-right. It's too late for room service so I just thought you might like a Co'Cola [p. 92].

As King has indicated, the good old boy's function is to protect women from black men, from other white men, and from themselves. Flynt (1979) has expained that the lynching of black men was to protect and defend white women from rape, although actual rape rarely occurred. Instead, sometimes the "nigger jes looked at her the wrong way." The women protect themselves by pretending that they do not hear comments or see gestures and by demonstrating a "freeze" position.

Some of the men in the middle-, and even more in the upper-classes, live in a society that is matriarchal. Grandmama (granny, Big Mama, MaMinnie) is the boss. She is the moral force behind the family, and she makes all the rules until she "passes away." Granny often traces the lineage to the Mayflower and is a member of the Daughters of the American Revolution or the United Daughters of the Confederacy. She probably attended college at one of the public or private "prestigious" women's institutions in the South (Agnes Scott, Mississippi State College for Women, Queens, Brenau, Wesleyan, Randolph Macon, et cetera.) She did not graduate, but she learned enough to have some idea about culture.

She works with the Women's Club, the Garden Club, and the Eastern Star. She probably learned to play bridge in college, which she plays at the country club on Wednesday mornings. Bridge is a cover for gossip. In addition, she learned all that Amy Vanderbilt ever knew about "mannuhs." It is important to her that her children and grandchildren have "mannuhs" and that they are always nice to everybody. That is an indication of blue blood in the South.

All of these factors are considered important by the middle- and upper-classes though not by the rednecks. In fact, the redneck views these factors as ridiculous, time-wasting nonsense. As has been mentioned, any kind of formal organization is a waste to the redneck. Social organizations are not needed because the neck can always go down to the local honky-tonk and down a few brews with his buddies, or they can set up a weekend of watching football together, a fishing trip, or a hunting trip. Political organizations are equally useless because the redneck has found himself politically powerless (Hickson 1976). Similar "wastes of time" include learning how to play complicated card games, learning how to "set a table," and other effeminate goings on, including "learnin' to like faggot [classical] music or play the piano."

It is important for the middle and upper classes to maintain their separation from the redneck. The middle class, however, often associates itself with the upper class. As Killian (1970) has indicated, middle-class members like to think of themselves as being from families of "good stock." Good stock becomes a difficult stratum to differentiate in the South because of the various combinations that one runs into, including "old blood and old money; old blood and new money; new blood and old money; new blood and new money; and that especially revered category, old blood and no money" (F. King 1975, p. 132).

Whereas there is a tendency for the middle class to identify with the working class in other parts of the United States, Southern middle-class people like to think of themselves as upper class. There is some reason for this, especially in small towns and rural areas where the rich must associate with middle class people or with no one at all.

Middle- and upper-class boys are supposed to attend college, and even when they have not done well in high school, they go "somewhere." Usually, the "bright" upper-class boys go to private colleges, often outside the South. The intelligent middle-class boys go to large state universities. The upper-class boys who do not do as well in high school end up in less prestigious schools where they can party and finish degrees in business, prelaw, or premed. By the time they finish, hopefully they will be more concerned about schooling. Some are and some are not. Most are not, but is does not matter because they can always go back to daddy's peach farm, cotton farm, tobacco farm, feed store, bank, or business—and most do.

Grocery markets are particularly bothersome to middle- and upper-class Southerners. Everyone goes to grocery markets, including blacks and rednecks. Middle- and upper-class people do not like having their privacy invaded, and having rednecks see their groceries is almost like being peered at by a "peeping Tom." For this reason, the middle- and upper-class shopper takes great care to appear organized and efficient. They do not check prices on cans.

They do, however, go to great lengths to have "someone wait on them" such as a butcher. They may ask : "Was this steak cut today?" or "Would you cut me a steak about such and such a size?" They may get someone to weigh their grapes, or they may ask if he has any bananas that are not "out." They are constantly vying for special attention to separate themselves from the blacks and the rednecks. When someone else gets special attention—for example, when one uses food stamps—the middle- and upper-class Southerner becomes very impatient, frustrated, and angry.

Even when a middle- or upper-class Southerner "knows" a redneck, the redneck is looked down upon. The superior one will stand and walk erect, in an exaggerated manner, avoid eye contact as much as possible, and hold conversation to the shortest time period possible. The only person the middle- and upper-class Southerner will have an extended conversation with (outside of her class) is the checker, but, in a sense, this conversation is simply an extension of "being waited on." It also occurs with tellers at the bank, clerks at the courthouse and post office, or any public service personnel.

Blacks

According to Newby (1978, p. 407), racism is "direct, unreflective action and mob violence." For the redneck, the black is, has been, and always will be his nemesis. As Benjamin P. Bowser, Raymond G. Hunt, and David C. Pohl (1981, p. 13) describe it, "Racism in America is a white problem." If racism is a problem for white Americans, it is even more so for Southern rednecks. In most of the South, blacks are the only ones keeping rednecks from being on the very bottom of the socioeconomic ladder.

James M. Jones (1981, pp. 27-28) delineates three types of racism: individual, institutional, and cultural. The South has traditionally provided a backdrop of institutional and cultural racism that has seduced individuals into their own brands of bigotry. Southern leaders have been elected because of their racism. Thus, the redneck lives in an environment where racism has been condoned, and his primary purpose has been to separate his own subculture from that of the blacks.

If antebellum times, the Civil War, and Reconstruction started such a racist dogma among rednecks, other twentieth century sociopolitical decisions enhanced it. The Supreme Court decision on school integration ignited the fuel. The Kennedy-Johnson "war on poverty" added fuel to the fire (Clark and Hopkins 1968). All the time, the blacks' socioeconomic position was improving while the rednecks' was not. Killian (1970, p. 114) has pointed out that "between 1959 and 1969 the Southern white share of total American rural poverty increased slightly."

"Poor whites have been in turn stereotyped by the dominant culture (as rednecks, Holy Rollers), discriminated against, and misunderstood" (Flynt 1979, p. xvii). In Northern cities, rednecks were given stereotypes not too distinct from those given to the blacks. Killian (1970, p. 107) indicates that poor Southern whites were considered as being clannish, as having low standards of hygiene and sanitation, as drinking heavily, and as brawling and having knife fights. One Chicago bartender said that they are the same as blacks, but "they're just niggers and they ain't even human. But a white man is human" (p. 108).

There are, of course, many similarities between rednecks and blacks in the South: their subcultures are intertwined, they work together side by side, they face poverty time and time again and through generations, they talk similarly, and they eat the same food.

The redneck's purpose, then, is to emphasize the differences. One of the basic differences is that the South assigns a great deal of importance to coming from "good blood," and regardless of the economic changes that a black may go through, he can never be white. The first attribute of having good blood is to be white. Of course, simply being white does not mean that one has good blood, but it is the necessary first prerequisite.

The redneck, then, focuses his attention on those aspects of blacks that differentiate the two groups. For example, they differ in their choice of music. While blacks prefer soul music, disco music, and rhythm and blues, the redneck likes the more sedate (or depressing) country and Western. Dancing is also different; while the blacks prefer the "Soul Train" orientation, the redneck does the two-step with a cowboy hat atop his head, or he refrains from dancing altogether.

There are also differences in verbal and nonverbal communication between the two groups. They have a different style of walking, and they maintain different sexual and marital patterns. Roebuck and Neff (1980, pp. 256-57) explain the reactions of rednecks:

As noted earlier, rednecks feel that their entire way of life is not only threatened but actively in the process of being replaced by "foreign" ways. Thus rednecks hate. They vent much of this hatred toward blacks, a familiar, weak, and highly visible "competitive" group that is safely and firmly at the bottom of the Southern pecking order. So far rednecks have focused little of their hostility toward their real enemies: the social system and the middle (managers, professionals, technocrats) and upper (owners) classes it serves at their expense.

Rednecks are aware that they have much in common with the Southern black. They realize that both groups are working class, virtually propertyless, economically insecure, marginal, powerless, disvalued and uneducated. However, it is always groups who are the most similar to a culturally stigmatized population who hate them the most. Whereas similarity ordinarily leads to attraction, when the similarity is threatening, the opposite occurs. Likewise, to minimize the threat, rednecks shy away from all associations with blacks other than the few (and increasingly exceptional) blacks who will still accept condescending treatment and otherwise acknowledge "their place" as inferiors.

Thus, the enemies of the redneck are formidable. They include all persons outside the South (foreign and domestic), the white middle and upper classes in the South, and blacks. The enemies are diverse. They are geographic enemies, class enemies, and radical enemies. The redneck has few friends—other rednecks. As Flynt (1979, p. 149) has evaluated the redneck situation: "Fatalism was a realistic appraisal of life experiences." With this evaluation of the political heroes and enemies of the redneck, we will attempt to evaluate their position in the political system.

ROLES IN THE POLITICAL SYSTEM

Flynt (1979, p. 124) claims that any solution to the problem of the Southern poor whites "must recognize unique problems that exist among Southern whites, including cultural isolation and racism bred by ignorance, fear, and powerlessness." The lack of power is a draining force on the redneck for a number of reasons. First, the machismo motive involves the need for power, and just as sexually impotent males have the need to show some prowess, political impotence has a similar underlying goal. However, rednecks have never had political power. They were disenfranchised after Reconstruction by the middle and upper classes' drives for literacy tests and poll taxes. They have since been "fooled" by Southern demagogues, who sided with the middle and upper classes after their elections. The once politically impotent have become so desensitized to politics that they are now virtually neuter.

The lack of power has also been manifest in the political conservatism that the redneck has maintained through the years. The past 25 years in particular have caused the redneck to resent the system. The Kennedy and Johnson years and their programs were the targets of rednecks. Rednecks, however, have not been particularly satisfied with Reagan's economic policies either. The redneck feels "shafted" by liberal Democrats and conservative Republicans alike. In comparison with other groups in the United States, the rednecks are overtaxed, and they resent the middle and upper classes' having less of a tax burden. They feel the impact of inflation and higher interest rates more than do others. They hate bureaucracy. They want government to take a laissez-faire approach to them as individuals.

The redneck's solution to his problem is to side with the moral majority and leaders such as Jerry Falwell. They usually side with the moral majority in cases such as the creation controversy in the public schools. They also verbally support Donald Wildmon's boycott of television programs that portray excessive sex and violence although often violating the boycott in their behavior. Without class consciousness they feel their problem can only be solved by individual effort and divine intervention.

The redneck would like to see the political system move in a direction of strict conservatism. Even with the support of the moral majority, however, most rednecks are now frustrated about achieving their goal. For all practical purposes, rednecks are outside of a political system that they know practically nothing about. Even when they move out of the South, their resistance to change continues.

INTRANSIGENCE TO CHANGE

Working-class Southern migrants to the North frequently visit their redneck kin "back home," the South. Northern exposure does not appear to have changed them in any way, and they are indistinguishable from their relatives who remain in the South. Many Northern friends from Ohio, Illinois, Michigan, Indiana, Pennsylvania, and New York tell us that rednecks (frequently called hillbillies, briars, hill jacks, ridge runners, stump jumpers, country boys, hicks, or white trash) remain rednecks through several generations and that many never change. They also report a constant flow of working-class whites to and from the South, a class that maintains its culture and identity by working together at the same factories and plants, residing in the same neighborhoods, attending the same churches, socializing at the same bars and restaurants, and marrying within the group.

Most Northern migrants we talked to (in the South and in the North) insisted that they would eventually return to the South, buy a little piece of land, and settle down. These findings about redneck migrants to the North lead us to believe that a working-class Southern culture has been, and is being, exported to the North. Most writers and scholars are primarily concerned with social change in the South as brought about by outside influences. We question this position and maintain that the South probably influences other regions to a greater extent than it is influenced by them. The more the South appears to be changing, the more it remains the same—that is, its central core.

SOCIAL STRUCTURE

Perpetuation of Class Differences

The redneck finds himself outside of the political system and at the bottom of the social heap. In the 1980s the redneck perceives the white race as unpopular. They feel blacks have gained priority in job opportunity. In addition, they feel that women have been given preference in business and industry.

In terms of class, the same two social class forms (upper class, lower class) of capitalism remain intact, though the content of each has changed. Upper-class Southerners are now members of the corporate wealthy class who own, manage, and control stocks, bonds, trusts, capital goods, real estate, et cetera, in financial, commercial, insurance, agricultural, and industrial corporations. Much, if not most, of the membership is tied in financially with outside as well as inside corporate interests. The upper echelon of the lower classes (referred to generally as the upper middle class) comprises owners of small and medium-sized businesses and corporations, large farmers, locally based construction firms, banks, and professionals. Frequently, friendship and kinship connections articulate this membership to that of the upper classes. These two strata share a similar life-style beyond the reach of the common man, though a wide differential in wealth delineates them. At the bottom are rednecks and blacks, who because of isolation and a dearth of economic knowledge, make no distinction between middle- and upper-class Southerners. Paternalism and racism still persist as a social form along class lines; however, the paternalism is gradually giving way to estrangement, distrust, and the separation of classes in other than secondary relationships. The underclasses continue to cooperate, but they do so with declining morale. This is especially true in the case of blacks.

The redneck has never identified his real enemy, the Southern upper class (an ownership class enmeshed with "outside" capitalists) and its supporting "middle class," though he is acutely aware of his insecurity in a land of plenty. On the other hand, the black appears more knowledgeable about class and race lines and acknowledges a tradition of slavery and racial segregation on which he has fashioned a culture—history, art, music, literature, and brotherhood. The redneck has been reluctant, unfortunately, to admit his structural underclass status and therefore has failed to identify with his own kind along social class lines. Though wary of and ambivalent toward the Southern big shots (middle and upper classes), he accepts their presence as in the nature of things and follows their preachments on political and economic ideology and policy. Powerless, economically and educationally deprived and stigmatized, the redneck accepts the economic and intellectual paternalism and noblesse oblige of the upper-class Southerner—a Southerner who has always taken the position that there is a differential ordering of men and that he is born to rule, though he acknowledges his responsibility to act decently toward those in the lower classes with the exception of white trash. This class doctrine of the upper-class Southerner is buttressed by his personal success story. Losers are born losers, that is, after the fact; winners are born winners, that is, after the fact.

Historically, the white upper class, with the help of the white middle class, has kept the redneck in his subservient place—by preventing an alliance between working-class whites and blacks. The middle and upper classes have, at times, encouraged racism among the rednecks. The motive for this was, and is, the preservation of a cheap, docile labor supply, which would be threatened should working-class whites and blacks realize their common interests, unite, and demand economic and political rights by way of organization. The planters in the antebellum and the Reconstruction periods, the Bourbons in the post-Reconstruction period (1876-1901), and later the large farmers and the owners and managers of businesses and corporations have utilized the "bloody shirt" antilabor technique—that is, an appeal to the white working man's racism.

In short, the upper-class Southerner has attempted with great success to indoctrinate the working-class Southerner with the fixed idea that any fraternization on his part with blacks would lead to social equality, miscegenation, and intermarriage (though in fact the latter two have always occurred in a veiled and peculiarly defined manner). The black is quick to point out that he has been marrying white men's daughters (with black mothers) for a long time. Through the present the trump card has been the threat of the sexually potent black male to the white man's woman—a potency reconstructed by the unwitting white man who now has second thoughts on the sexual myth he invented and disseminated. This ploy and its effectiveness since the Civil War is documented in the history of the sharecropping and crop-lien system and in the comparatively weak labor movement in the South. The Southern Farmers' Alliance (1874), Colored Farmers' Alliance (1896), Knights of Labor (1878-1893), the People's Part of the United States (1891), the Socialist party of America (1897), the American Federation of Labor (1886-1955), and the CIO and AFL-CIO (1955) have all been destroyed or attenuated in the South.

Unionization and Labor

The illegal and violent history of plant, factory, community, legislative, court, and law enforcement struggle against organized labor in the South through the early 1960s and labor's small gains in parts of the Southwest (for example, Texas and Oklahoma) have been well documented. To date, labor unions have not made a major commitment to organizing the South. Unionization faces an uphill fight because of a number of regional conditions and techniques. First, the local power structure (as well as plant ownership and management) throughout the South opposes unionization via local newspapers, churches, legal firms, businesses, schools, municipal officials, community leaders, and law enforcement personnel. Business and community organizations utilize antiunion firms, police repression, and violence. Management consultants from large specialized firms (for example, Modern Management Methods of Chicago) are hired to "cool out" employees who press for unions. Another method to prevent labor contracts is "surface bargaining," negotiating in bad faith to obstruct the unionization process (for example, as used by J. P. Stevens Mills in Rosnake Rapids, North Carolina). Two other management techniques used to prevent unionization are running prospective employees through a psychological screening process to weed out potential troublemakers (for example, Michelin at its Greenville, South Carolina, plants) and using "job enrichment" techniques to convince employees that unionization is unnecessary (for example, General Motors in several Southern plants).

The Southern region affords two major types of labor, both utilizing a redneck membership: traditional low-skill, low-wage labor in such industries as textiles and furniture, which are often semirural and employ substantial numbers of blacks and women; and high-wage primary labor, that is, those in the auto, rubber, and electrical manufacturing plants. Employers of workers in the first and most numerous category use cruder methods of repression (for example, police and imported goon squads) to intimidate their employees. Management techniques used on the second category of workers are more sophisticated.

Recent research (Montgomery 1981) discloses that three interrelated conditions prevailed in the South from 1800 through the early 1930s that doomed labor-organizing efforts and strikes in this region to an end of violence and defeat. Given these conditions, past is likely to be prologue. The first obstacle was the crushing poverty of the region that created a labor surplus, which swamped most efforts to form enduring unions and made large numbers of hungry, determined strikebreakers constantly available. Second, the tradition of white supremacy and the division and manipulation of the white and black workers by farm, factory, and mill owners proved a barrier to union organization and engendered bloody labor violence. Machine-tending jobs were reserved for whites, while both groups were thrown into bitter competition for unskilled labor jobs. Blacks were frequently used as strikebreakers but infrequently employed in textile mills, the primary employer of industrial wage earners during this period. Third, state and local government and social and political "elites" induced outside industrial entrepreneurs and capital investment by offering cheap money (interest rates), taxation, labor, coal, power, land, and water. Finally, state and local law enforcement officers and local elites used violence and illegal vigilante tactics to suppress strikes.

A recent in-depth interview study (Botsch 1981) of young (all under 35) nonunion furniture workers in North Carolina throughout the 1970s indicates the insidious and persistent difficulties of unionization in the South. These blue-collar workers expressed ambivalent feelings toward labor unions. They liked union wages, pensions, hospitalization, job protection, and other benefits but thought unions throughout the United States had too much political power, were out of hand, and had too much coercive power over the individual worker. They maintained a set of rationalizing myths that many Southern workers have about unions—for example, the myth that the cost of living differences between the North (where one finds unions) and the South compensate for regional wage differences; and that the differentials between union and nonunion wage scales and other union benefits are offset by union dues. Another obstacle to unionization was the workers' expectations: they did not envision a long, tedious struggle for better working conditions; they blamed union failures in the South on "weak unions" but did not realize that unions can be no stronger than the collective will of union workers; they were interested only in quick union benefits for themselves as individuals rather than in long-term working-class benefits; and they were afraid of losing their jobs for "talking union" and not being able to find another job (a verified fear).

Robert E. Botsch found that the most formidable attitudinal obstacle to unionization among these workers was the possession of traditional Southern values, values central to their self-concepts, that is, *individualism* and "antipathy toward any external coercion." Not joiners, they were proud of the fact that they participated very little in formal organizations (such as church, fraternal organizations, and political parties) and that they had practically no experience in collective action. They admired private-oriented men who avoided politics and public scrutiny. Their citizen role models were religious men who enjoyed private morality, minded their own business, were good neighbors, went to church, gave to charities, and avoided collective action. These workers expressed abhorrence toward the use of force by any agencies other than themselves, especially any coercion that could be applied toward them. Much of their self-esteem was based on being able to make it on their own without anyone else's help, and they voiced pride in their ability to survive and cope as individuals. The poor, they felt, could really make it on their own if they tried hard enough. Though angry about their perceived deprivations, they credited themselves and no one else for the vicissitudes of life. Many praised their parents and grandparents for their individual ability to survive without outside help.

The so-called self-reliance of these men was reflected in their work behavior. Nearly all had very mobile work records. They moved from one plant to another in efforts to secure slightly better wages in each move. Virtually all were opposed to the use of compulsion or force of any kind by private organizations, including labor unions, and advocated the right-to-work laws. Many thought that union membership would eventually come about as the result of inspirational leadership and moral suasion. Botsch thought otherwise. He noted that local owners regularly broke National Labor Relations Board rules and regulations, tied up cases in protracted hearings and court battles, paid legal fees and fines—all in the cause of avoiding collective bargaining or coexistence with labor unions. The workers in his study remain free to work for low wages and to worry about losing their jobs. Finally, he found the local power structure to be aggressively antiunion.

One could not ask for a better set of conditions and attitudes more detrimental to unionization. Our observations and impressions of Southern wage earners throughout the South confirm Botsch's findings. Even should more positive attitudes toward unionization develop, the Southern work force is badly undereducated, poorly paid, and isolated economically, socially, and geographically from the town and business community without either economic security or occupational alternatives (Newman 1981). In short, the future of unionization in the South appears dim. Again we see the persistence of the Southern poor folk culture.

Influence of Religion

Southern religion has complemented and supported paternalism and racism, and the triumvirate still fosters a set of cozy and supportive relationships for the upper class. The upper class initiated a Christian mass movement on the eve of the Civil War extolling slavery and the "aristocracy" to convince the redneck to fight its war. Socially rejected in peacetime, the redneck has always been welcomed when war is imminent or in progress. During the Civil War, through the clergy the gentry convinced the redneck for the first time that he, too, was a member of God's chosen people and that the Confederacy had been commissioned by God as the conservator of the Bible and the system of slave labor (entrusted to the Southern people for the benefit of the world). Abraham Lincoln was identified with the King of Egypt, and Jefferson Davis was another Moses leading his people to victory. After the war the redneck flocked to the evangelical and fundamentalist churches, which mush-roomed throughout the South in the latter part of the nineteenth century and the beginning of the twentieth. Since then the redneck has remained religiously orthodox and has defended America's most reactionary economic values and institutions.

Influence of Southern Writers and Intellectuals

Southern writers and intellectuals have provided the redneck (via a trickling-down effect from upper-class membership and conservative institutions, for example, the public school system) with a hazy, false ideology that has prevented him from developing a clear class con-sciousness and a realistic approach to race relations. Novelists of the 1940s and 1950s (William Faulkner, Thomas Wolfe, Robert Penn Warren, Eudora Welty, Carson McCullers, Flannery O'Connor, Truman Capote, William Styron) and literary critics (John Crowe Ransom, Allen Tate, Cleanth Brooks) exerted a strong conservative intellectual force, espec-ially in Southern universities and literary quarterlies. During the 1940s throughout the 1960s, Southern writers converged on New York City from all over the South and moved into positions of power and influence in the journalistic world—for example, Turner Catledge, a Mississippian, the former executive editor of the New York *Times*; and Clifton Daniel, a North Carolinian, the one-time managing editor of the New York *Times*. Willie Morris, a Mississippian, edited *Harper's*; Harold Hayes, a North Carolinian, edited *Esquire*; and Clay Blair, a Virginian, edited the *Saturday Evening Post*. These writers, for the most part, were defensive on the issue of race and the South in general. They loved the South, celebrated its virtues, and disclaimed "the intruders in the dust," that is, outsiders who desired changes via legislative and legal reforms. They appealed to traditional paternalism, claiming the bond between black and white was stronger and more intimate in the South than anything existing in the relations between the two races in the North. There was love as well as guilt, and if given time and left alone, the South would eventually solve its race problems on its own.

In the late 1960s a wave of Southern journalists supplanted the former generation of Southern novelists, poets, and critics. These Southern WASPs (white Anglo-Saxon Protestants) who claimed to be liberals (and to believe in peace, justice, love, cooperation, and art) attracted attention and managed to succeed handsomely in editorial offices all over New York City because they were bright and talented, could write, were disarmingly ambitious, and worked hard. These "new Southern liberals" were called "good ol' boys" by the New Yorkers who worked with them because they were gracious Southerners, mannerly, quaintly charming, cliquish, and unknowingly conservative. However, the self-professed liberal position they assumed on racial and economic issues was (and is) considered dated and ludicrous by New York liberals who had long outdistanced this Southern tact—for example, the "good old boys" *reluctantly* and uneasily accepted the necessity for federal intervention in racial discriminatory cases in the South, the necessity for strict governmental controls of the oil cartel, and the necessity of accepting some fruits of the Civil Rights movement (Roebuck and Neff 1980, pp. 257-61).

THE REDNECK'S WORLD VIEW

The redneck is present centered, lives in the here and now, and is too busy "just making it" for any prolonged serious concern about his or his family's future. Meat and bread must be put on the table today, and all sorts of bills have to be paid at the end of the month. What is going to happen a year or more from now is distant, problematic, and unworthy of serious consideration. He lives in a concrete physical world at work, home, and leisure where thought, emotion, and action center on making, "fixing," operating, moving, lifting, handling, sorting, gauging, measuring, transporting, driving, planting, and harvesting mundane things. The objects and utensils surrounding him are of the practical workaday variety, for example, engines, trucks, trailers, pliers, saws, boats, guns, lumber, pipes, belts, and tools. He interacts in this milieu with his own kind and thinks and talks about things in an isolated and restricted social world: going to work, shoptalk, wages, bosses, time off, hunting, fishing, boating, trucking, cattle, physical strength, endurance, alcohol, beer joints, making it, war, cheap sex, fighting, sports, kinfolk, wives and children, good eating, and outside and inside enemies. He rails about "niggers," Yankees, "furners," labor unions, big government, big business, government workers, social welfare and welfare recipients (free loaders), and the screwed-up world in general.

The redneck not only lives in a nonintellectual world, but he is rabidly antiintellectual and antiaesthetic. He fears and dislikes those things he knows little about and perceives them as above him and beyond his reach—for example, any kind of theory or symbolism, sophisticated art, classical music, haute couture, ballet, the legitimate stage, and literature. He does not like jazz or rhythm and blues because "it's nigger music." Nothing is accepted from popular culture unless, like country music, it fits into his life-style. Education and book learning to the redneck are for other kinds of people. To hear him tell it, he is always been too busy "making it" for all that education stuff. As one redneck reported: "Now what' in the hell is all that Shakespeare shit and algebra doing for anybody. I shore cain't use none of that ejacation shit."

The redneck takes his fundamentalist religion as a given without thinking or talking about it in any analytical way. Certainly his religion fits in with and influences his fatalistic, individualistic, and physically oriented working-class life-style. It also gives him solace, a purpose for living, and ties him in with his immediate and extended family and with his friends and peers. Essentially, the redneck is preoccupied with his family and friends, work, and some leisure time to spend as he chooses—hunting, fishing, drinking, socializing, or just "takin' it easy." He lives in a small, closely knit, fearful, changing world. Increasingly besieged by inside and outside enemies, and with a poorly developed class consciousness, he is enmeshed in a poor white folk subculture that has endured since antebellum times.

Things do change. And should the labor movement ever develop in the South, the rednecks' consciousness may change. One could point out that without a change in the rednecks' attitudes, the labor movement will never become strong. In any event the redneck himself will have much to say and do about the future. But without enlightened leadership, he remains as he is.

ELEVEN

CONCLUSION

Our research indicates that Southern rednecks are white, Anglo-Saxon, blue-collar, fundamentalist Protestants who have lived in the region for a significant portion of their lives. They comprise a socially and politically isolated working-class group articulated to a class system based upon materialism, traditionalism, paternalism, racism, and religiosity—a class system that has changed little in form since antebellum times and that shows little evidence of future modification. Severed from blacks because of race and from other whites because of social class differences, rednecks—individualists by choice—stand alone. They are looked down upon by the Southern upper classes, whom they do not trust, and misunderstood by outsiders, whom they consider foreigners. Uneducated and ignorant about Southern history, the economic and political system, and labor relations and disappointed with past demagogic would-be leaders, rednecks distrust inside or outside organizers and formal organizations. Their perceived enemies list is long: Yankees, blacks, foreigners, middle- and upper-class Southerners, labor unions, big government, big business, socialists, progressive movements, do-gooders, new ideas, and modernity of any stripe.

Rednecks encompass a rigid, marginal group nurtured in a semi-traditional society who face an unwanted, perplexing, and dynamic world. They react to the problems of change by falling back on an enduring Southern poor white folk culture that includes "the savage ideal." Obviously, this remarkable culture is not conducive to class consciousness, economic well-being, or upward social mobility. On the other hand, it

187

provides them with a strong sense of place, time, family, and continuity along with a tolerable self-concept.

Rednecks love the outdoors for both work and recreational activities and hold a whimsical life ambition to live on their own farm and "work it." They prefer a fundamentalist religion supportive of individual needs and tuned in to their personal problems. Traditional and reactionary in the sexual sphere, rednecks desire wives from similar backgrounds to themselves who will accept their macho image of real men and husbands. They wish to stay in the South, and when they leave, they maintain their traditions elsewhere—and look forward to an eventual return to kith and kin.

Though rednecks place great emphasis on working for an honest living, work is not as central to their life scheme as it is for many middle- and upper-class Americans. Work is primarily a necessary means to survival, a means of avoiding the shackles of welfare and the federal government. Rednecks want to be free, and they are would-be twentieth century frontiersmen. They dream that their children will grow up to be better off economically than themselves, which does not necessarily mean to be either more educated or middle class, because rednecks reject most middle-class values. They just want their children to be freer than themselves—an impossible dream, given current circumstances.

The redneck is proud of his background and wishes to be left alone. He is not all bad. He is dependable, loyal to his own kind, and straightforward. In sum, he is what he wants to be, and his future, barring outside interference, will be determined primarily on what he wants to be.

Who knows, the redneck may soon feel himself less alienated than before in light of the current trend in the United States toward the radical Right as evidenced by reactionary politics, a failing, anachronistic, capitalistic economic policy, a disenchanted (with liberalism) electorate, religious and moral fundamentalism, the hardening of ethnic and class lines, and the return to a primitive pop culture. A proliferation of examples indicate such a trend. At the political and economic level, there are white middle-class, small businessmen, lower echelon professionals, tradesmen, pensioners, small farmers and rural dwellers, and blue-collar wage earners who reject liberalism—and seek a strong leader, "law and order," national patriotism, cultural and moral traditionalism, and the consolidation of their economic and social status against the intrusion of lower class and minority memberships. These groups appear to be involved in a con-servative populist movement. The Reagan administration is attempting with some success to dismantle social, educational, and welfare programs that are necessary to the security of the middle and lower classes. Big business is being deregulated, and a contradictory fusion of monetarism and supply-side economics has led to a depression marked by inflation and unemployment. A tax policy that favors the rich at the expense of the middle and working classes worsens the economic situation. The return to a primitively oriented criminal justice system, weakened labor unions, and the loss of some civil rights movement gains (busing, equal opportunity employment) offer other illustrations.

Members of the Moral Majority are riding high with significant victories against the separation of church and state, abortion for women, pornography, liberal congressmen, and certain freedom of the press rights. The Ku Klux Klan is very much alive again, and a brand of conservative populism reminiscent of that preached by George Wallace is on the upsurge in the South.

The Sun Belt has arrived and is implanting its cultured cachet on the rest of the nation—double knit suits, synthetic clothing (as opposed to natural fabrics), country-and-western music, cowboy dress style, fundamentalist evangelical religious television programs, nostalgia, hick movies, nationalism, and a primitive (frontier) individualistic stance. The region's high technology and communication system fosters the spread of such a pop culture. (Though the Sun Belt extends beyond the Confederate South, the Confederate South remains this region's primary cultural cradle.)

Some scholars think this drift toward the Right will result in a radically-right third political party. They speculate that such a political party might lead to corporate statism° (Phillips, 1981: 27-32). Certainly the redneck would find a place in such a system.

°A highly centralized economic security state run by the federal government and big business with special welfare provisions for the needs of farmers, wage-earners, pensioners and the middle class. The focus of such a state capitalism is on production, economic growth, trade, reindustrialization, and national defense. Its ideology rests on nationalist pride, moral traditionalism, work, family, neighborhood, and personal economic security.

REFERENCES

Aaron, Henry. 1978. *Politics and the Professors: The Great Society in Perspective.* Washington, D.C.: Brookings Institution.

Agee, James. 1941. *Let Us Now Praise Famous Men.* Boston: Houghton Mifflen.

Anderson, Jack. 1974. *The Political Economy of Social Class.* Englewood Cliffs, N. J.: Prentice-Hall.

Ashbaugh, Carolyn, and Dan McCurry. "On the Line at Oneita." In *Working Lives: The Southern Exposure History of Labor in the South,* edited by Marc Miller. New York: Pantheon.

Averill, Patricia. 1973. "Esoteric-Exoteric Expectations of Redneck Behavior and Country Music." *Journal of Country Music* 4:34-38.

Birdwhistell, Ray L. 1970. *Kinesics and Context: Essays on Body Motion Communication.* Philadelphia: University of Pennsylvania Press.

Blumer, Herbert. 1969. *Symbolic Interactionism: Prespective and Method.* Englewood Cliffs, N. J.: Prentice-Hall.

Boney, F. N. 1971. "The Redneck." *Georgia Review* 25:333-42.

Botkin, B. A., ed. 1977. *A Treasury of Southern Folklore: Stories, Ballads, Traditions, and Folkways of the People of the South.* New York: Bonanza.

Botsch, Robert E. 1981. "You Can't Have It Both Ways: The Difficulties of Unionization in the South." In *Perspectives on the American South: An Annual Review of Society, Politics and Culture,* edited by Merle Black and John Shelton Reed, 1:173-86. New York: Gordon and Breach.

Bowser, Benjamin P., Raymond G. Hunt, and David C. Pohl. 1981. "Introduction." In *Impacts of Racism on White Americans,* edited by Benjamin P. Bowser, Raymond G. Hunt, and David C. Pohl. Beverly Hills, Calif. Sage.

Bruns, Hal. 1973. "Chicago, Hillbilly Ghetto." In *Power in the Affluent Society,* edited by Hara H. Meissner. New York: Harper & Row.

Bunch, Ernest J. 1978. *The Hell You Say.* Fort Valley, Ga.: MRW.

Burgoon, Judee K., and Thomas Saine. 1978. *The Unspoken Dialogue: An Introduction to Nonverbal Communication.* Boston: Houghton Mifflin.

Caldwell, Erskine. 1932. *Tobacco Road.* New York: Scribner's.

Cash, Wilbur J. 1941. *The Mind of the South.* New York: Knopf.

Chalmers, David M. 1965. *Hooded Americanism: The First Century of the Ku Klux Klan, 1865-1965.* Garden City, N. Y.: Doubleday.

Clarion Ledger (Jackson, Miss.), October 13, 1981.

Clark, Kenneth B., and jeanette Hopkins. 1968. *A Relevant War against Poverty.* New York: Harpertorch Books.

Coles, Robert. 1972. *Farewell to the South.* Boston: Little, Brown.

_____. 1971. "Understanding White Racists." *New York Review of Books,* December 30, 1971, pp. 12-15.

Collins, Randall. 1979. *The Credential Society: An Historical Sociology of Education and Stratification*. New York: Academic Press.

Complete CB Slang Dictionary. North Miami, Fla.: Merit.

Daniels, Jonathan. 1938. *A Southerner Discovers the South*. New York: Macmillan.

Davis, David Brian. 1975. *The Problem of Slavery in the Age of Revolution, 1770-1823*. Ithaca, N. Y.: Cornell University Press.

Degler, Carl N. 1974. *The Other South*. New York: Harper & Row.

Demerath, Nicholas J., III. 1965. *Social Class in American Protestantism*. Chicago: Rand McNally.

Dickey, Charley. 1981a. "Puttering for Doves." *Field and Stream* 86 (December): 52, 110.

_____. 1981b. "Save Gas on Rabbits." *Field and Stream* 86 (December): D-E.

Dotter, Daniel, and Michael Moore. 1979. "A Phenomenology of Redneckery: An Anatomy of a Work Culture." Paper read at the Mid-South Sociological Association Meetings in Memphis, Tenn. November 4, 1979. Mimeographed.

Dunbar, Anthony P. 1981. *Against the Grain, Southern Radicals and Prophets, 1929-1959*. Charlottesville: University Press of Virginia.

Eakins, Barbara Westbrook, and R. Gene Eakins. 1978. *Sex Differences in Human Communication*. Boston: Houghton Mifflin.

Ekman, Paul, and Wallace V. Friesen. 1975. *Unmasking the Face: A Guide to Recognizing Emotions from Facial Cues*. Englewood Cliffs, N. J.: Prentice-Hall.

Emmerich, J. Oliver. 1973. *Two Faces of Janus: The Saga of Deep South Change*. Jackson: University and College Press of Mississippi.

Faulkner, William. 1932. *Light in August*. New York: New Directions.

Flynt, J. Wayne. 1979. *Dixie's Forgotten People: The South's Poor Whites*. Bloomington: Indiana University Press.

_____. 1969. "The Ethics of Democratic Persuasion and the Birmingham Crisis." *Southern Speech Journal* 35:40-53.

Fogel, Robert William, and Stanley L. Engerman. 1974. *Time on the Cross: The Economics of American Negro Slavery*. Boston: Little, Brown.

Form, William H. 1976. "Conflict within the Working Class: The Skilled as a Special-Interest Group." In *The Uses of Controversy in Sociology*, edited by Lewis A. Coser and Otto N. Larsen, pp. 51-73. New York: Free Press.

Frady, Marshall. 1980. *Southerners: A Journalist's Odyssey*. New York: New American Library.

_____. 1968. *Wallace*. New York: World.

Genovese, Eugene D. 1974. *Roll Jordan Roll: The World the Slaves Made*. New York: Pantheon.

_____. 1965. *The Political Economy of Slavery: Studies in the Economy and Society of the Slave South*. New York: Pantheon.

Goffman, Erving. 1971. *Relations in Public: Microstudies of the Public Order*. New York: Harper & Row.

Goldberg, Herb. 1979. *The New Male: From Self-Destruction to Self-Care.* New York: Signet.

Greeley, Andrew M. 1972. *The Denominationalism Society: A Sociological Approach to Religion in America.* Glenview, Ill.: Scott, Foresman.

Greet, William Cabell. 1935. "Southern Speech." In *Culture in the South,* edited by W. T. Couch, pp. 594–615. Chapel Hill: University of North Carolina Press.

Griffin, Susan. 1971. "Rape, the All American Crime." *Ramparts,* September, 1971.

Hamilton, Charles G. 1958. "Mississippi Politics in the Progressive Era 1904-1920." Ph.D. dissertation, Vanderbilt University.

Harte, Thomas B. 1972. "The Rhetoric of Pox: Invention in George Wallace's Speech at Cape Girardeau, Missouri." *Central States Speech Journal* 23:202-05.

Helper, Hinton Rowan. 1968. *The Impending Crisis of the South: How to Meet It.* Edited by George M. Frederickson. Cambridge, Mass.: Belknap Press.

Hickson, Mark, III. 1980. *NVC: Studies and Applications.* Mississippi State, Miss.: Communication Applications.

Hickson, Mark, III. 1976. "Saul Alinsky: American Marxian Strategist?" In *Marxian Perspectives on Human Communication,* edited by Mark Hickson III and Fred E. Jandt, pp. 36-43. Rochester, N. Y.: PSI.

Hickson, Mark, III, Larry Powell, Sidney R. Hill, Jr., Genetta B. Holt, and Hank Flick. 1979. "Smoking Artifacts as Indicators of Homophily, Attraction, and Credibility." *Southern Speech Communication Journal* 44:191-200.

Hirschman, Charles, and Kim Blankenship. 1981. "The North-South Earnings Gap: Changes during the 1960s and 1970s." *American Journal of Sociology* 87:388-403.

Hollander, A. N. J. Den. 1935. "The Tradition of 'Poor Whites.' " In *Culture in the South,* edited by W. T. Couch, pp. 403-31. Chapel Hill: University of North Carolina Press.

Holloway, Harry. 1969. *The Politics of the Southern Negro.* New York: Random House.

Hopkins, Harry. 1934. *Harry Hopkins Papers.* Hyde Park, N. Y.: Franklin D. Roosevelt Library.

Hudson, Charles. 1972. "The Structure of a Fundamentalist Christian Belief System." In *Religion and the Solid South,* edited by Samuel S. Hill, Jr., pp. 122-42. Nashville, Tenn.: Abingdon Press.

Hundley, Daniel R. 1979. "The Southern Bully." In *Relations in Our Southern States,* edited by William J. Cooper, Jr., pp. 223-83. Baton Rouge: Louisiana State University Press.

Jacobs, Robert D. 1980. *"Tobacco Road:* Lowlife and the Comic Tradition." In *The American South: Portrait of a Culture,* edited by Louis D. Rubin, pp. 206-26. Baton Rouge: Louisiana State University Press.

Jehlen, Myra. 1978. *Class and Character in Faulkner's South.* Secaucus, N. J.: Citadel Press.

Johnson, Charles S., Edwin R. Embree, and Will W. Alexander. 1935. *The Collapse of Cotton Tenancy.* Chapel Hill: University of North Carolina Press.

Jones, Bill. 1966. *The Wallace Story.* Northport, Ala.: American Southern.

Jones, James M. 1981. "The Concept of Racism and Its Changing Reality." In *Impacts of Racism on White Americans,* edited by Beverly Hills, Calif.: Sage.

Kelly, Edith S. 1923. *Weeds.* New York: Harcourt.

Key, V. O., Jr. 1949. *Southern Politics in State and Nation.* New York: Vintage.

Killian, Lewis M. 1970. *White Southerners.* New York: Random House.

King, Florence. 1975. *Southern Ladies and Gentlemen.* New York: Bantam.

King, Richard H. 1980. *A Southern Renaissance: The Cultural Awakening of the American South, 1930-1955.* New York: Oxford University Press.

Kirwan, Albert D. 1951. *Revolt of the Rednecks: Mississippi Politics in 1876-1923.* Lexington: University of Kentucky Press.

Knapp, Mark L. 1978. *Nonverbal Communication in Human Interaction.* 2d ed. New York: Holt, Rinehart, and Winston.

Kolko, Gabriel. 1962. *Wealth and Power in America.* New York: Praeger.

Kousser, J. Morgan. 1974. *The Shaping of Southern Politics: Suffrage Restriction and the Establishment of the One-Party South, 1880-1910.* New Haven, Conn.: Yale University Press.

Lachicotte, Alberta. 1967. *Rebel Senator: Strom Thurmond of South Carolina.* New York: Devin-Adair.

Lampman, Robert. 1962. *The Share of Top Wealth-Holders in National Wealth.* Princeton: Princeton University Press.

Langley, Roger, and Richard C. Levy. 1977. *Wife Beating: The Silent Crisis.* New York: Pocket.

"Latest on Unions' Drive to Organize the South." 1977. *U.S. News & World Report,* January 10, 1977, pp. 72-74.

Lawrence, Ken. 1975. "The Roots of Class Struggle in the South." *Radical America* 9:15-37.

Le Masters, E. E. 1975. *Blue Collar Aristocrats: Life-styles at a Working Class Tavern.* Madison: University of Wisconsin Press.

Long, Huey Pierce. 1933. *Every Man a King: The Autobiography of Huey P. Long.* New Orleans: National.

Lundberg, Ferdinand. 1968. *The Rich and the Super Rich.* New York: Bantam.

Lyle, Katie Letcher. 1980. "Southern Country Music: A Brief Eulogy." In *The American South: Portrait of a Culture,* edited by Louis D. Rubin, pp. 140-60. Baton Rouge: Louisiana State University Press.

McDavid, Raven I. 1967. "Needed Research in Southern Dialects." In *Perspectives on the South: Agenda for Research,* edited by Edgar T. Thompson, pp. 113-24. Durham, N.C.: Duke University Press.

McLaurin, Melton Alonzo. 1978. *The Knights of Labor in the South.* Westport, Conn.: Greenwood Press.

McWhiney, Grady. 1973. *Southerners and Other Americans.* New York: Basic.

Madigan, Charles. 1981. "Sun Belt Opportunities Rated among Poorest in the Nation." *Clarion Ledger* (Jackson, Miss.), December 13, 1981, p. 16A.

Makay, J. J. 1970. "The Rhetorical Strategies of Governor George Wallace in the 1964 Maryland Primary." The *Southern Speech Journal* 36:164-75.

_____. 1968. "George Wallace: Southern Spokesman with a Northern Audience." *Central States Speech Journal* 19:202-08.

Marshall, F. Ray. 1967. *Labor in the South.* Cambridge, Mass.: Harvard University Press.

Mayfield, Chris. 1981. Introduction to *Growing up Southern: Southern Exposure Looks at Childhood, Then and Now,* edited by Chris Mayfield, pp. ix-xii. New York: Pantheon.

"Measuring Poverty Now." 1976. *U.S. News & World Report,* November 8, 1976, pp. 57-58.

Mell, Mildred. 1943. "The Southern Poor White: Myth, Symbol, and Reality of a Nation." The *Saturday Review of Literature,* January 23, 1943, pp. 13-15.

_____. 1938. "Poor Whites of the South." *Social Forces* 17:153-67.

Mertz, Paul E. 1978. *New Deal Policy and Southern Rural Poverty.* Baton Rouge: Louisiana State University Press.

Meyer, Jerry. 1981. "Tree Stand Tactics." *Field and Stream* 86 (December):20.

Miller, Caroline. 1933. *Lamb in His Bosom.* New York: Harper.

Mitchell, Broadus, and George Mitchell. 1930. *The Industrial Revolution in the South.* Baltimore: John Hopkins University Press.

Mitchell, Steve. 1976. *How to Speak Southern.* New York: Bantam.

Molloy, John T. 1975. *Dress for Success.* New York: Peter H. Wyden.

Montgomery, David. 1981. "Violence and the Struggle for Unions in the South, 1880-1930." In *Perspectives on the American South: An Annual Review of Society, Politics and Culture,* edited by Merle Black and John Shelton Reed, 1:35-74. New York: Gordon and Breach.

Morgan, Marabel. 1973. *The Total Woman.* New York: Pocket.

Morris, Richard B., Henry Steele Commager, and Jeffrey B Morris. 1976. *Encyclopedia of American History.* New York: Harper & Row.

Murray, Michael D. 1975. "Wallace and the Media: The 1972 Florida Primary." *Southern Speech Communication Journal* 40:429-40.

Naylor, Thomas H., and James Clotfelter. 1975. *Strategies for Change in the South.* Chapel Hill: University of North Carolina Press.

Newby, I. A. 1978. *The South: A History.* New York: Holt, Rinehart and Winston.

Newman, Dale. 1981. "The Myth of the Contented Southern Mill Worker." In *Perspectives on the American South: An Annual Review of Society, Politics, and Culture,* edited by Merle Black and John Shelton Reed,1:187-204. New York: Gordon and Breach.

Nixon, Herman C. 1938. *Forty Acres and Steel Mules.* Chapel Hill: University of North Carolina Press.

Odum, Howard. 1936. *Southern Regions of the United States.* Chapel Hill: University of North Carolina Press.

Offen, Carol, ed. 1977. *Country Music: The Poetry.* New York: Ballantine.

O'Neill, George, and Nena O'Neill. 1972. *Open Marriage.* New York: Avon.

Owsley, Frank Lawrence. 1949. *Plain Folk of the Old South.* Baton Rouge: Louisiana State University Press.

Parmley, Ingram. 1981. "Stalking the Good Ole Boy." In *Perspectives on the American South, An Annual Review of Society, Politics, and Culture,* edited by Merle Black and John Shelton Reed, 1: New York: Gordon and Breach.

Patman Committee. 1972. "Investments and Major Interlocks between Major Banks and Major Corporations." In *American Society, Inc.*, edited by M. Zeitlin, Chicago: Markham.

Percy, William. 1941. *Lanterns on the Levee*. New York: Knopf.

Phillips, Kevin. 1982. "Post-Conservative America," *New York Review of Books* 29, number 8:27-32.

Phillips, Ulrich Bonnell. 1929. *Life and Labor in the Old South*. Boston: Little, Brown.

Potter, David M. 1973. *The Impending Crisis, 1848-1861*. New York: Harper & Row.

———. 1968. *The South and the Sectional Conflict*. Baton Rouge: Louisiana State University Press.

Powdermaker, Hortense. 1939. *After Freedom: A Cultural Study in the Deep South*. New York: Viking.

Powell, Larry. 1975. "Hank Williams: Loneliness and Psychological Alienation." *Journal of Country Music* 6:130-35.

Ransom, John Crowe, Donald Davidson, Frank Lawrence Ousley, John Gould Fletcher, Lyle H. Lanier, Allen Tate, Herman Clarence Nixon, Andrew Nelson Lytle, Robert Penn Warren, John Donald Wade, Henry Blue Kline, and Stark Young. 1930. *I'll Take My Stand*. New York: Harper and Brothers.

Raper, Arthur F. 1936. *Preface to Peasantry: A Tale of Two Black Belt Counties*. Chapel Hill: University of North Carolina Press.

Raper, Arthur F., and Ira Reid. 1941. *Sharecroppers All*. Chapel Hill: University of North Carolina Press.

Raphael, Ray. 1976. *Edges: Backcountry Lives in America Today on the Borderlands between the Old Ways and the New*. New York: Alfred H. Knopf.

Rawlings, Marjorie Kinnan. 1938. *The Yearling*. New York: Watts.

Reed, John Shelton. 1972. *The Enduring South: Subcultural Persistence in Mass Society*. Lexington, Mass.: D. C. Heath.

Roberts, Elizabeth Maddox. 1926. *Time of Men*. New York: Viking Press.

Robinson, Michael J., and Clifford Zukin. 1976. "Television and the Wallace Vote." *Journal of Communication* 26:79-83.

Roebuck, Julian B. 1948. "Domestic Service in the South." Master's thesis, Duke University.

Roebuck, Julian, and Wolfgang Frese. 1978. *The Roundabouts, A Case Study of an After Hours Club*. New York: Free Press.

Roebuck, Julian B., and Ronald L. Neff. 1980. "Multiple Reality of the 'Redneck': Toward a Grounded Theory of the Southern Class Structure." In *Studies in Symbolic Interaction*, edited by Norman K. Denzin, 3: Greenwich, Conn.: JAI Press.

Roebuck, Julian B., and Stanley C. Weeber. 1978. *Political Crime in the United States: Analyzing Crime by and against Government*. New York: Praeger.

Rubin, Zick. 1973. *Liking and Loving*. New York: Holt, Rinehart and Winston.

Ryscavage, Paul M. 1970. *The Poor in 1970: A Chartbook*. Washington, D.C.: Office of Economic Opportunity.

Sacks, Harvey. 1979. "Hotrodder: A Revolutionary Category." In *Everyday Language: Studies in Ethnomethodology*, edited by George Psathas, pp. 7-14. New York: Irvington.

Sanchez, Billie Sue. 1978. "Marriage Deferment and Achievement: Antecedents and Consequences among Rural Youth." Master's thesis, Texas A & M University.

Savin, Nina. 1981. "The Official Redneck Handbook." *Fashion for Men*, Fall/ Winter, pp. 75-78.

Scheflen, Albert E. 1965. "Quasi-Courtship Behavior in Psychotherapy." *Psychiatry* 28:245-57.

Scheflen, Albert E., with Norman Ashcraft. 1976. *Human Territories: How We Behave in Space-Time*. Englewood Cliffs, N.J.: Prentice-Hall.

Schwartz, Charles F., and Robert E. Graham, Jr., eds. 1956. *U.S. Office of Business Economics, Personal Income by States Since 1929: A Supplement to the Survey of Current Business*. Washington, D.C.: U.S. Government Printing Office.

Segrest, Mab. 1981. "Delicate Conversations." In *Growing up Southern: Southern Exposure Looks at Childhood, Then and Now*, edited by Chris Mayfield, pp. 82-88. New York: Pantheon.

Sennett, Richard, and Jonathan Cobb. 1973. *The Hidden Injuries of Class*. New York: Vintage.

Sheehy, Gail. 1976. *Passages: Predictable Crises of Adult Life*. New York: Bantam.

Sherrill, Robert. 1969. *Gothic Politics in the Deep South: Stars of the New Confederacy*. New York: Ballantine.

Shostak, Arthur B. 1976. "Politics, Conflict, and Young Blue-Collarites: Old Dissensus and New Consciousness." In *The Uses of Controversy in Sociology*, edited by Lewis A. Coser and Otto N. Larsen, pp. 74-94.. New York: Free Press.

Siegman, Aron Wolfe. 1978. "The Telltale Voice: Nonverbal Messages of Verbal Communication." In *Nonverbal Behavior and Communication*, edited by Aron W. Seigman and Stanley Feldstein, pp. 183-243. Hillsdale, N.J.: Lawrence Erlbaum Associates.

Silver, James W. 1964. *Mississippi: The Closed Society*. New York: Harcourt, Brace, and World.

Simmel, Georg. 1950. *The Sociology of Georg Simmel*. Edited and translated by Kurt H. Wolff. New York: Free Press.

Sims, Barbara B. 1974. " 'She's Got to Be a Saint, Lord Knows I Ain't: Feminine Masochism in American Country Music." *Journal of Country Music* 5:24–30.

Sims, Patsy. 1978. *The Klan*. New York: Stein and Day.

Smith, Lillian. 1949. *Killers of the Dream*. New York: Norton.

"The Southern Regional Council's Report." *Clarion Ledger*. Jackson, Mississippi, October 13, 1981, p. 21.

Sorensen, Theodore C. 1965. *Kennedy*. New York: Harper & Row.

Stambler, Irwin, and Grelun Landon. 1969. *Encyclopedia of Folk, Country, and Western Music*. New York: St. Martin's Press.

Stamp, Kenneth M. 1960. *The Era of Reconstruction, 1865-1877*. New York: Knopf.

Sterling, Tom. 1981. "Waterhole Whitetails." *Field and Stream* 86 (December): F-H.

Stillman, Don. 1980. "Runaways." In *Working Lives: The Southern Exposure History of Labor in the South*, edited by Marc Miller, pp. 217-28. New York: Pantheon.

"Sudden Drive on Poverty—Why?" 1964. *U.S. News & World Report*, January 20, 1964, pp. 36-40.

Tarrants, Thomas A., III. 1979. *The Conversion of a Klansman: The Story of a Former Ku Klux Klan Terrorist*. Garden City, N.Y.: Doubleday.

Terkel, Studs. 1974. *Working*. New York: Avon.

Thomas, Emory M. 1979. *The Confederate Nation, 1861-1865*. New York: Harper & Row.

Thourlby, William. 1978. *You Are What You Wear: The Key to Business Success*. Kansas City, Kans.: Sheed Andrews and McMell.

"A Nation within a Nation," *Time*, May 17, 1968, pp. 24-35.

Tindall, George Brown. 1967. *The Emergence of the New South, 1913-1945*. Baton Rouge: Louisiana State University Press.

Toby, Jackson. 1974. "Violence and the Masculine Ideal: Some Qualitative Data." In *Violence in the Family*, edited by Suzanne K. Steinmetz and Murray A. Strauss, pp. 58-65. New York: Dodd, Mead.

Toplin, Robert Brent. 1975. *Unchallenged Violence: An American Ordeal*. Westport, Conn.: Greenwood.

Townsend, James L. 1980. *Dear Heart*. Atlanta, Ga.: Peachtree.

Tuchman, Barbara. 1978. *A Distant Mirror: The Calamitous 14th Century*. New York: Alfred A. Knopf.

Turner, Jonathan, and Charles E. Starnes. 1976. *Inequality: Privilege and Poverty in America*. Pacific Palisades, Calif.: Goodyear.

"25 Million Poor in U.S.—Really." 1971. *U.S. News & World Report*, May 24, 1971, pp. 40-43.

University of Michigan, Survey Research Center. 1960. *1960 Survey of Consumer Finances*. Ann Arbor, Mich.: Survey Research Center.

U.S., Bureau of Statistics. 1978. "Conference Papers Presented at the Thirteenth Meeting of the Industrial Relations Research Associates, December 28-30, 1977." *Monthly Labor Review* 101 (April):28-30.

U.S., Bureau of the Census. 1973. *1970 Census of Population*. Vol. 1. Washington, D.C.: Government Printing Office.

U.S., Congress, Senate, Select Committee on Nutrition and Human Needs. 1969. *Nutrition and Human Needs*, 90th Cong., 2d sess. - 91st Cong., 1st sess. Washington, D.C.: Government Printing Office.

Veblen, Thorstein. 1902. *The Theory of the Leisure Class: An Economic Study of Institutions*. New York: Macmillan.

Warren, Robert Penn. 1963. *All the King's Men*. New York: Time.

Wilkinson, Sylvia. 1980. "Red-Necks on Wheels: The Stock Car Culture." In *The American South: Portrait of a Culture*, edited by Louis D. Rubin, pp. 129-39. Baton Rouge: Louisiana State University Press.

Williams, Donald E. 1961. "Protest under the Cross: The Ku Klux Klan Presents Its Case to the Public, 1960." *Southern Speech Journal* 27:43-55.

Williams, Juanita H. 1977. *Psychology of Women: Behavior in a Bio-Social Context.* New York: W. W. Norton.

Wilson, John. 1978. *Religion in American Society: The Effective Presence.* Englewood Cliffs, N.J.: Prentice-Hall.

Wohlenberg, Ernest H. 1976. "A Regional Approach to Public Attitudes and Public Assistance." *Social Service Review* :491-505.

Wolfe, Thomas. 1929. *Look Homeward Angel.* New York: Grosset & Dunlap.

Woofter, Thomas Jackson, Jr. 1936. *Landlord and Tenant on the Cotton Plantation.* Works Progress Administration Research Monographs, vol. 5. Washington, D.C.: Works Progress Administration.

Woodward, C. Vann. 1951. *Origins of the New South, 1877-1913.* Baton Rouge: Louisiana State University Press.

INDEX

ABOUT THE AUTHORS

JULIAN B. ROEBUCK is Professor of Sociology at Mississippi State University. He previously served as a research analyst with the District of Columbia Department of Corrections, Washington, D.C.; Associate Professor of Sociology at San Jose State University, San Jose, California; and Associate Professor of Sociology at Louisiana State University, Baton Rouge, Louisiana.

He has published several books and articles in the fields of criminology, deviant behavior, and race relations.

Roebuck holds an A.B. degree from Atlantic Christian College, an M.A. from Duke University, and a Ph.D. from the University of Maryland, College Park, Maryland.

MARK HICKSON, III, is Professor of Communication at Mississippi State University. He previously served as Visiting Professorial Lecturer at the American University, Washington, D.C.

Dr. Hickson has published widely in the field of communication. His articles and reviews have appeared in *Communication Quarterly*, *Psychological Reports*, the *Southern Speech Communication Journal*, *ETC*, *Speech Teacher*, the *Journal of Communication*, and the *International Journal of Communication Research*.

Dr. Hickson holds B.S. and M.A. degrees from Auburn University and a second M.A. (Sociology) from Mississippi State University. He received his Ph.D. from Southern Illinois University, Carbondale.